The Two
Walter Raleighs

The Two Walter Raleighs

*Famous Father, Rebellious Son
and a Shared Tragedy*

FRED B. TROMLY

McFarland & Company, Inc., Publishers
Jefferson, North Carolina

ISBN (print) 978-1-4766-7240-3 ♾
ISBN (ebook) 978-1-4766-3346-6

LIBRARY OF CONGRESS CATALOGUING DATA ARE AVAILABLE

BRITISH LIBRARY CATALOGUING DATA ARE AVAILABLE

© 2019 Fred B. Tromly. All rights reserved

No part of this book may be reproduced or transmitted in any form or by any means, electronic or mechanical, including photocopying or recording, or by any information storage and retrieval system, without permission in writing from the publisher.

Front cover: portrait of Sir Walter Ralegh and Walter Ralegh by an unknown artist, oil on canvas, 1602, 78½" × 50⅛" (© National Portrait Gallery, London)

Printed in the United States of America

*McFarland & Company, Inc., Publishers
Box 611, Jefferson, North Carolina 28640
www.mcfarlandpub.com*

For Annette

Table of Contents

Acknowledgments ix
Preface 1
Introduction 5

ONE • What's in a Son's Name? 9
TWO • The Son of His Father—and His Mother 21
THREE • Wat as Second Self 37
FOUR • Imagining a Son on the Gallows 52
FIVE • Disinheritance and Corruption of Blood 61
SIX • A Paterfamilias Undone 71
SEVEN • Instructing and Neglecting a Son 88
EIGHT • Escape to Oxford 102
NINE • Continental Drifting with Ben Jonson 116
TEN • A Son in Arms 132
ELEVEN • From Thomasine to Guiana 148
TWELVE • Destiny 163

Conclusion: Last Words and Silences 178
Chapter Notes 193
Bibliography 209
Index 217

Acknowledgments

I would like to extend my thanks to the staff at McFarland, and especially to Charlie Perdue for his commitment to my work.

As readers will surmise from its notes, this book would have been impossible without the labor of many scholars, four of whom were remarkably generous in their help. Mark Nicholls offered crucial encouragement at a time of hesitation and responded gamely to countless annoying questions. Andrew Thrush saved me from many mistakes and introduced me to valuable resources, notably the rich biographies commissioned by the History of Parliament Trust. Helen Bradley kindly removed a large roadblock by volunteering to translate two crucial documents in difficult law Latin. Years ago, Judith Owens and I discovered a shared interest in the two Walter Raleghs, which has led to a fruitful exchange of ideas and an enduring friendship.

Many gallant people have responded to requests for help in their areas of expertise. I warmly thank Mark Ashley-Miller, Bob Barnett, Dr. Anna Beer, Cindy Chant, Professor Pauline Croft, Dr. Christine Dunbar, Dr. Catharine MacLeod, James Murdoch, Didi Pollock, Professor Wilfrid Prest, Dr. Daniela Prögler, Dr. Tim Stretton, David Swinscoe, and Dr. Martine Zoeteman. None of the errors in the pages to follow should be laid at any doorstep but my own.

Valuable institutional help has come through many persons and is acknowledged in notes. One outstanding contribution, however, must be named here: that of Nigel Taylor in the manuscripts division of the National Archives (London), who counselled my wife and me in the handling and searching of awkward, weighty King's Bench rolls.

Closer to home, I want to single out the staff at some libraries at the University of Toronto—the Robarts Library, the Centre for Renaissance and Reformation Studies, and the Thomas Fisher Rare Book Library—for unfailingly courteous and thoughtful service.

Too numerous to name, my old friends in Peterborough and newer ones in Toronto expressed a supportive interest in this project and cheered on my sometimes fitful progress. Over the years, they have provided vital oxygenation.

Then there is family. With the happy exception of Mary Gould, my sister-in-law here in Toronto and solver of many problems, online and off, we are far-flung: Seattle, Winnipeg, Corrales, Plano, Albuquerque, Ojai, Denver, and Brooklyn. Fortunately, our closeness extends over the distances. That being said, the geographical separation of my precious grandchildren—Maxim, Sasha, and Henry—feels especially pronounced and exceptionally unjust. My daughters-in-law, Katya Peshkova and Stephanie Pena-Sy, have generously shared their children, and my sons Luke and Ben have always been a source of loving support, laced with a good dose of tonic sarcasm. The dedication cherishes a pilgrim soul.

Acknowledgments for Illustrations

Special thanks are due to His Grace, the Duke of Rutland and His Grace, the Duke of Bedford, for making images of precious art works in their collections available to me.

A number of individuals have aided in the sometimes tedious process of preparing electronic images and arranging permission for their use. I wish to thank Nicola Allen, Archivist, Woburn Abbey; Peter Foden, Archivist for the Duke of Rutland; Paul Fox, National Portrait Gallery; Joanna Langston, Director, Portrait Miniatures, Christie's; Lisa Lucassen, Erfgoed Leiden en Omstreken; Sean Mooney, National Gallery of Ireland; Natalya Rattan, Fisher Rare Book Library, University of Toronto; and the staff of the Heinz Archive at the National Portrait Gallery.

Although the location of the portrait of Lady Ralegh in Mourning with her son Carew remains unknown, I am grateful for the help of many people who contributed to my quest to discover it, especially Alexis Ashot (Director, Old Masters Group, Christie's), Dr. Catharine MacLeod (Curator of Seventeenth Century Painting, National Portrait Gallery), Andrew O'Hagan, Rupert Thomas, and Aliette Boshier.

Preface

The genesis of this book lies in the painting that serves as its cover. In the course of writing a volume on fathers and sons in Shakespeare, I found the double portrait of Sir Walter Ralegh and his son Walter to be intriguing but couldn't give it as much attention as I wished. Later I discovered that the relationship between the two Walter Raleghs had never been examined in any detail. This omission struck me as odd, given the popularity of the elder Ralegh as a biographical subject and the obvious importance to him of his same-named son. I resolved to learn as much about their interactions as I could, and it soon became clear that the story of this father and son—both of whom died exactly four hundred years ago—still resonates. Despite the historical displacement of fixed patriarchal norms, the two Walter Raleghs vividly exemplify a family dynamic that persists to this day: an imposing father's desire to identify his son and heir with himself stimulates the son's fierce rebellion. In its modern versions the conflict is often happily resolved, but the only way the Raleghs could come together was in the tragic story they lived and in the violent deaths they shared.

Names

With regard to the famously varied spelling of the surname, "Ralegh" respects the clear preference of both Walters. However, attention must also be paid to the whims of modernity and needs of potential readers, and consequently on the title page and cover this book refers to the now more-common and readily found "Raleigh." As I learned long ago when my same-named father and I spent the better part of an afternoon paging "Fred Tromly" from opposite ends of a cavernous airport terminal, shared names within a family can beget terrible confusion. To distinguish between the two Walter Raleghs without making them sound like a family law firm, the pages that follow usually refer to the father simply as "Ralegh" and to the son as "Wat." The plain "Ralegh" intends no disrespect—I have no desire to strip him of the knighthood he so richly merited. But "Ralegh" may help to avoid the Victorian clichés that repeated references to "Sir Walter Ralegh" might activate, and the inevitable countless repetitions of his name make brevity a virtue.

For Walter junior, the inevitable name to use is "Wat." Not only is it the name by which he was known within his family, but its youthfulness is poignantly appropriate for a person who did not live to grow into mature adulthood. With regard to addressing Ralegh's wife and Wat's mother—the former Elizabeth Throckmorton—a question of tact arises. Since she was a formidable, well-born woman who deployed her status effectively, it feels more appropriate to refer to her (usually) as "Lady Ralegh" rather than the tempting but perhaps overly familiar "Bess." Another rejected alternative—to refer to her as "Elizabeth"—runs the risk of confusing her with a much more imperious woman who bore the name, a woman to whom Ralegh and his wife gave offense and paid dearly.

I have opted to refer to some prominent figures, most notably the ubiquitous Robert Cecil, by family name rather than (Elizabethan-style) by the office they were holding at a given moment. Cecil, unlike Ralegh, was always in ascent from one high post to another, and it would be pointlessly confusing to refer to him by the governmental position he was currently occupying. For similar ease of identification, usually I refer to titled aristocrats as they are best known today; hence Ralegh's friend and fellow resident of the Tower is more often "Henry Percy" than "the ninth earl of Northumberland," but the second earl of Essex is usually simply "Essex," and never "Robert Devereux."

Spelling

In quotations, I have retained Elizabethan spelling, which has more life and certainly more individuality than our timidly prescriptive language of today. Occasionally problems of comprehension arise, and sometimes I have briefly glossed archaic or misleadingly spelled words within square brackets. Many difficulties will evaporate if the reader sets Webster aside and sounds out words phonetically. For Lady Ralegh's extremely inventive orthography, this is a necessity. I have silently updated Elizabethan usage with regard to "i" and "j" as well as "u" and "v."

Documentation

The lives of the two Walter Raleghs are so asymmetrical—the father's intensively studied and the son's largely unknown—that different approaches to documentation are called for. Ralegh's life has been the subject of many scholarly biographies, and it is not necessary to cite sources for well-established facts. For readers wishing more detailed commentary on many aspects of Ralegh's life, the best and most easily available place to start is the scrupulously researched work by Mark Nicholls and Penry Williams, first appearing as the "Sir Walter Ralegh" entry in the *Oxford Dictionary of National Biography* and later expanded into their adroitly written and more fully documented book, *Sir Walter Raleigh: In Life and Legend* (London: Continuum, 2011).

Of Wat Ralegh's short life, however, relatively little is known, and a number of the oft-repeated statements of supposed fact about him in biographies of his father are incorrect. Wat left fewer traces than one would wish—this graduate of Oxford appears not to have left a single piece of extant writing (except for his firm signature, which is reproduced in this volume). The dearth of evidence makes Wat's surviving traces precious, and I have attempted to bring to bear everything that is relevant. Especially with regard to Wat's relationship with his father, the documentary evidence has been supplemented with what I hope is judicious, adequately-flagged inference—based on a lifetime of experience as a son, a father of sons, and a student of Elizabethan culture.

Endnotes

Finally, and they are a final consideration, are the endnotes. I assume that they will be passed over by readers, since they usually do not convey information beyond supplying the specific source I have drawn on to make a point. There will, however, be readers who wish to explore sources of information for themselves, or who desire assurance that evidence actually exists for statements I have presented as facts. The endnotes are for them.

Introduction

Following his execution in 1618, the abundance of material circulating about Ralegh prompted a Londoner to observe that "We are so full still of Sir Walter Raleigh that almost every day brings foorth somewhat in this kind."[1] Four hundred years later, the flow of ink shows no sign of subsiding. This is a charismatic man who lived as if he were on a stage and memorably died on one. His activities were numerous and notable: dashing suitor of Queen Elizabeth, courtier, soldier, privateer, poet, explorer, colonist, propagandist for empire, historian, parliamentarian, horticulturist, chemist, and, finally, noble victim of King James. But there is a cost in chronicling this fascinating public activity. Biographers have allowed his emotional life—and especially his family relations—to slip into shadow. Indeed, some of the older biographies treat his family as if it were an embarrassing blemish in a life that was otherwise exemplary in its heroism. Fortunately, some successful expeditions into this domestic *terra incognita* have been undertaken in recent years, most notably a pioneering biography of his devoted and indomitable wife, Lady Elizabeth (Throckmorton) Ralegh.[2] But much remains unexplored.

The emptiest territory on our map of Ralegh is surprisingly central: his complex relationship with his son and heir, Walter junior ("Wat" within his family and in the pages to follow). This inattention is serious because his love for his eldest son and namesake may have been the most deeply felt personal attachment of his life. Certainly the aim of leaving Wat an ample patrimony was one of this restless, many-sided man's most abiding commitments.

Of course Wat invariably makes an appearance in biographies of Ralegh, but always too fleetingly to reveal his importance to his father. Beyond these brief accounts, which are based largely on oft-repeated anecdotes, he is scarcely known at all. The degree of Wat's present obscurity can be inferred from Wikipedia's Disambiguation feature for "Walter Raleigh," where Sir Walter is distinguished from a Stuart clergyman (his nephew) and a Victorian literary critic as well as from an essay, a hotel, and a renowned steam locomotive—but not from his namesake. A late-seventeenth-century painting epitomizes and in a small way contributes to Wat's displacement.[3] It copies the charming and revealing Elizabethan portrait of the two Walter Raleghs that serves as this book's cover, but with one major change: while closely reproducing the image of the father, it removes the son completely. The aim of the present volume is to return Wat to the picture.

Despite the extreme brevity of his life (from late October 1593 to 2 January 1618), Wat Ralegh left many more traces than his father's chroniclers have found, or perhaps desired to find. New documents have come to light concerning his alarming feuds and duels, which often led to his incarceration and were frequent enough to qualify as addictive. His truculence was not confined to male opponents, for new evidence shows that he was convicted of assault against Thomasine Ostler, a feisty young widow with close family connections to the King's Men, Shakespeare's theatrical company. Following this conviction, Wat was confined to the Marshalsea prison for failure to pay his hefty fine, and—not for the first time—his father came to the rescue. Wat was freed through Ralegh's intervention, as previously unknown legal documents reveal, and he fled England by joining his father's ill-starred second expedition to Guiana (1617).

The life of Wat Ralegh that comes into focus is certainly not the life his father had envisioned for him. To be sure, he attended Oxford and graduated with a B.A., as Ralegh wished, and we now know that as well he matriculated at Leiden, one of the most respected universities in Protestant Europe. But Wat appears to have engaged in very little academic study at either institution. His energies were dedicated to the pursuit of "violent exercises," as his Oxford tutor complained in an inadequately examined exchange of letters with his worried father. Ralegh's deep engagement with his son—always marked by grave concern for his future—is apparent in the fascinating range of writing he addressed to Wat: an eloquent exhortation before his own expected (but delayed) execution, a poem beginning jauntily and ending with a gallows, and an odd treatise of paternal advice. His concern is also to be found in contexts where it is not explicit, such as the digressive essay condemning dueling that he inserted in his *History of the World* at the start of Wat's extended eruption of swordsmanship.

For the first nine years of Wat's life, the name he shared with his father encouraged the two of them (and especially Ralegh) to imagine the boy's future life as a natural, even inevitable, extension of his father's. In this same-named, mutual identification, Wat would inherit honor and wealth from his father, and Ralegh would live beyond the grave in the accomplishments of his son. In a letter to his wife, Ralegh compresses the dream into a few pregnant words: "He is parte of me and I live in him."[4] In the early years, the paternal fantasy of replication was promising, as Wat inherited his father's grey eyes, curly hair, and well-knit body.

As the years went by, however, it became increasingly evident to Ralegh that Wat was refusing the path laid out for him. There is a distinct, perhaps timeless familiarity to their relationship: an imposing but loving father attempts to leave a traditional patrimony for a son who wishes to escape from his progenitor's long shadow. Also, in a disturbing twist, Ralegh realized that his son was beginning to exhibit some embarrassing similarities to his own youthful self, embarrassing because they reflected behavior of his own that he no longer wished to acknowledge, thus giving "I live in him" a darker, unintended meaning. Ralegh would have blanched had he heard an Elizabethan equivalent to Nietzsche's dictum that "What was silent in the father speaks in the son, and I have often found the son the unveiled secret of the father."[5]

After Ralegh's conviction for treason, serious divisions between father and son began to open up. What may have been a conventional frostiness between father and adolescent son was exacerbated as Ralegh was tried for treason and found guilty, allowing the government to strip away from him his wealth, estate, and social standing. Over time, their division became transformed into distance between them, with Ralegh remaining confined to the Tower while Wat moved to Tower Hill, then to Oxford and ultimately the Continent. It is difficult to say what the lad was searching for unless it was distance itself, a life entirely his own. His thirst for individuality is clear, whether he is indulging in the pleasures of "straunge company" at Oxford, mocking religious customs in France, or developing impressive skills as a self-possessed duelist in the low countries. Wat defined himself against others, and his father's well-intentioned (if misguided) attempts to provide direction for him served only to strengthen his resistance to paternal authority.

One benefit of returning Wat to the picture is that his lively presence illuminates the person behind the carefully poised image presented by his father. Ralegh is never more familiarly human than in the rapidly changing and increasingly challenged role he played in the family as father and husband. To a degree increasingly difficult for us to imagine, paternal authority and patrilineal values permeated the culture that shaped Ralegh's early hopes for his son and his understanding of his wife. But with his downfall at the accession of King James—not long after the double portrait was painted—Ralegh's place of pride in his society and in his family suffered greatly. During her husband's long, crippling imprisonment in the Tower of London, Lady Ralegh vigorously assumed many aspects of the traditional paternal role of defender and breadwinner for the family, which now included a baby boy, Carew. Wat Ralegh grew into adolescence in a world for which he and his suddenly superseded father were not prepared.

As one traces the intricately interwoven lives of the two Walter Raleghs, an ironic pattern insistently declares itself: the father's unwavering concern for his son results in unintended and unfortunate consequences for both of them. Their story unfolds as a tragedy in which Ralegh strives mightily to create an outcome that his very actions serve to undermine. In a resolution that smacks of the theatre, Wat ended a period of bitter filial estrangement by agreeing to join his father's desperate expedition in search of a goldmine in Guiana, an attempt to undo an earlier voyage that had failed when Wat was a toddler. Supportively but ill-advisedly, Ralegh placed his undisciplined, much-loved son in command of a troop of soldiers on the vessel that he had built for the expedition and christened the *Destiny*. In a way they could not have foreseen, father and son had finally become one, their lives entwined in a single, shared tragedy. The present book is an attempt to honor their relationship by understanding it.

• ONE •

What's in a Son's Name?

On November 1st, 1593, a company made its unhurried way through the rolling green hills of Dorset, from Sherborne Castle to the small village of Lillington some three miles to the south. Sir Walter Ralegh was conveying his infant son—probably no more than two weeks old—to be baptized and duly christened.[1] Presumably Lady Ralegh was not present, since after childbirth women were expected to lie in for a month before being ritually "churched" and thus allowed (or perhaps forced) to re-enter the public world. Twenty-five years later, this father and son would undertake another journey—a desperate naval expedition—without Lady Ralegh. Only a broken husband, facing imminent death, would return to her.

An important moment in the baptismal ceremony was the godparents' response to the minister's query about the name of the infant. Often the name they supplied was that of the godparent of the child's gender, symbolizing the spiritual kinship between them. Thus, although the identities of godparents usually were not recorded in parish registers, sometimes they can be deduced. It is a safe inference, for instance, that Hamnet and Judith Sadler were the godparents of Hamnet and Judith, the twins born in 1585 to their Stratford-upon-Avon friends, the Shakespeares. At Lillington, however, the identity of the godfather cannot be inferred since the infant received his father's given name. The Bishop's Transcript of the (no longer extant) register records the baptism of "Walter the sonne of Sir Walter Rawley."[2]

It may seem odd that the usually self-dramatizing Ralegh chose for the ceremony the out-of-the-way parish church of St. Martin of Tours rather than the ancient, magnificently fan-vaulted Abbey in Sherborne, where they lived. To be sure, the church at Lillington was—and remains—beautifully situated and sturdily picturesque, small in scale but with a powerful barrel vault surmounted by a substantial square tower topped by gargoyles. The fifteenth-century baptismal font at which Wat was christened still survives, and it, too, is attractive in its ageless simplicity. But Ralegh chose the venue not for its aesthetics but rather for its removed location. Since he held the lease to the manor at Lillington—a gift from Queen Elizabeth—he exercised considerable authority in the village, and the event could be as private as he wished. Ralegh had good reason to think the spectacle of a conventionally lavish ceremony would have angered his queen, since only a year earlier he and his wife had deceived her, resulting in their disgrace at court, imprisonment in the Tower, and—upon being freed—banishment from the royal presence.

The Raleghs' infant son was born into a childless household, and Wat remained its only child until the birth of a brother conceived in the Tower of London a dozen years later.[3] For the first half of his life, then, Wat was his parents' sole living child, and thus he was always Sir Walter's heir apparent, the primary focus of their hopes and fears. But he was not the first child born to the Raleghs. In late March 1592, Lady Elizabeth Ralegh had given birth to a male infant named Damerei, who lived for only half a year and may have been carried off by the fierce visitation of the plague that killed many people and closed London's theatres. Wat's birth must have been especially welcome because Damerei's entry into the world was associated with—and had helped to bring about—calamitous consequences for the Raleghs. His birth was catastrophic for his parents' fortunes because it provided incontrovertible evidence of the disloyalty they had committed against their royal benefactor.

It is no exaggeration to say, as Ralegh's enemies were eager to remind him, that his great success at court was entirely the gift of the queen. He was a younger son from an established family that was respected among the West Country gentry but not wealthy. Ralegh's attempts to make his own way were marked by courage and ambition, but little initial success. At only fifteen or sixteen he joined Protestant forces in the brutal civil war in France, and upon returning home he took up the hunt for plunder on the seas, an enterprise in which his extended family had considerable experience. But Ralegh's ship found no prizes, and after a spell at Oxford and a fruitless attempt to insinuate himself at court, he joined the land service as a captain in the bloody subjugation of Ireland.

In his late twenties, he was ambitious, brave, and well-acquainted with danger but had not found a way to make his mark. His opportunity came when he was sent from Ireland bearing documents for policy-makers at court, and he made the most of it. By dint of being tall and well formed, Ralegh may have caught the queen's attention, but he held it with his sharp mind. As a rival courtier acknowledged, he had "a strong wit naturally, and a better judgment, with a bold and plausible tongue whereby he could set out his part to the best advantage ... and he had gotten the Queen's ear in a trice."[4] Soon he was enjoying the fruits of royal favor.

Courtiers were expected to pay their respects to the queen in a display of conspicuous courtship, and Ralegh played the part to perfection, being unmarried, strikingly handsome, and an accomplished poet to boot. In quick succession he received an impressive array of royal gifts and grants, including a knighthood, some forty thousand acres of land in Ireland, and the very lucrative patent for licensing vintners to sell wine, which became a significant source of income for this critic of drunkenness. Perhaps the zenith of Ralegh's meteoric rise occurred in 1591, when he became the captain of the guard, a long-coveted position that carried the responsibility of protecting the queen and offered the correlative reward of privileged access to her. Though he was roundly hated by better-born but less successful rivals, he had little to fear so long as he continued to enjoy Elizabeth's favor.

Within a year, however, Ralegh had outraged and alienated the queen. Unbeknownst to her, he had entered into an intimate relationship with another Elizabeth, a gentlewoman of the queen's privy chamber, Elizabeth Throckmorton. Queen Elizabeth invariably punished courtiers and ladies in waiting who entered into a blatant sexual relationship without her blessing, but the wrath that she directed at Ralegh and his secretly married wife was unprecedented. (That the queen herself arranged the relationship to keep her beloved Ralegh close to her is a recent invention of Hollywood.[5]) The queen had good reason to feel betrayed by Elizabeth Throckmorton, who had served her for seven years in a role that demanded and amply rewarded devotion, but Ralegh's humiliation of her would have stung more deeply. The lovers had not only hidden their relationship successfully, but, to make matters worse, Lady Ralegh had somehow contrived to conceal her pregnancy for her full term. An impressive portrait of the queen, the Rainbow Portrait at Hatfield House, depicts her wearing a gown decorated with ears and open eyes, signifying her all-knowing wisdom. In this instance, however, her omniscience was greatly exaggerated.

As if this effrontery were not sufficiently damning, the Raleghs compounded their offense by continuing their brazen charade even after the infant's birth, and when their deception was exposed they failed to throw themselves on the queen's mercy. For his part, Ralegh wrote impassioned, incoherent verses to her as the chaste but mutable moon-goddess Cynthia, employing his familiar but now inadvisable guise of faithful, spurned lover.

Perhaps he was writing for her eyes when, in a letter to his hard-headed colleague Sir Robert Cecil, he wondered if "All thos tymes past—the loves, the sythes [sighs], the sorrowes, the desires, can they not way [weigh] doune one frail misfortune."[6] As his euphemistic reference to his "frail misfortune" reveals, Ralegh was never inclined to accept responsibility for his failures, be they financial, military, or familial.

In August of 1592, Queen Elizabeth imprisoned the Raleghs—in separate quarters—in the Tower of London, a brief foretaste of the long imprisonment that her Scottish successor would impose on Ralegh. But his stay proved to be relatively brief. He had been in the Tower for a month when Elizabeth freed him under very special circumstances—she needed his expertise to protect the crown's share of an uncommonly rich prize seized in a privateering expedition he had organized. But Lady Ralegh had no such luck, and she was not released for another three months. By dint of redoubled effort, Ralegh struggled to regain his former stature, and with some success. Significantly, the queen did not replace him as captain of the guard and allowed him to occupy the post again five years later. But her animus toward her rival with the same name never abated. Lady Ralegh was never again admitted into the royal presence, nor did she ever express regret for her actions, much less apologize.

Why did the Raleghs risk their privileged positions and much of their livelihood by entering into their prohibited relationship? In the first place, Ralegh fell victim to an error that was common among the favorites of the queen—he exaggerated greatly his sway over her. But passion must have played its unruly part, and, more than usual, the court was the site of what an historian called "aristocratic concupiscence." In 1591, the attrition among Elizabeth's maids of honor was very high. By the end of the year she "lost half of her complement of maids," and their "mother"—the matron assigned to watch over them—was dismissed for corruption.[7]

But, beyond these common issues in the court environment, there may be more to the liaison—and subsequent marriage—of Ralegh and Bess Throckmorton. It is likely that the two of them shared a restive chafing, perhaps even a degree of resentment, at what must have seemed a commitment to endless service for the queen. He had been acting as her attentive suitor for a decade, and Elizabeth Throckmorton had waited attendance on her for almost as long, becoming in the process "the eldest of the maids of honour."[8] For the queen's female servitors, remaining plausibly maid-like—or at least unmarried—was a condition of employment. The emotional cost of this commitment to unmarried life was glaringly obvious to Bess Throckmorton when—perhaps around the beginning of her sexual involvement with Ralegh—the queen's long-time confidant Blanche Parry "died a maid in the eighty-two years of her age," after fifty-seven years of service.[9] For a woman who desired a full life and whose twenties were slipping away, such sacrificial devotion would not have been attractive.

For his part, Ralegh was approaching forty, an advanced age for a man who had taken—and would continue to take—many risks on land and sea. (That he was born to a fifty-year-old father—living a safe existence in the West Country—was no reason for him to dally.) In his traditional (male) view, the primary value of a family was as a means through which a man could perpetuate himself. Thus, in the *History of the World*, he declared that the desire to preserve our being—"to be that which we are"—expresses the law of nature that is manifested in "the desire of issue, with care to provide for them."[10] For Ralegh, the simple truth of the matter is that, since "the Father after his death lives in his children," it follows that (at least for a man) "the desire of life comprehends the desire of children." Begetting children was in his view a biological imperative, a means of sustaining selfhood. The most significant expression of this impulse, being the closest to himself, would be replication in a son.

As most Elizabethan gentlemen did, Ralegh conceived of a family's extension through time in patrilineal terms. In his *Instructions to His Son*, written in his long imprisonment in the Tower, he flatly expressed to Wat the patrilineal credo that "Wives were ordained to continue the generations of Men, not to transferre them, & diminish them, either in continuance, or abilitie; and therefore thy house and estate which liveth in thy Sonne, & not in thy Wife, is to be preferred."[11] This conception of women as ancillary to issues of male estate appears in Ralegh's only surviving will and last testament, which (as we will see) takes account of Lady Ralegh only in the most minimal terms. It is the continuity of the "generations of Men" that marks the prosperity of one's "house and estate." But, as we will have frequent occasion to observe, Ralegh was attracted to and chose to marry a very forceful woman, and a central thread of his story is provided by the dissonance between his generally patriarchal assumptions and the actual circumstances of his life.

In the patrilineal dispensation, fathers saw themselves and their sons—especially eldest sons—as ancestors in the making, links in a chain extending a family's name and estate from the distant past into an endless (male) future. Of course, this vision of a never-ending continuum of fathers and eldest sons was often punctured by familial realities, most egregiously failure in the male line. Through a legal instrument called an entail, would-be patriarchs attempted to guarantee their chosen succession by fixing the future ownership of their estates, but often to no avail. When the skeptical philosopher Michel de Montaigne remarked that "We take these male entails too much to heart. And we look forward to a ridiculous eternity for our names," his comment was as true for England as for his native France.[12]

Ralegh believed that, for better or worse, a father's actions will be judged by—and thus help to shape—the future generations of his offspring. Just as ancestors' fame serves as a spur to the virtue of their posterity, their shame will also live in the minds of their progeny. Thus, in his *Instructions to His Son*, Ralegh warns Wat against excessive drinking because "after thy death thou shalt only leave a shamefull infamy to thy posterity, who shall study to forget that such a one was their Father."[13] This patrilineal understanding of family relations was easily transferred to all history, and so in his "Preface" to the *History of the World* Ralegh remarks that "it is not the least debt that we owe unto History, that it hath made us acquainted with our dead Ancestors; and, out of the depth and darknesse of the earth, delivered us their memory and fame."[14] His emphasis on fame indicates that he has male lineage (and possibly himself) in mind when he speaks of "Ancestors." Later in the seventeenth century an admirer of Ralegh quotes this passage at the beginning of his exclusively patrilineal history of his own family.[15] In this outlook, to speak of "male ancestors" would have been a redundancy—ancestors were progenitors, forefathers.

It is surprising that, despite his emphasis on patrilineal continuity, Ralegh seems to have had little connection with his own father, a gentleman also bearing the given name of Walter. Indeed, there is nothing to indicate that, between his return from France in the mid–1570s and his father's death in 1581, Ralegh ever had dealings with him, or that the two even came into direct contact. Given his frequent comments on how ancestors beget either honor or shame in their descendants, it is interesting that Ralegh mentions his father only rarely, and then in factual contexts. Thus, in a farewell letter to Lady Ralegh before his expected execution in 1603, he speaks of two possibilities for his final resting place. His second choice is to be buried "in Excester [Exeter] church near my father and mother," but his preference is to be interred at his beloved estate at Sherborne in Dorset.[16] He had acquired and greatly improved the Sherborne property in the hope that it would become the ancestral seat for Wat and his progeny, and his preference is to be interred as a patrilineal originator rather than a son and mere member of an established line. With some justice, Ralegh saw himself as a founder rather than an inheritor because he had created his estate without the benefit of a patrimony.

Ralegh had been denied an inheritance by an essential protection of patrilineal continuity, the observance of primogeniture. But he was not soured on the custom. Common throughout most of England, the custom of settling the paternal estate upon the eldest son exerted a strong pull in the West Country, where the time-honored project of the landed gentry was twofold: to protect their often modest estates from division among their children and to augment them through advantageous marriages.[17] (Daughters and younger brothers had to be content with, respectively, dowries and testamentary bequests that would not appreciably diminish the family's precious holdings of land.) Ralegh's father was the eldest son in an old and well-connected but not especially wealthy family, and he inherited several estates when he came of age. The elder Ralegh's assets steadily diminished over his long life, and upon his death there was little to bequeath to his many sons, to say nothing of his daughters and third wife.

The child who would become Sir Walter Ralegh was the last of his father's four sons and thus last in the primogenitural sweepstakes. They had been born in two pairs (their mothers being the elder Ralegh's first and third wives) separated by roughly two decades. In accordance with tradition, the senior Walter concerned himself with providing a patrimony for his eldest son, George, who inherited two manors upon his father's death in 1581.[18] When George died in 1597 (having outlived his younger brother John and his father's third wife) the family properties passed on—finally—to the future Sir Walter and his older brother Carew. But the cupboard was almost bare for the younger sons in their crucially formative years.

The only record of the elder Ralegh's provision of financial support for his two younger sons dates from their childhood. In 1560, when little Walter was six and Carew ten, Walter Sr. purchased—in his own name and in theirs—an interest in the tithes of fish and larks at the nearby manor of Sidmouth (Devon).[19] This investment appears to have made a modest but dependable annual return, and eighteen years later the three Raleghs disposed of their interest in these tithes—which had cost £7 s.10—for £60. This was surely a welcome infusion of cash but (after being split three ways) not exactly a princely patrimony for the young men.

Ralegh always knew that he would have to make his own way and that the struggle would not be easy. In a shrewd assessment, a contemporary courtier derived Ralegh's restlessness from this primal privation, saying of his early career that "he stayed not long in a place, and being the youngest brother and the house diminished in its patrimony, he foresaw his own destiny, that he was first to roll through want and [the] disability to subsist before he could come to a repose...."[20] Ultimately, he could come to a (forced) repose only within the walls of the Tower, but even then his mind ranged imperiously through time and space in *The History of the World* that he constructed.

Evidence of Ralegh's conception of himself as a self-begotten founder who began with nothing is apparent in the "Epistle Dedicatorie" that John Hooker, a supplicatory West Country historian, addressed to him in the second edition (1587) of Raphael Holinshed's *Chronicles*. Hooker's dedication begins by asserting the ancient origins of the Ralegh line, claiming that a noble ancestor, Sir John de Raleigh, had "maried the daughter and heire to sir Roger D'amerei," who was "a noble man and of great linage."[21] (Ralegh probably derived the name of his first son, Damerei, from this passage.) Hooker proceeds to say that the family's splendid beginning was followed by a decline in which "by little and little the honour and estimation of your noble and worthie ancestors seemed at length to be buried in oblivion, and as it were extinguished and to be utterlie forgotten as though it had never beene." But "it hath pleased God" to resurrect the family through Ralegh, who is likened to the biblical Joseph (another dispossessed but heroic son who eclipsed many older brothers) as "a hope to restore the decaied house of your sept [line] and familie." This is less conventional praise of a family line than diminishment of his immediate predecessors to create a contrasting glorification of Ralegh himself. We can safely assume that Hooker's dismissal of Ralegh's closest forebears met with the approval of the heaven-sent patron.

The most immediate of these undistinguished progenitors was Sir Walter's father, yet another Walter Ralegh, who spent his time in the pursuit of what a biographer terms "the usual activities of a landed gentleman" from the West Country, such as financing privateering and piracy (a distinction without much difference), engaging in lawsuits, and discharging various public duties such as levying troops and organizing local coastal defenses.[22] His undertakings, unlike those of his restive son, were not distinguished by conspicuous risk-taking or creativity. It is revealing that, despite the elder Ralegh's three-year service as acting Vice-Admiral of Devon and his ownership of several privateering vessels, his biographer remarks that "there is no evidence of his actually going to sea."[23] The senior Ralegh's naval battles were fought for the spoils of privateering and confined to the High Court of Admiralty. The son's ambitious, questing nature seems to have been entirely absent from the father, and their difference in temperament must have been exacerbated by the considerable gap in age that separated them. The senior Walter was fifty years old when his namesake was born, and he was already comfortably retired when his son boldly came of age.

Two anecdotes about the elder Walter Ralegh, both related in the updated edition of Holinshed's *Chronicles* that John Hooker dedicated to Sir Walter, depict inglorious behavior that his honor-obsessed son would not have been proud of. During the religious struggles of Edward VI's reign, Hooker writes, "a certeine gentleman named Walter Raleigh" came upon an old woman who, with rosary beads in hand, was on her way to celebrate mass. Ralegh's father sharply reprimanded her, warning that "as a good Christian woman and an obedient subject" she should follow the reformed church lest she be punished.[24] Unfortunately for Ralegh, the aggrieved woman aroused her gathered fellow-parishioners and "in all hast[e] like a sort of wasps they fling out of the church" in pursuit of the haughty gentleman. Ralegh was forced to take refuge in a chapel and, had he not been rescued by some mariners who accompanied him, "he had beene in great danger of his life, and like to have beene murdered." In another unflattering episode chronicled by Hooker, the elder Ralegh was later imprisoned in a church tower during the West Country uprising, and upon gaining their freedom he and some friends helped themselves to many valuable articles of worship, which they may or may not have returned after being confronted with their theft.[25]

Notwithstanding his patrilineal orientation, Ralegh may well have come to realize that his vital inheritance came from his mother's side of the family. When Katherine Gilbert married Ralegh's father, she was a widow with three sons, all of whom were in the process of distinguishing themselves in military, exploratory, and intellectual pursuits. The remarkable Sir Humphrey Gilbert is the best-known of the three, and in many ways he provided a template for his younger and ultimately more famous half-brother: many years of dedicated service to the queen, experience in the French civil wars (his first cousin had married a Huguenot leader), ruthless deeds in Ireland, and a commitment to colonial expansion. Humphrey Gilbert's personal mottoes—*Quid Non* ("Why not") and *Mutare vel timere sperno* ("I scorn change or fear")—expressed an attractive insouciance, and his well-publicized willingness to risk his life for fame and country made a deep impression on his half-brother. After comparing Katherine Gilbert Ralegh's five sons to the two undistinguished sons born to the elder Ralegh's first wife, a modern biographer of the family entertains "little doubt that she contributed much more to the genius of her famous youngest son than did his father."[26]

The single recorded story about Ralegh's mother indicates a courage and principle that make her husband look, at best, distinctly conventional.[27] In his *Actes and Monuments*, the protestant martyrologist John Foxe recounted how "the wife of Walter Ralegh, a woman of noble wit and godly opinions," visited in prison an uneducated woman named Agnes Prest, who had been condemned to die at the stake for supporting the reformed religion. In this visit, Katherine Ralegh showed courage of conviction at a dangerous time. Upon returning to her husband, Katherine reported that Agnes Prest spoke "so godly and earnestly" that "if God were not with her she could not speak such things." In evident wonderment, Katherine added that "I was not able to answer her, I who can read and she cannot." It is easy to see the openness to experience that would come to characterize her son's energetic mind.

The distance of Sir Walter from his father, which has gone curiously unexamined by biographers, raises questions about the significance of the name that he chose to give his new son and heir. In a broad historical perspective, Ralegh's bestowing his own name on his son could be seen as unremarkable because the sixteenth and seventeenth centuries witnessed a steadily rising incidence of fathers naming a son (often a first son) after themselves.[28] Moreover, "Walter" was one of the most common forenames in the recent family line, being borne by both Sir Walter's great grandfather and father. So there was ample precedent for Ralegh to name his son after himself, as his father had done. But he did so with a characteristic twist of his own: it was to his sole living son that he gave his own name. By contrast, the elder Walter Ralegh had been in so little haste to attach his given name to a child that he waited until the arrival of a fourth son—twenty seven years after the birth of his first—to do so.

By naming his last son "Walter," the father of Sir Walter was honoring and continuing one of the family's venerable Christian names, a name that happened to be his own. With Sir Walter, however, the impulse for bestowing his own name on his child seems considerably more self-referential, and certainly less emphatically patrilineal than the "Damerei" he bestowed on his first son. Ralegh appears to have named *his* son Walter after himself, the familiar name more an affirmation of his own creative vitality than obeisance to his same-named forebears, including his father. Following his recent calamity at court, Ralegh's conferring of his own name was probably part of his vigorous campaign to reassert his identity and reclaim his prior standing. But a dimension of egotism is involved in Ralegh's choice that goes beyond the recovery of his former status.

It is never far from patriarchal thinking, especially in an age of royalism and primogeniture, that one's male heir may—probably *should*—become a second self, participating in and extending one's essential being. An eldest son is easily conceived of as a sort of crown prince who inherits his regal progenitor's domain and extends his reign. Perhaps Ralegh's fancy was fed by the magical potency widely attributed to names (*nomen est omen*), which inclined him to imagine that a shared name might become self-fulfilling, or at least an encouragement for Wat to replicate his father. Certainly, there is abundant evidence of a father's dream of replication in the double portrait of Ralegh and Wat, in which the boy's close mirroring of the man's pose appears to be unprecedented in British painting, to say nothing of the letter to his wife (written shortly before his scheduled execution) in which he asks her to "let my sonne be thy beloved for he is parte of me and I live in him, and the difference is but in the number and not in the kinde."[29]

Apparently Ralegh did not foresee the likely negative consequences (for Wat) of naming his heir after himself. Even without the added burden of carrying his father's given name, Elizabethan sons faced the expectation to model themselves on and indeed to measure up to their fathers, an expectation voiced in the pulpit and hinted at in humanist proverbs such as *Patris est filius* ("He is his father's son") and *Qualis pater, talis filius* ("Like father, like son").[30] But for "Waltherus Ralegh filius"—as Wat would sign an important legal document underneath his father's and mother's signatures—the weight of the paternal name would prove to be burdensome, preceding him and invariably creating expectations (especially unpleasant after Ralegh's conviction for treason when Wat was ten). Perhaps his own father's lack of notable accomplishment blinded Ralegh to the pressure he was placing on his son by giving him a paternal name so widely celebrated and despised. Wat was to suffer the fate lamented by Theodore Roosevelt, Jr.: that he would never have a name of his own.[31]

The poet and dramatist Ben Jonson memorably articulated the challenge facing sons of famous fathers when he observed that "Greatness of name in the father oft-times helps not forth but o'erwhelms the son; they stand too near one another. The shadow kills the growth…."[32] In the case of the two Walter Raleghs, the "greatness of name in the father" extends to the son's given as well as his family name, and it may be that Jonson had in mind Wat's uneasy existence within his father's encompassing shadow. He knew the two Raleghs—and especially Wat—very well. A decade before his comment, as we will see in due course, Jonson had served as the tutor and markedly dissolute chaperon of Wat on an eighteen-month, ill-advised tour of the Continent.

But Wat's shared name only intensified a deeper problem: that his father's fame was overwhelming because it derived from his remarkably varied and passionate engagement with the world. His father's precedence was ubiquitous. While there is no documentary evidence that Wat ever directly articulated his dilemma, we may catch a glimpse of it in an image created by Franz Kafka, a young man with a father perceived to be overbearing. In his impotently angry and apparently undelivered *Letter to His Father*, Kafka remarked that "Sometimes I imagine the map of the world spread out and you stretched diagonally across it. And I feel as if I could consider living in only those regions that either are not covered by you or are not within your reach."[33] Kafka's imagination opened up regions far beyond the little familial and mercantile world controlled by his father, but the boundless energy of Wat Ralegh's father had left few realms—geographical or intellectual—untouched and uncolonized. No matter the goal to which Wat might address himself, the father whose name he bore was likely to have been there first.

• Two •

*The Son of His Father—
and His Mother*

Indulging in a novelistic gesture, one of Ralegh's first biographers assured his readers that after their wedding Sir Walter and Elizabeth Ralegh "lived together ever after in the most exemplary degree of conjugal harmony."[1] Certainly their marriage stood the test of time, and in many ways it grew stronger over the years. But the biographer's phrasing misrepresents an important reality: that the time in which they actually "lived together" amounted to a distinct minority of their married life. For fully half their married years, the walls of the Tower separated them, even if family stays of considerable length were sometimes allowed. If we add to this central separation his long voyages to Guiana before and immediately after his incarceration by James, together with the myriad commitments that carried him away on military engagements and affairs of state too numerous to list, the Raleghs lived apart for upwards of three-quarters of their married days. Even when they were together, distance left its mark.

With the obvious exception of Ralegh's two incarcerations in the Tower, these separations were largely volitional on his part, suggesting a centrifugal impulse away from domestic relation. The first detachment occurred soon after their clandestine wedding, when the newlyweds went their separate ways, or rather when Ralegh went his. While his wife prepared for imminent childbirth at the London home of her nervous brother Arthur Throckmorton, Ralegh threw himself into organizing a major expedition against Panama and the Spanish treasure fleet. In his mind, the expedition and the childbirth had a strategic connection; he hoped the fury of the queen at learning of his and his wife's betrayal would be ameliorated, or perhaps even forgotten, in her pleasure at receiving the tribute of plundered wealth. But perhaps the design had a less conscious attraction as well: it would allow him to escape—at least for the moment—from the looming crisis born of contradictory commitments to two quite formidable Elizabeths. (Compared to facing the queen's wrath, marauding in the Caribbean represented relative safety.) In the event, the queen was probably still unsuspecting of the marriage when she recalled her favorite before he could put himself at martial risk, but the conflation of pursuing public expeditions and fleeing domestic engagement is clear.

Ralegh's ability to escape from emotional uncertainty by throwing himself into a major project was soon to manifest itself again. By the time the Panama expedition returned to England, the queen had discovered his secret and imprisoned him in the Tower. Fortunately for him, the fleet returned with an enormously valuable prize, a Spanish treasure ship (the *Madre de Dios*) stuffed with luxury goods. After the ship's return, the valuables were quickly being pillaged—pirates will be pirates—at the expense of the queen, a major investor in the expedition. Ralegh was quick to buy his freedom, promising the queen no less than £80,000 from his share if he were allowed to leave the Tower and to oversee the distribution of the loot. In a letter to a friend, Robert Cecil perceptively observed Ralegh at work, noting that his "heart is broken, as he is extremely pensive, unless he is busied, in which he can toil terribly."[2] For Ralegh, immersion in laborious projects was always a salve for anxiety and sorrow.

In what was perhaps an unspoken exchange, Ralegh apparently had agreed to marriage and Elizabeth Throckmorton had agreed to keep the marriage secret. For both of them, subterfuge was necessary, yet Ralegh's avoidance of his wife and newborn child was so thorough as to be almost indistinguishable from downright denial. When Damerei Ralegh was born (29 March 1592) in Arthur Throckmorton's London residence, Ralegh was in the city arranging his expedition. He was not present at the delivery, and his brother-in-law's diary makes no mention of his presence in the days afterwards. More notably, when the baptism of Damerei was celebrated two weeks later, Ralegh was not present. His absence is especially significant, since someone had persuaded his rival, the earl of Essex, to risk the queen's eventual anger by standing as one of Damerei's godfathers.[3] (The other godfather was the baby's uncle Arthur.) Only a single occasion can be documented in which Ralegh actually saw his son before the baby's unrecorded death. On 28 May 1592 the infant's wet nurse brought her charge to Durham House, where Ralegh interrupted his preparations for Panama by making his firstborn's acquaintance.[4] Clearly Damerei must have embodied a much more exigent, felt reality for his mother than he did for his detached and distracted father.

Two • The Son of His Father—and His Mother

A valuable glimpse into Ralegh's denial of his wife and child is afforded by a letter he wrote to Sir Robert Cecil, a colleague who carefully archived his correspondence and will appear in many of the pages to follow. Cecil was an important backer of the Panama expedition, and most of the letter involves arrangements for financing the fleet, which was being prepared to sail. As if it were an afterthought, Ralegh closes by delivering to his colleague a categorical, bold-faced lie. Realizing that (well-founded) rumors about himself and Elizabeth Throckmorton were making the rounds, Ralegh flatly dismisses the possibility "of a marriage and I knowe not what."[5] After beseeching Cecil "to suppress what you can any such mallicious report" (an interesting request given his own suppression of the truth), he ends with a foolish and desperate lie: "For I protest before God there is none on the face of the yearth [earth] that I would be fastned unto." (Though for some time they maintained a collegial relationship, Cecil knew that Ralegh's word could never be trusted.) In the context of the forthcoming expedition, Ralegh's choice of the vivid "fastned" indicates an element of wishfulness in his denial—to be married is to be held fast to a commitment offering little horizon for adventure. And desires die. A decade and a half later, he was to warn his son Wat that "if thou marry for Beauty, thou bindest thy selfe for all thy life for that which perchance will neither last nor please thee one yeer…."[6]

It is fair to say, with no implication of philandering, that Ralegh did not behave as if he were married. There is no evidence that, during the four months in which Lady Ralegh remained in the Tower after his release, he acknowledged his wife's existence, much less attempted to intervene on her behalf. More revealingly, as Lady Ralegh's biographer noted, when she was finally freed from the Tower, it is likely that the person responsible for winning her freedom was her brother, not her husband.[7] Nor did she appear in the text of his letters, even though anyone who mattered would have known of their dalliance and marriage. Even if we assume that many of his letters from this disrupted time were lost, it is significant that Lady Ralegh was not acknowledged in Ralegh's extant correspondence until some three years after their marriage, and that in a postscript (to Cecil) following a discussion of another expedition.

Since no early letters between the Raleghs survive—and indeed precious few survive from their later years—it is impossible to know how in their early days they represented their feelings for each other. Luckily a letter from the Tower survives in which Lady Ralegh writes to her good, well-connected friend Elizabeth Heneage, vividly expressing her unequivocal commitment to her husband at this trying time. It may be that her correspondent had implied a criticism of Ralegh, for Bess resoundingly states her loyalty to him. Her pride in being his wife is palpable when she declares that "I never desiared nor never wolde desiar my lebbarti [liberty] with out the good likeking [liking] ne [nor] advising of Sur W R."[8] After asking her friend to visit her, she ends the letter by observing memorably (of herself and Ralegh) that "wee are trew with in ourselfes I can asur you." If she felt slighted by her husband's failure to acknowledge her, or doubted his commitment, she shows no sign of it. Despite her imprisonment, which was followed by a permanent banishment from Elizabeth's court, she possessed great strength of character, facing the future with confidence in herself and her husband. Her faith would be tested but never broken.

Wat Ralegh was born to a marriage that had survived severe strain and suffered deep bruises in the process. Certainly the birth of a second son so soon after the death of Damerei was cause for parental rejoicing and hope for a new future. But the tension in the Raleghs' relationship between the vitally energetic outreach of his ambitions and her commitment to a domestic inwardness persisted. Effectively banished to his native West Country, Ralegh might well have been content to cultivate his gardens and his family—if he had not been Ralegh. Instead, a furious desire to recreate his premarital good fortunes took hold of him. Since he was now *persona non grata* at court, his chances for fame and wealth lay beyond England in dangerous expeditions (military and exploratory) that took him from his family for months on end. And even when Ralegh remained in England, he was often not to be found at the family's Dorset home. Increasingly, he spent time at Durham House, his center of operations in London, where he dwelt while supervising the financial and logistical preparations for his voyages.

A major distraction of Ralegh from his home and family came only too quickly. When Wat was only three months old, his father threw himself into organizing an expedition to search for gold and glory in Guiana. It is not known what Lady Ralegh said to her husband about his plan, but she was sufficiently worried to write a very frank letter Sir Robert Cecil, a supporter of the Guiana expedition. She entreats Cecil that "I hope for my sake you will rather draw sur watar [Sir Walter] towardes the est then heulp hyme forward toward the soonsett [sunset]."[9] Or as she says in plain English (and still resolutely phonetic spelling), "I humbelle beseech you rather stay him then furdar [further] him." Rather bitterly, this mother of a recently deceased infant proceeds to contrast "you greate counselares [who] ar so full of new councels" with their helpless wives like herself, who "have bought sorrow at a high price." As she says rather drily, her fear is that new undertakings "will but multiply misseri, of wich we have allredi felte sufficiant." Fearful of angering her husband and despairing of changing his mind, she has resorted to pleading with his patron to restrain him. In the event, Ralegh did return safely to his intact family after an expedition lasting seven months, but without the golden success that he continued to pursue.

Lady Ralegh's premonition of danger approaching her unprotected family came true even before Ralegh's Guiana expedition could lift anchor. Once again, the evidence comes in the form of a letter to Robert Cecil, this time from Ralegh himself. The letter (dated 20 September 1594) marks a watershed in Ralegh's surviving correspondence because it contains his first written references both to Lady Ralegh and to Wat. As with his earlier letter to Cecil, which ends with his denial of being "fastned" to a wife, Ralegh dwells mainly on arrangements for an upcoming expedition (to Guiana) but adds an agitated postscript: "I had a post this morning from Sherburne. The plauge [plague] is in the town very hote. My Bess is on[e] way sent, hir sonne another way, and I am in great troble ther withe."[10] (At eleven months, Wat would likely still have been on the breast, and it appears that his wet nurse fled with him in one direction while Lady Ralegh—for whatever reason—fled in another.) Since Damerei had died during a visitation of the plague, it is easy to imagine the "great troble" that Ralegh felt, and yet the planning for the voyage went ahead as he prepared to sail still farther away from a family already beyond his intervention.

There is no doubt that the Raleghs deeply loved their little son, Wat, but for the two of them that love took very different forms. Like that of many of his male peers, Ralegh's concern was oriented to the patrilineal future, more focused on providing a patrimony for his mature years than engaging with him as a child. Yet despite Ralegh's lack of involvement in the everyday life of his infant, it would be a mistake to think he was negligent in his concern. With some justice, he would have defended the Guiana expedition as an attempt to provide for the future wellbeing of his son and his house, whereas Lady Ralegh clearly saw it as a threat to her family. It is telling that Ralegh's letter about the plague refers to his wife as "*my* Bess" but to their endangered infant as "*hir* sonne," which suggests his realization that her bond with him is more intimate than his own. In legal documents, however, Wat is invariably *my* son.

After their banishment from court, the Raleghs drew emotional sustenance from two sources: their new dwelling at Sherborne and Wat, who was born there. For Ralegh in particular, the two were very closely related—as his son and heir, Wat was (he thought) the destined owner of the estate he was struggling to possess outright. Before Sherborne, Ralegh remained the landless younger brother he had always been, notwithstanding a brilliant decade at court. He did not possess an estate in England, an ignoble deficiency not remedied by the queen's grant of thousands of acres in Ireland. In the first blush of his success, he had attempted to buy the manor in Devon that had been his birthplace and (rented) childhood home, but its owner was obdurate in his refusal to negotiate.[11] Clearly, Ralegh required an estate commensurate with his power and dignity, an estate that would provide a suitable patrimony for a son who would be his link to patrilineal immortality.

In the late 1580s, a beautifully situated property at Sherborne in northern Dorset caught Ralegh's eye. The location was perfect—a day's ride from London while firmly anchored in his native West Country. Sherborne also had the considerable virtue of being on the main road from London to Plymouth, the port of departure for many maritime expeditions. Despite the dilapidated condition of the Norman castle, Ralegh saw the potential of the property and successfully urged the queen to prise it from its owner, the bishop of Salisbury. The saga of the Raleghs' dealings over the Sherborne estate stretches over more than twenty years, with twists and turns best appreciated by students of Tudor property law. For now, suffice it to say that the family engaged in complex legal maneuvering concerning the possession of Sherborne: first in a successful campaign culminating in their ownership, followed by an unsuccessful attempt to retain it after Ralegh's full conviction for treason, and finally (when there was no alternative) seeking the most favorable terms before relinquishing it to King James and his favorites.[12]

For Ralegh, Sherborne became (like so much else) a grand project in which he could invest his energies, dreams and always insufficient cash. After he realized that making the old castle comfortably livable was a hopeless task, he changed course, and at the meadowland site of a hunting lodge and adjacent deer park the Raleghs built an elegant, beautifully situated residence. The Lodge (as they always called it) could not have been more unlike the vast, palace-like prodigy houses that Ben Jonson dismissed as "proud, ambitious heaps."[13] The Raleghs' new home was considerably more modest and graceful than the grander building—expanded by the Digby family in the seventeenth century—that now occupies the site. Originally, the building was rectangular in form, being three stories high and with each story defined by a row of large, square headed windows cut into the limestone exterior. A few years later, the Raleghs made the building more imposing and more vertical by adding a fourth story and, at each corner of the house, a hexagonal tower. The light-filled, cakebox verticality of the building was fundamentally altered when Sir John Digby added a long two-story wing to each tower, turning the shape of the whole into a letter H.

Much of the building's beauty derived from its harmony with the setting on the River Yeo (later dammed up by Capability Brown), and Ralegh took particular pleasure in developing the grounds and gardens, a task he entrusted to his gifted half-brother Adrian. Ralegh had scientific, horticultural interests (which he later cultivated in a garden in the Tower), and his gardens had a practical function as well as providing comfort and recreation. When he discussed Sherborne in his will, Ralegh's love for the property is clear in his itemized improvements such as "newe erected buildinges in the said parke, gardens, orchardes, walkes, fishe pondes, conduit pipes of lead, tymber, trees, newe planted trees or hedges in the same parke...."[14]

In Ralegh's mind, the Sherborne estate was inextricably linked to Wat, as it was his birthplace and also destined to be the fixed point of the family's patrilineal future. To establish that future, he took single-minded pains to ensure that his son would inherit the little Dorset kingdom with a clear title. Although he took care to prevent his wife from knowing the degree to which he was favoring the rights of his son over herself, there was nothing illegal in his testamentary arrangements. But the fact that he kept them from Lady Ralegh indicates an element of bad conscience on his part. In his various overseas ventures, Ralegh saw himself as operating in a separate sphere from his wife, a sphere she did not need to know about. But with regard to the details of his last will and testament, he could hardly convince himself that her engagement was intrusive or irrelevant.

A telling indication of Ralegh's marginalization of Bess occurs in another letter he wrote to Sir Robert Cecil—without the vast archive of correspondence compulsively preserved by the Cecils, we would know a good deal less about the Raleghs. Sir Walter sent this letter (December 1594) shortly before his setting sail for the "soonset" of Guiana on the voyage that Lady Ralegh had implored Cecil to prevent. Ralegh had borrowed money from a widow Smith, and (his finances being stretched very thin) he feared that she might undertake a suit against him to recover her money. With respect to a possible writ being served by the sheriff of Dorset, Ralegh tells Cecil that he is not too worried because "all the intrest is in my soonn," meaning the equity in Sherborne (still only sublet from the queen) could not be alienated from the one-year-old Wat.[15]

Ralegh immediately reveals his discomfort and his primary reason for writing: "yet the discreditt wilbe great if I be driven to shew that conve[y]ance.

And besyds by that means my wife will know that shee cann have no intrest in my livinge, and so exclayme." For the widowed Lady Ralegh to "have no intrest in my livinge" means that, in addition to losing Sherborne, she would have no legal grounds to claim a share of his fixed income. He has conveyed the title of Sherborne to Wat without telling his wife, and he fears she will vent her angry denunciation ("and so exclayme") if she learns of the arrangement. His hope is to keep his dealings secret, perhaps as earlier he had attempted ineffectually to conceal his relationship with Bess from the queen. Ralegh could be a commanding presence, and John Aubrey rightly referred to the "awfulness and ascendency in his Aspect over other mortals."[16] But a modern historian's observation about his regard for his wife is equally true: "it would appear that he stood in some awe of her."[17]

Three years after this clandestine conveyance of Sherborne to little Wat, Ralegh preferred his son to his wife in a more calculated and pervasive way, instructing his lawyer to draw up his last will and testament without her knowledge. He signed this document on the day (10 July 1597) he set sail on a military expedition to Cadiz, in the course of which he would be wounded in a daring assault inside the harbor. Had she known of the will, Lady Ralegh would have had plenty to exclaim against, for in addition to being slighted in its provisions she was (tacitly) denied a role in its administration. It was common for a testator to appoint his wife to serve as his executor, since she would be the person best acquainted with the family's finances and possessions. For that reason courts sometimes named the widow to be executor if her husband had died intestate. Indeed, one of Ralegh's motives for drawing up the will may have been to remove himself from intestate status, thus preventing the possibility that Lady Ralegh could become his executor. He was careful to name his four-year-old son to fill that critical function, with Ralegh's friends to fill the role until Wat came of age.

Ralegh, foreseeing that he might not live until Wat reached his majority, named four overseers to administer the will if his death necessitated their action. Significantly, he did allow Lady Ralegh an indirect voice in the proceedings, since two of the four administrators were her kinsmen, one of them being her loyal brother Arthur. But the witnesses who actually signed the document (perhaps the only persons, apart from his lawyer, who knew of its existence) were all close associates of Ralegh with no connection to his wife or her family. Presumably the administrators related to Lady Ralegh would have learned of the will only in the event of Ralegh's death, in which case he would be safely beyond her wrath.

Following an initial reference to "Walter Ralegh esquire, my son and heire apparent," the centrality of Wat in the will is unmistakable. Indeed, no one else seems to matter very much. Unlike many wills of the time, Ralegh's does not acknowledge his wife with a customary phrase like "well-beloved," nor does it reflect her wishes or gesture toward their shared life together. Few assets are mentioned that are not earmarked for Wat upon his marriage or his reaching the age of majority; avoiding any diminishment of his son's legacy, Ralegh makes relatively few bequests to relatives and loyal followers, with nothing set aside for the poor or for his own funeral. And some of these few bequests are in fact provisional, to be granted only if Wat dies without leaving an heir. Thus, Ralegh bequeaths a fine set of Chinese porcelain to "my right honorable good frinde Sir Roberte Cecill," but he is to receive it only if Wat "shall happen to dye without heire of his bodye before he be of full age" (383). No one mentioned in the will, and indeed no one at Elizabeth's court, was more crucial to Ralegh's political and economic fortunes than Cecil, who must queue up behind little Wat and his children in order to lay his hands on the coveted porcelain.

The patrilineal orientation of the will is never in doubt, beginning with Ralegh's declaration that all his lands and castles, both in England and in Ireland, should go to "the heires males of my bodye lawfully begotten," descending to his wife "Dame Elizabeth" only "for defaulte of such yssue" (381–82). Within its traditional bias, the will treats Lady Ralegh in fairly customary terms, allowing her the "occupation" and "profit" of Ralegh's considerable holdings in Dorset (notably Sherborne) and Somerset until Wat marries or comes of age. Similarly traditional is the division of household stuff and valuables into two equal parts between Wat and Lady Ralegh (excepting her pearls), with his half going to his mother if he should die before having come of age without an heir. Also, Lady Ralegh is to receive £500 per annum from Ralegh's monopoly on wine licensing and sales, but (again) only until Wat's marriage or majority. Another significant bequest to Lady Ralegh was a leased house and property at Haselbury Plucknett in Somerset, which Ralegh apparently intended as a "dower house" in which she could live after his death.[18] But, once again, he favors Wat with a significant qualification—the valuable adjoining woods are to go to him.

In the will, Ralegh's attitude toward his wife is consistent with the distinctly cool admonishment he was to give to Wat later in his *Instructions to His Son*: "Yet always remember, that thou leave not thy Wife to bee a shame unto thee after thou art dead, but that shee may live according to thy estate; especially, if thou hast few Children, and them provided for."[19] Ralegh's equitable view that Wat's widow should enjoy a level of support commensurate with the status she had enjoyed as a wife is followed with a familiar proviso: that his son's children should first be "provided for." Moreover, one senses Ralegh's lack of sympathy for this abstraction; preventing the poverty of Wat's future wife matters because it avoids a shameful reflection on the honor of her husband.

Alongside the (perhaps grudging) decency of its settlement for Bess, Ralegh's will reveals his fear that she may take advantage of Wat's being underage to carry off or sell assets that should eventually go to him. This suspicion is related to Ralegh's decision not to name her as his executor, and it is by no means peculiar to him. Henry Percy, the earl of Northumberland and later fellow prisoner with Ralegh in the Tower, reminds his son and heir that after his own father's death his mother had stripped the house bare, except for "wainscots, or things revited [riveted] with nails, for wyves commonly are great scratchers after there husbands deaths if things be loose."[20] In a similar spirit, near the end of the will, Ralegh declares that Bess shall not make grants of any of the properties temporarily entrusted to her or despoil them, including the prized fish ponds and lead pipes mentioned earlier.

But why would Lady Ralegh want to lay waste to this carefully tended paradise before her much loved son came of age? Sir Walter's worry is surely based less on suspicions of avarice on her part than on fears that a rapacious second husband might coerce her into plundering Wat's estate before he took possession. (Twice in the will Ralegh characterizes Bess as "my nowe wife," which seems really to mean "the wife whose husband I now am.") Six years later, as we will see in the letter he sent to Lady Ralegh before his expected execution, Ralegh remained deeply and still more explicitly concerned about the damage that a second husband might do to Wat's interests.

The best gloss on Ralegh's testamentary strategy appears in the *Instructions* he would write for Wat a decade later. In his dicta on choosing a wife, Ralegh accepts as a foregone conclusion that a widowed wife with an estate will marry again, and so he encourages Wat to "leave thy Wife no more then of necessitie thou must, but onely during her widdowhood...."[21] Should she marry again, the "necessitie" of providing decent support no longer obtains. In the event, Ralegh's misgivings about his wife's loyalty to Wat could not have proved more groundless or more unjust. Although she outlived her husband by almost three decades, Lady Ralegh never remarried. Moreover, for many years she struggled resolutely to protect Sherborne for the children whom he feared she might sacrifice to a new husband.

Despite his father's fixation on providing a patrimony for him, the central reality of Wat's childhood is that it was lived in the company of his mother. Indeed, his presence must have been especially important to Lady Ralegh since her husband was often far away. We get a taste of her loneliness in a letter she sent to Robert Cecil when Ralegh was away on his Guiana expedition—this was the voyage which she had sought to prevent by pleading with Cecil to dissuade her husband from sailing toward the sunset. In this letter she laments Ralegh's absence and declares that—without the company of her friend Lady Cecil—life is "an hermit's sell [cell] most fit for me and my mind at this time; beeng for a tim thus desevered [dissevered] from him that I am."[22] Her striking characterization of Ralegh as "him that I am" suggests her sense of incompleteness or emptiness without him. Ironically, her phrase is reminiscent of the shared identity that her husband was to insist on with their son.

Born and bred in the Midlands, Lady Ralegh evidently felt little sense of connection with the West Country, where she was living in de facto exile. At times, even her Sherborne estate must have seemed foreign since it had been the gift of the now alienated queen to her husband and thus was a monument to a relationship that antedated and nearly destroyed her own. Even in the brief periods when Ralegh actually was in residence at Sherborne, Lady Ralegh may have felt a certain isolation. As social historians have observed, it was not uncommon for the lady of a great country house to find herself without close companionship.[23] Whether or not her lord was at home, the wife of the manor could find that the decorum of privacy left her socially isolated, and perhaps definitely not welcome in the male conviviality of her own great hall. Small wonder that, despite the many improvements she and her husband made, the estate may have seemed alien, or at least not fully her own home. Moreover, as we know, Ralegh himself did not look upon Sherborne as hers.

Many of her days would have been spent in the company of her son in a domestic intimacy that left virtually no historical record. Decades would pass before it was common for parents to write circumstantial diary entries about their children, such as John Greene's poignant observation in 1649 that "my boy Alexander, being almost two year old, cannot go yet alone, but by holding he can go about the house. He hath twenty teeth ... and I do a little fear that his right shoulder grows a little bigger than the other, which we observed last Michaelmas."[24] Though Lady Ralegh surely would have followed Wat's developmental milestones attentively, there are no such accounts of his teething or first steps, no recorded parental observations about his growth and skills.

When the demands of office and ambition allowed, Ralegh resided at Sherborne, and there is no reason to think he avoided his little child, as some contemporary fathers did. For instance, the great French philosopher Michel de Montaigne said of his children that "I have not willingly suffered them to be brought up near me."[25] In wealthy Elizabethan families, even the most indulgent father maintained a certain distance from his small children. Little boys (along with their sisters) lived in the nursery, which was exclusively the province of care-giving women: mothers, nurses, and serving maids. The children's clothing in the nursery reflected this female ambience; for boys as well as girls, the usual outfit consisted of a long-skirt frock with little gender variation in the early years. It was not until they were six or seven that boys left the nursery and were symbolically "breeched," putting off the largely unisex robe and donning the doublet and breeches that signified entrance into a distinctly masculine sphere. As an historian of dress remarks, "Breeching a boy was the outward sign of his passage from the care of women—of mother or nurse within the home—to preparation for his future as a man."[26]

After being breeched, well-born boys traditionally moved into the social and educational ambit of men. Sir Thomas Elyot, a respected authority on education in Ralegh's youth, bluntly opined that "After that a child is come to seven years of age, I hold it expedient that he be taken from the company of women."[27] Absent fathers were especially concerned about sons who were at home without a tutor. Even a devoted husband like Sir Robert Sidney, who rarely could leave his post as governor of Flushing, insisted (to his wife's displeasure) that his son Will required a tutor when he turned seven.[28] A more pointed concern was expressed by Henry Percy, who worried that his heir Algernon was spending too much time in what he disparaged as "nursery societe," where he was subject to the "mutche pamperings and other humors that are incident to over tender mothers."[29] Presumably it was to prevent the ill-effects of prolonged maternal tenderness that Percy regularly brought young Algernon (and his tutor) to stay with him for long visits in the Tower.

It is unlikely that Ralegh shared his friend Percy's opinion—or if he did he must have been very frustrated—for Wat appears to have lived with his mother until he went up to Oxford at fourteen. Indeed, for long periods of time Lady Ralegh functioned as a single parent. Before his father's imprisonment in 1603, when the ten-year-old lad and his mother shifted their primary residence first to the Tower and then to a nearby house, Wat appears rarely to have been absent from Sherborne and more rarely from his mother. A deep bond must have developed between mother and child— he an only child, she an often lonely spouse—and her devotion to Wat continued long after his death. Oddly, in his extant writing Ralegh never acknowledges the crucial role his wife played in the raising of their son—neither criticizing her for cloistering him nor praising her for nurturing him.

For most Elizabethan boys of privilege, the transition to breeches marked the beginning of his formal education, and this may have been so for Wat. But there is precious little evidence to indicate how and where he was taught. The town of Sherborne was fortunate to possess an excellent grammar school (which continues to exist today), and it would have made good sense for the Raleghs to have sent Wat to it, especially given his father's frequent absences. But apparently they did not take advantage of the opportunity. It is intriguing that, at roughly the time Wat would have begun grammar school (1600), Ralegh and Sir Robert Cecil recommended a client of theirs to be master of the Sherborne school, but no surviving records indicate that either Wat or Cecil's son Will (who was visiting the Raleghs) ever enrolled.[30] Perhaps the Raleghs did not think it appropriate for their scion to be rubbing shoulders with local boys who were not of his water.

Since there is no reason to think that Wat was sent away to a boarding school (as young Philip Sidney had been sent to the Shrewsbury School), the likelihood is that he was tutored within the Ralegh household, probably beginning not long after his breeching. When Robert Cecil's son Will was spending the summer of 1600 (Wat's seventh year) *chez* Ralegh, Sir Walter reassured his learned colleague that his son is "better keipt to his booke then any wher elce," and it may be that a tutor had been provided to make sure that Will (and his younger playmate Wat) was for periods of time not anywhere else.[31] Given the virtually total absence of household records for the Raleghs at Sherborne, the lack of evidence of a tutor's presence is not proof that such a person did not exist. Perhaps various people played the role for short stints. It is only in the Tower, where John Talbot took on the task of preparing Wat for Oxford, that we can be sure he was tutored in a sustained fashion.

The key fact of Wat's education before university is the absence of a classroom and other students. Then, as now, the results of schooling in the home were mixed. One of the best advertisements for the practice was Robert Cecil himself. As a child he had been self-conscious and frail (a consequence of inherited scoliosis), and his parents created at Burghley House a protective environment in which their bookish boy could be educated.[32] Robert Cecil's scholarly father, Lord Burghley, was Chancellor of Cambridge University and a pedagogue manqué, while his mother Mildred was one of the four celebrated Cooke sisters, all of whom were exceptionally well educated. Being fluent in both Latin and Greek, Mildred Cecil was very able to monitor her son's progress. Lady Ralegh's education, however, was much more typical of the social arts usually stressed for her gender. To judge from her resolutely phonetic spelling (she once spelled "ocean" as "oscion"), her virtues did not include much reading in English, much less acquaintance with Latin. Worse yet, her impressively self-educated husband was too frequently absent to provide continuity and depth for Wat's learning. To judge from Wat's subsequent failure to distinguish himself at Oxford—according to his tutor, Daniel Featley, the only way he exerted himself was in "violent exercises"—it would appear that he had not benefited much from home tutoring.[33]

Given her close, supportive bond with Wat, Lady Ralegh may have resembled the stereotypical mother that Elizabethan pedagogues disparaged as given to "cockering" their sons. These were mothers who failed to challenge their educable sons and instead acceded to their emotional demands, neglecting to punish their transgressions. An uncommonly nasty misogyny is obvious in a common illustration of excessive maternal coddling: when a young thief on his way to the gallows is tenderly embraced by his mother, he responds by biting off her nose and charging that her failure to discipline him was responsible for his crimes.[34] It is revealing that the charge of cockering children was often brought by schoolmasters who found the sympathy of mothers for their sons' troubles an obstacle to the discipline they prided themselves on dispensing. (They may have felt that fathers were equally permissive, but it was much easier to lay blame on mothers.)

This conventional construction of the harmful, indulgent mother has often been attached to Lady Ralegh. One biographer attributed Wat's future troubles to the fact that he "had grown up without his father's advice and restraint, very much spoiled by his adoring mother."[35] The obvious riposte to this charge is to say that the customary absence of fathers made the engagement of mothers all the more important. Certainly there is not enough evidence to support the simplistic division between paternal "advice and restraint" and maternal "adoration." For one thing, it is not clear how much restraint Ralegh demanded of Wat. It is notable that the word "obedience" never occurs in Ralegh's expressions of advice to his son, nor does the concept of discipline. The traditional precept is articulated by Sir Henry Sidney, who admonished his young son Philip to "Be humble and obedient to your master, for unlesse you frame your self to obey others, yea and feele in your selfe what obedience is, you shall never be able to teach others how to obey you."[36] For him, and evidently for his father as well, obedience was no virtue if it meant taking orders from self-proclaimed superiors.

If Wat's fitful household schooling had ill effects on him, the cause was less likely an excess of maternal affection or absence of paternal discipline than a deficiency of social interaction. Ben Jonson foresaw the general problem when, without singling out mothers for blame, he lamented that many children were harmed by being overly indulged in the home. To remedy the problem he prescribed public school: "To breed them at home, is to breed them in a shade; where in a school they have the light, and heat of the sun."[37] Notwithstanding lurid instances of brutality in the early modern classroom, which recent scholarship has dwelt on, in many grammar schools a healthy culture of fellowship and good cheer prevailed. Richard Mulcaster, the noted Elizabethan schoolmaster and pedagogue, championed the value of the public grammar school over private tutoring on the Aristotelian grounds that "Education is the bringing up of one, not to live alone, but amongest others, (bycause companie is our natural cognisaunce [distinguishing mark]."[38] For Mulcaster, the enemy of reclusive education, the classroom itself works to exercise the mind because "the child is not alone, and there must he learne that which is laid unto him in the hearing of all and censure of all." Wat never participated in the richly various society of a school, where individuals engaged in shared activities and were expected to abide by common rules.

For Wat, the negative effects of a missing school cohort were magnified by a more pervasive social isolation. An only child until he was thirteen, in his early years he never had to share his parents' affection and attention with a sibling, nor did he have the formative experience of playing with siblings. Despite the company of his mother and her attendants, the ensuing solitariness was never mitigated by the comforts of belonging to an extended family. More seriously, Wat's social privilege appears to have contributed to an isolation that made it easy for him to grow up without participating in a group that would have required him to recognize the claims of others and the corresponding need to restrain his own freedom. Before the fatal Guiana voyage, his battles were single combats fought in the name of his personal honor.

Wat's familial and social isolation at Sherborne could not have been more unlike the childhood of his father, who learned resilience amongst the push and shove of brothers, half-brothers, and cousins. Ralegh's upbringing was further enriched by the web of kinship for which the West Country was noted. The Elizabethan proverb that "all Cornish gentlemen are cousins" was not far from the literal truth for the West Country in general; throughout his letters Ralegh refers to dozens of people as "my cousin," the family connection sometimes having come about as remotely as four or five generations earlier.[39] Unlike his father, who was raised among many people with whom he could identify and against whom he could measure himself, for Wat there was but a single, preeminent figure for comparison, the imposing and often absent man for whom he was named. His life would be marked by the tension between an increasingly distant father who claimed a shared identity with him and an always affectionate mother who could not serve as a role model.

• THREE •

Wat as Second Self

At the close of the sixteenth century there were many reasons why an ambitious man like Ralegh might hope to replicate himself in a son, but a single positive example inevitably would have come to mind: that of Lord Burghley (William Cecil) and his son Robert. Burghley's careful grooming of Robert resulted in an outcome that was (for them) conspicuously happy, a successful fusing of paternal instruction with filial propensity. One of the most powerful men in England, Burghley taught his son to follow his own progress through some of the highest offices of the land, including a seat on the Privy Council, the master of wards, and eventually the lord high treasurer. Father and son worked in seamless harmony, with Burghley transferring to Robert increasing amounts of his workload as age and illness took their toll. To their rivals, "it had long been clear that Cecil was a repository for Burghley's hopes," and there were murmurs about a "*Regnum Cecilianum*," as if they were an alternate king and crown prince.[1] As a competitor tartly observed, Robert Cecil had learned his father's lesson all too well, since Burghley "was like an aged tree that lets none grow which near him planted be, and it is well followed by his son at this day."[2]

Eight years older than Robert Cecil but increasingly junior to him in governmental authority, Ralegh would have been envious of the many advantages that Burghley had provided for his frail, hunchbacked son. He hoped to bequeath to Wat similar benefits of power and privilege, benefits that he had lacked himself. To Ralegh's dismay, however, Wat turned out to be much more similar to Burghley's older, scapegrace son William than to the extraordinarily talented and tractable Robert. Ralegh's dream of a shared identity with his son, like that of many a father, was undone by time and untoward filial growth, beginning in Wat's early childhood with paternal hopes for replication and foundering in adolescence on the rocks of filial resistance. The common arc of early mutual identification giving way to friction and to the disappointed withdrawal of both father and son holds true for the two Walter Raleghs.

As we have seen, Ralegh was often absent in his child's early years, and there is little evidence of their interaction at that time. Interestingly, Ralegh's only recorded memory of Wat's infancy inadvertently reveals an impulse to prove their shared identity by attributing his own feelings and ideas to his son. It is a projection that casts more light on himself than on the son whom he nominally describes. In the *Instructions to his Son* that he wrote for the adolescent Wat, Ralegh asks him to "Remember when thou wert a sucking Child, that then thou diddest love thy Nurse, and that thou wert fond of her, after a while thou didst love thy dry Nurse, and didst forget the other, after that thou didst also despise her; so it will be with thee in thy liking in elder yeeres; and therefore, though thou canst not forbeare to love, yet forbeare to linke...."[3] With regard to nursing arrangements, there is no reason to doubt that the Raleghs hired wet-nurses to suckle their infants (even if Ralegh was later to disparage what he called the "milke of a strange Dugge"), and certainly Wat would have been transferred to the care of a so-called "dry nurse" after being weaned.[4]

Questions arise, however, with Ralegh's characterization of Wat's behavior, especially with his observation that the child came to "despise" each of his nurses after his initial "love" for her. The spiteful rejection of love objects seems oddly adult behavior to attribute to an infant, especially in the primal act of nursing, but Ralegh's interpretation becomes clear when its immediate context in the *Instructions* is taken into account. The behavior he attributes to Wat tidily serves to illustrate the statement he made in the sentence preceding the recollection: that "the desire dyeth when it is attayned, and the affection perisheth, when it is satisfied."[5] Later, in the *History of the World*, his commitment to the idea appears again: "For as in other men, so in Kings, the passion of love growes old, and weares out by time."[6] Ralegh's belief appears to be retroactively shaping his memory of Wat rather than being informed by it.

With this dubious recollection, Ralegh is not only imposing his ideas on the past behavior of his infant son but also attempting to shape the now-adolescent Wat's future attitude to sexuality. At the close of the anecdote about Wat's love-turned-to-hate relations with his nurses, he declares that "so it will be with thee in thy liking in elder yeeres." This prophesy is alarmingly cavalier in its insistence on the impossibility of his son's enjoyment of an enduring erotic relationship. Ralegh's dictum is clearly not an inevitability, and it is worrisome (with regard to Wat) because it appears to reveal his inability or unwillingness to imagine his son living a life different from his own.

A more explicit, and much more troubling, identification of Wat with himself also touches on sexuality—that of father, son, and mother. Soon after Ralegh was sentenced to death for treason (when Wat was ten), he wrote a long and frequently touching letter to Lady Ralegh, in which he proposes she replace him in their marriage with a substitute, namely Wat. He begins the letter with a rather conventional preamble urging his wife and child to "comfort your selves, trust God and be contented with your poore estate," but for the remainder he speaks very personally and sometimes discontentedly.[7] Abruptly, he shifts to the issue of remarriage, which figured implicitly in the will he had drawn up five years earlier. Now he declares that Lady Ralegh should "forbeare not to marry againe" (his double negative amounting to rather less than a positive assertion) because "It is nowe nothing to me." Not surprisingly, this denial of interest rings hollow, for Ralegh immediately insists that for the sake of Wat she avoid a sensual second marriage: "To witnes that thowe didest love me once take care that thowe marry not to please sence [sense] but [to] avoide povertie and so preserve thy child." His injunction for her to marry without the pleasure of "sence" is balanced ambiguously between his opening request for an affirmation of their past love and his closing request that Wat's well-being be her only priority.

At the end of the letter, the identity of the two Walter Raleghs becomes much more explicit and comes disconcertingly close to a kind of paternally sanctioned incest—the Oedipus complex stood on its head. Suddenly returning to the topic of remarriage, he counsels Lady Ralegh that "whosoever thowe chuse againe after me, lett him be but thy politique husband, but let my sonne be thy beloved for he is parte of me and I live in him, and the difference is but [merely] in the nomber and not in the kinde."

More emphatically than earlier, Ralegh assumes she will remarry, and once again he advances the idea of her taking a second husband with whom marriage should be merely "politique" (concerned with financial and social advantage) rather than "sence" (passion). In his earlier plea, his formulation had begun with himself and ended with Wat—but now he explicitly replaces himself in the marriage with his son, who should be her "beloved" since "he is parte of me and I live in him." In this formulation, the differences between a husband's and a son's love are elided—the restraint that Ralegh proposes for his wife becomes evidence of her continuing fidelity to the father and son who may be two in number but are one in "kinde" (essence). Ralegh's invoking of his intimate bond with Wat entails a kind of bondage for Lady Ralegh.

While it is important to note Ralegh's sexual jealousy of a second husband (chosen by Bess), it is his insistence on his union with Wat that is most revealing. The complex relationship with a wife is juxtaposed against the perfect union of father and son. The statement that "He is parte of me and I live in him" is memorable in its intertwining of form and meaning, a connection relevant to its topic. In form, Ralegh's progression of "he" "me" "I" "him" exemplifies the rhetorical figure of chiasmus, A B B A, creating a sense of tight, unified enclosure, everything in its inevitable place. This connectedness is intensified by the rhyme of "He" and "me," and also in the mirroring of the first half of the sentence by the second. It is as if Ralegh has inserted a perfect ten-word poem in his long and conflicted letter.

In conjunction with its uncommonly evocative structure, the statement is remarkably personal. Being deeply patrilineal, if not downright patriarchal, Elizabethan culture stressed the central importance of the bond between father and son. But Ralegh's words suggest that the two are so interdependent as to be virtually one. It is common enough for Elizabethan fathers—less so for mothers—to assert their "part" in their children, but his formulation implies a deeper connection. When Sir Robert Sidney and his wife Barbara had a disagreement about their children—she wanted to bring them with her on a visit to him in the Low Countries, and he thought she should leave them at home—he put his foot down, saying "you must remember I have part in them, as well as you, and therefore must have care of them."[8] In a conventional manner, Sidney seems to be thinking of their children in terms of joint ownership and joint responsibility, with himself and his wife each possessing a "part" of them (but clearly not an equal part).

For Ralegh, however, this familial sense of relatedness seems to be on the verge of becoming a metaphysical or even theological union. Tacitly denying his wife's part in Wat, he asserts that the difference between himself and Wat "is but in nomber and not in the kinde." As the earlier part of the sentence indicates, the "kinde" to which they belong involves more than their common gender; in Elizabethan England, the word often denoted a specific quality that determines the essential identity of a thing or person.[9] There is a certain Sir Walter Raleghness that joins them. The father does not own a part of his son—he inhabits his son.

But balanced and mutually mirroring as it is, Ralegh's "he is parte of me and I live in him" does not imply the complete equality or shared identity of the two Walters. The second half—"I live in him"—is more conventionally patrilineal than the first, and less problematic. Fathers can live in their sons in many forms and degrees, and so long as they do not attempt to live *through* their sons the idea is benign. But the presence of Wat in his father is more ambiguous. In addition to indicating an organic connection between father and son, "he is parte of me" may suggest a containment of the son within the larger, all-encompassing being of the father. This interpretation is supported by Ralegh's understanding of the Christian trinity, in which his dominant focus is always on the omnipotence and omniscience of the Father at the expense of the conjoined and equal manifestations of the godhead in the Son and the Holy Spirit. As John Aubrey aptly noted, in his scaffold speech Ralegh "spake not one word of Christ, but of the great and incomprehensible God, with much zeale and adoration, so that … he was an a-christ, not an atheist."[10] Indeed, there is a sense in which Wat did turn out to be merely part of his father, in that he re-enacted only a piece of his complex, many-sided—both loving and demanding—progenitor.

In Wat's early years, this emphasis on their likeness would have been gratifying for both Walter Raleghs, and Lady Ralegh certainly would have been happy to emphasize their similarities. For Wat, as for most Elizabethan boys, a key moment in this mutual identification would have come with Wat's transition from gown to breeches. As noted earlier, the breeching of a boy, usually in his seventh year, symbolized his passage from the care of women to the discipline of men; it became the boy's duty to concentrate on imitating models of masculinity within the family and beyond.[11] In miniature, Wat began to look and dress like a man in the making, which would have increased Ralegh's pleasure at seeing an inchoate but still recognizable image of himself—a mirroring powerfully insisted upon in the double portrait of father and son painted a year or two later.

A reference to the newly masculine-attired Wat appears in the likely year of his breeching (1599) and may be connected to it. A list of expenses for gifts made by Henry Percy, the earl of Northumberland, includes six shillings for a "white curled feather" given to "Walter Reighley his son."[12] Sometimes breechings became social occasions to celebrate the child's first appearance as a man in the making, and it is pleasing to imagine this gorgeous ostrich feather gracing the hat of the proud little boy. Whether or not it was associated with the actual breeching, this feather was given by a man who was a friend of Ralegh's and must have known that Wat was a boy who enjoyed putting himself on display—an early indication that he was indeed his father's son.

The fortunate survival of a handful of letters written in the following year brings to life a very happy spring and summer at Sherborne, when the Raleghs served as a surrogate family for Will Cecil, the only son of Robert Cecil. Three years earlier, Bess Ralegh's friend Lady Cecil had died, leaving a sad, sickly boy whose grief-stricken, workaholic father was paying him and his sister too little attention. (Ralegh wrote a consolatory letter sternly urging Cecil to forgo his grief and to "establishe" his children, but to little avail.[13]) Since their always fragile (and dependent) relationship with Robert Cecil was beginning to deteriorate, the Raleghs must have calculated that taking in little Will would ingratiate them with his father as well as do the lad a good turn. In addition, the prospect of bringing to Sherborne a surrogate brother only two years older than Wat would have been attractive. And if the boys were to establish a strong, lasting friendship, a doting parent could hope that their future connection might resemble Ralegh's still profitable relationship with Cecil.

For Will Cecil himself, but not for the hopes of his hosts, the Ralegh cure proved to be a great success. After only a week had passed, Ralegh reported to Cecil that "your beloved creature" was "better in health and strenght then ever I knew hyme" and stressed that "His stomake that was heretofore weake is altogether amended...."[14] Six months later—not long before his father removed the boy from his adoptive family—Lady Ralegh was happy to confirm punningly to Cecil that "My cossin Will is heer, very will, and looketh will and fat with his batheing."[15]

But the best evidence for the boy's recovery at Sherborne was provided by Will himself in a charming note he sent "To the right hon. my loving friend Sir Walter Ralegh, knight," who must have been in London. Speaking for Wat as well as for himself, Will declares with peremptory familiarity that "You being absent, we are like soldiers that when their Captain are [sic] absent they know not what to do: you are so busy with idle matters. Sir Walter, I will be plain with you. I pray you leave all idle matters and come down to us."[16] In sharp contrast, Will wrote at the time a dutifully turgid Latin letter to his father, beginning "Honoratissime pater" ("most honored father").[17] It looks as if Ralegh joined in the boys' (probably military) play with high spirits. At Sherborne a little masculine society was taking shape, or being played at, with Ralegh as its captain. Recently established in doublet and breeches, Wat could begin to play—under the tutelage of an older playmate—the part of a warrior. And the old soldier could play at being a boy again. Wounded at Cadiz four years earlier and now walking with a stick, Ralegh must have enjoyed—and envied—the eager vitality he no longer possessed.

Three • Wat as Second Self

In October, six months later, Will's happy stay at Sherborne came to an end when Ralegh sailed to Jersey to assume his new post of governor. Notwithstanding the revival of Will's spirits, the relationship between Ralegh and Robert Cecil was steadily deteriorating, and Cecil removed Will from the Raleghs in order to install him in another noble house, perhaps thereby facilitating his forthcoming betrayal of his son's cherished hosts. Though there is no record of subsequent connections between his family and Will, Ralegh's hopes to be remembered by him died slowly. Fourteen years after his Sherborne stay, Will assumed his deceased father's title of earl of Salisbury, but there is no reason to think he showed any favor to Ralegh. Will's marriage to a daughter of Thomas Howard, first earl of Suffolk and one of Ralegh's most passionate enemies, did not presage a *rapprochement*.

Just as it made him more attractive to his father, Wat's advance into boyhood must have fostered his appreciation of his tall, handsome father's social and political stature. When Ralegh was away, his mother must have told him enthralling tales of his father's adventures, and a sense of his father's importance would have been confirmed by the respect Ralegh commanded wherever he went in the West Country. Perhaps Ralegh was recalling the pride of his former days when he observed in the *History of the World* that "great men do study not only to hold their own but also to command and insult upon inferiors...."[18] In October of 1600, at the end of the summer of Will Cecil, Wat had a taste of his father's formal command of subordinates. Lady Ralegh speaks of how "little Wat and my selfe brought him [Ralegh] abord the shipt" that took Ralegh to Jersey to assume the governorship; Wat's ferrying of his father to his ship was probably his first journey on water, and the thrill must have been magnified by Ralegh's ceremonious welcome on board the impressive ship.

The richest evidence for Ralegh's sense of shared identity with Wat—and Wat's largely responsive identification with him—is of course the full-length portrait of father and son painted two years after Ralegh's leave-taking for Jersey, when his son was eight. Although the painter has not been identified and there is no surviving contract, we may be sure that it was Ralegh who commissioned this highly unorthodox portrait. At the time, double portraits of a father and son were rare in England (though commoner on the Continent), and in English portraiture it was extremely rare, perhaps even a breach of familial decorum, for a living wife to be excluded from a portrait of her husband and her son.

A likely inspiration for the portrait was not a painting but rather a funeral monument that Ralegh knew very well, the double tomb of Sir

John Horsey II and Sir John Horsey III in Sherborne Abbey (c. 1565). The Horseys were the most powerful family in the area, having gained (and later sold) the Abbey through connections with Henry VIII and much shrewd dealing. The tomb is a monument to patrilineal relationship, and the architectural surround is festooned with elements from the Horsey coat-of-arms, most notably the heads of the horses (a rebus pun) that surmount the impressive structure. Innovatively, the wife of neither of the deceased Horseys is represented, and instead of the customary husband and wife we see father and son lying side-by-side. The similarity of the same-named father and son could hardly be more emphatic—they share the same long-faced (one is tempted to say equine) features, and they lie in exactly the same posture, identically outfitted in anachronistic fifteenth-century armor designed to conceal their nouveau riche status. In Ralegh's imaginative animation of the monument, the dynastic architectural surround is removed, placing the entire focus on the similarity of the living father and son who stand side by side in identical poses.

The portrait of the two Walter Raleghs is above all an act in which the father lays exclusive claim to the son who is his same "kinde." The absence of Lady Ralegh is especially significant—not only was she very much alive at the time, but also she was of course the parent who had been almost entirely responsible for Wat's care over the years. Her elision occludes the female past and orients the painting to the male future. Unlike most contemporary paintings of children, this portrait gives no indication of a feminized domestic world, and there is a notable absence of the household pets or toys that in many contemporary paintings occupy the attention of children. The business at hand is serious: becoming a man.

For several years Wat had been wearing breeches and doublet, and his sporting of an adult-looking sword suggests a completed transition from the world of women. Since only gentlemen were allowed to wear one, the sword was a sign of superior social status, and of course it marked the arrival of manhood as well. Though it was not uncommon for adolescents to be depicted wearing swords, the eight year-old Wat is certainly on the young end of the spectrum. (The eight-year-old James VI of Scotland also wears a sword in a standing portrait, though rather less confidently.[19]) Perhaps Wat's bravado indicates that his blade may have been given to him recently, and in this regard the placement of his age directly underneath his sword's

Opposite: **Ralegh's vision of a shared identity with an imitative son was soon to change. Double Portrait of Sir Walter Ralegh and Walter Ralegh Junior (anonymous, 1602) (courtesy the National Portrait Gallery, London).**

hilt is suggestive. That father and son share a fellowship of the sword is emphasized by the exactly parallel arrangement of their similarly embroidered sword-belts; indeed, these belts are the only identical item worn by both Raleghs. The sword will prove to be a prominent feature in Wat's brief life.

Like their similarly hung swords, the elegant clothing of father and son suggests their shared spirit. As we would expect, Ralegh's clothes are considerably more costly and sumptuous than Wat's, but not more stylish. Not only is the father's doublet richly embroidered with seed pearls, with a white satin vest underneath, but also the black feather in his hat is affixed by a pin containing a large ruby and pearl drop. Wat is tricked out as elegantly as his father, although his white ostrich feather is nowhere to be seen—perhaps it was a casualty of his military service with Will Cecil at Sherborne. He wears "Venetians" (fashionable silk breeches closed at the knee), which are beautifully matched in design and color with his silver-braided silk jacket.[20] From the large beaver hat in his hand to the blue bows on his shoes, he dresses with his father's panache. Both figures are at home in their finery, uncommonly poised and self-contained. They are both (in Shakespeare's phrase) the lords and owners of their faces.

This tight focus on father and son is of a piece with the painting's depiction of a very limited, almost claustrophobic, space. We do not see the window from which daylight makes its way from the left, and the two Walter Raleghs are hemmed in by the substantial table on which Sir Walter rests his right hand and by the heavy curtain hanging not far behind them. The curtain does not extend all the way to the left edge of the picture, and the painter easily could have created greater spatial depth by depicting a familial living area or (as in a full-length portrait of Henry Prince of Wales) by including a window that opens on to a garden.[21] But instead of a suggested social sphere or a glimpse of the green world, we see simply a space that is undefined and darkly opaque. This painting is entirely occupied by (and with) *this* father and son.

Although it depicts an exclusively male universe, the portrait does not have a conventional patrilineal focus. Unlike the Horsey monument, it does not assert (or pretend) that the father and son belong to a long family line. Significantly, there is no coat of arms in the painting, and no allusion to the family's past. Nor are there trees or other symbols of organic growth over time. Instead, a legend at the top left gives the date (1602), supplying Ralegh's name (but not Wat's) and recording the offices of state he was holding at the time. Like Ralegh's bestowal of his own name on his son, the painting celebrates the replication of the father in the son rather than the honor of the family line.

The most striking and most original feature of the painting is of course Wat's imitation of his father's pose. If a close precedent for this replication exists in Elizabethan portraiture, it has never been pointed out in the numerous discussions of the portrait. Viewed without reference to his son—as in the seventeenth-century copy at Knole House that deletes Wat—the depiction of Ralegh is conventional; in many English and Continental full-length portraits the subject stands with his right hand resting on a table. As well, the subject's left hand is often, like Ralegh's, resting on his hip with his elbow extended—a pose recently dubbed the "Renaissance elbow."[22] In early modern portrait painting, this gesture coded as masculine, often conveying an aristocratic or military assertion of control. In family portraits, the gesture can characterize strength and authority, as in the husband who guards his wife or the older brother who extends protection to his younger sibling.[23] In some English portraits of single figures, the composition includes symbolic possessions (often ceremonial armor) that indicate the sitter's mastery and are displayed underneath his elbow, the space occupied by Wat.[24]

Although the portrait's full-length format ensures that Ralegh towers over his son, Wat is a surprisingly independent and undeferential figure. Given his subordinate place in the composition, it is remarkable how forcefully Wat draws the viewer's eye—his intensity and vitality are missing in his rather grey father. The indistinctness in Ralegh's features may be due in part to the heavy restoration of paint in his face, but even before the painting was retouched, Wat's fresh and lively face must have been its center of interest.[25]

Wat shows no sign of obedience, much less genuflection, even though holding one's hat in one's hand was an indication of filial deference. Indeed, in his intense engagement with the viewer he seems oblivious to his father. When the painting is seen hanging in its current (but not permanent) residence in the Long Hall at Montacute House, Ralegh seems to be looking to the horizon, apprehending something only he can see. By contrast, the lad stands at the viewer's eye-level, meeting and even challenging the spectator's gaze. There is something distinctly mischievous, perhaps even truculent, in Wat's expression, as careful viewers have attested.[26] The double-portrait proudly claims Wat as Ralegh's son, while hinting at difficulties to come (or so it seems for those who know their story).

In the year the painting was completed (1602), the Raleghs were at the top of fortune's wheel. Certainly, Ralegh had good reason to congratulate himself for ensuring Wat's future prosperity. Given how large Sherborne loomed in his imagination and calculation, it is easy to forget that

Ralegh had been holding it merely as a sublet from the queen, who had leased it from the Bishop of Salisbury. Moreover, the queen's lease (and Ralegh's tenure) was good only for the duration of her life; at the end of her rule it would revert to the crown and to the whim of the new monarch, whoever that might be. In September of 1599, Queen Elizabeth finally took the decisive step. She extracted the Manor of Sherborne from the Bishop of Salisbury and in a Conveyance of Freehold granted it to Ralegh and to his heirs in perpetuity.[27] Troubled by dark intimations of her mortality, she was evidently making a final bequest to her newly restored but no longer intimate friend.[28]

Finally, Ralegh had captured (or at least been granted) the grand prize of the Sherborne estate outright, and he had every reason to think that in due time it would belong to Wat, as he had long imagined. The Raleghs celebrated by purchasing a number of estates and lands in the area and also sinking a good deal of money into Sherborne manor itself. In 1600 they hired Simon Basill, Surveyor of the King's Works, who made the building considerably more imposing by adding "five turrets to turn it into a hexagon with a flat balustrade platform on the roof top."[29] Ralegh would soon learn, however, that his quest to establish Wat had been futile, in good part because of his own behavior.

A prosperous estate requires a healthy income, and in the year of the portrait Ralegh joined in a rather unsavory plot that he hoped would provide a wealthy heiress for Wat to marry. When the prosperous Staffordshire landowner William Bassett died in 1602, he left (in addition to his widow) a single surviving child, a three-year-old daughter named Elizabeth. Being underage, she was deemed to be a ward of the queen and thus became subject to the machinations of Robert Cecil, the master of wards.[30] After refusing the plea of Bassett's widow Judith that she be allowed to be her daughter's guardian, in May of 1602 Cecil sold the wardship to his brother-in-law, Lord Cobham, who immediately transferred it to his (then) good friend Ralegh for an unspecified fee or reciprocity. For a hefty annual fee to be paid to him, Ralegh magnanimously granted Judith Bassett the "custody of the body" of her little daughter, but he retained the benefits of her wardship, among which were a yearly payment and the right to arrange her marriage.[31] Not surprisingly, the Raleghs deemed Wat to be the perfect match for this child who was, they reckoned, worth £3000 a year, and a betrothal was planned.

In light of the two Raleghs' future lives, the painting is terribly poignant. It was painted on the verge of disaster—at the height of identification between father and son, and, not coincidentally, at the height of the family's fortunes. Following his attainder for treason in 1603, Ralegh forfeited the wardship of Elizabeth Bassett along with the rest of his possessions and offices. In December 1603 Robert Cecil saw to it that the wardship went to Sir Roger Dallison, a pliable client of Henry Howard, earl of Northampton.[32] Howard served as a commissioner at Ralegh's trial and was proving to be a devoted enemy. But the Raleghs did not surrender their dream of this lucrative marriage easily. In 1605, Elizabeth Bassett's mother Judith and her third husband demanded that Lady Ralegh and John Shelbury, the family lawyer, appear in the Court of Wards to clarify "the true grantee of her [Elizabeth's] wardship and marriage, which have several claimants."[33] The Raleghs' lawyer duly testified, but the plaintiffs were unable to proceed because Lady Ralegh "would not appear or make answer." Her family may have lost its own claim, but she was never one to give ground to enemies.

Ultimately, however, the Howards had their way. When Elizabeth Bassett was married in 1613, the victorious suitor, Mr. Henry Howard, was the third son of Thomas Howard, earl of Suffolk—another great enemy of the Raleghs. It is surely no coincidence that, a little more than a year after the wedding of young Henry Howard and Elizabeth, Wat was to engage in a bloody duel with a henchman in Suffolk's service who was likely a companion of Henry's. Half a century later, the loss of Elizabeth Bassett still rankled the Raleghs. Voicing the family's grievances, Wat's brother Carew numbers among Ralegh's accomplishments that "he had the daughter and heyre of Bassett to his ward, to marry to his son; her estate worth 3000 *li per. an.* who was taken from him, and married to Mr. Henry Haward...."[34] After Howard's early death, Elizabeth married the wealthy earl of Newcastle, who (Carew continues) "professed he would never have married her, if young Walter Raleigh had been alive; conceiving her before God to be his [Wat's] wife, for they were married as much as children could be...." (He does not pause to ponder how much a ten-year-old and a four-year-old could—or should—be married.) Carew's (unverified) quotation of the earl sounds like a family article of belief, attesting to the lasting pain of the lost Bassett inheritance.

In the year following the idealized double portrait and the family's apparent acquisition of Elizabeth Bassett, Ralegh was convicted of high treason, and the mutual identification between him and Wat, like much else in their lives, must have been deeply wounded. In the ruins of what had been their shared good fortune, it became much more difficult for the two Walter Raleghs to see themselves in each other. The change of attitude would have been more sharply unsettling for Wat than for Ralegh, as his idealized view of a triumphant father no longer squared with the helpless, imprisoned figure he saw before him. Although devaluation of the father is a common stage of adolescent development, for Wat it came early and with shocking force. On Ralegh's part, the identification with Wat became steadily (if less dramatically) difficult to sustain. It would be a serious understatement to say that Wat failed to live his (short) life according to his father's plan.

It goes without saying that widening gaps of difference pose problems for fathers and sons, but it is less obvious that, in conjunction with these differences, perceived similarities can be even more troubling. In the Renaissance, the great age of education, fathers were especially sensitive to the imputation that the moral failures of their sons were their own responsibility. For their part, sons could feel an ambivalent mixture of both deep connectedness and also resistance to the paternal presence. This filial ambivalence pervades Shakespeare's plays, and it lies just below the surface of a fascinating passage in Montaigne's essay titled "Of the Resemblance betweene Children and Fathers." In an observation blending awe and alarm, the great skeptic wondered, "What monster is it, that this teare or drop of seed, wherof we are ingendred, brings ... in it the impressions, not only of the corporall forme, but even of the very thoughts and inclinations of our fathers?"[35] His term "monster" (Fr. *monstre*) suggests that the father's presence within the son is at once both marvelous and unnatural, and on the same page he comments revealingly that he is also "indebted" to his father for the excruciating attacks of gallstones that were afflicting him as they had his progenitor.[36] The suggestion is that the son is mysteriously, wonderfully formed—but perhaps at the same time deformed—by his begetter's ghostlike inhabitation. Wat Ralegh was not inclined to philosophy and he died young, but his actions indicate that he must have chafed under the pressures and expectations of being his father's son.

Nowhere is the contrast between the father's dream of oneness with his son and the inescapable reality of difference more poignant than in a letter sent to Ralegh by the Oxford tutor whom he would hire for Wat (1608). The tutor ends his letter by declaring to Ralegh that Wat is "your richest treasure and most your owne, bearing the image not onely of your body but mind too."[37] A few years earlier, such an affirmation of their shared identity would have been music to Ralegh's ears. But the very fact that he has hired a tutor to oversee his son *in loco parentis* indicates a gap between paternal expectation and filial performance. Indeed, the tutor acknowledges having received a letter expressing Ralegh's anxieties about the "most dangerous evils" that threaten Wat's character. If this adolescent son is indeed the true image of his father and at the same time prone to dangerous tendencies, the value of the replication may appear—even to Ralegh—to be problematic. Some sense of the discrepancy between ideal and reality appears to occur to the tutor, for he adds that he will strive to "brighten it [the father's filial treasure, i.e., Wat] by art, and mak the image and shapes of your virtues more clearely to appear in it." When he read the tutor's facile commitment to restore in Wat his father's image—something he himself had not been able to achieve—Ralegh must have felt a rueful disappointment.

• FOUR •

Imagining a Son on the Gallows

The three surviving pieces that Ralegh addressed to Wat—a riddling poem that ends with the boy's execution, an eloquent exhortation to fare bravely in the world, and a treatise of sober instruction—do not lend themselves to generalization.[1] Yet, varied as they are, these three works share an important similarity: they all came late to the public eye. It is likely that, before Ralegh's death in 1618, none of them appeared in print or circulated in manuscript—a common means of informal publication. The only one that reached print before the twentieth century was Ralegh's *Instructions for His Son*, which appears to have had little or no circulation in manuscript between Ralegh's death and its print publication in 1633. Before the advent of modern editing, the other, shorter pieces—the dark poem for Wat and the exhortation to him—appeared only in a few manuscript anthologies which seem not to have been compiled before the second decade of the seventeenth century.[2] It was only after the author's death, when his personal papers were rather casually dispersed, that these addresses to his son began to circulate. Their belated appearance suggests that Ralegh had no interest in making his words to Wat available beyond his immediate family, or perhaps even beyond Wat himself. When Ralegh penned them he had no reason to concern himself with readers other than his son, and thus he felt no external pressure to say anything he did not feel.

The primary emotion informing these stylistically varied pieces is a deep anxiety about what the future holds for a son who is clearly showing signs of waywardness. As sudden shifts of tone and thought in each piece suggest, Ralegh's attitude toward Wat's prospects is unsettled and equivocal. At bottom, his ambivalence about his son cannot be separated from his identification with him, which is increasingly becoming a source of paternal

Four • *Imagining a Son on the Gallows*   53

concern as well as pride. The problem is that the father can imagine Wat's future only in terms of his own proud but checkered past, a past that does not bode well for the son and heir who, he fears, may come to share his own imprisonment and condemnation. When the pieces are read though this prism, it comes as no surprise that (between the lines) they tell us as much about the father's history as the son's prospects.

The most intriguing of these pieces, and likely the earliest of the three, is a lyric poem which has no title and is usually referred to by its opening words, "Three Things There Be." It has been called "one of the strangest poems ever written by a father for a son," probably because it is an affectionate poem that imagines Wat's execution by hanging.[3] Not surprisingly, the mixing of what are usually thought of as mutually exclusive emotions characterizes the poem, and often critics respond to this tonal mingling by employing the language of oxymoron to describe it in formulations such as its being a "wittily gruesome lyric" or expressing a "grim theme in a whimsical but personal manner."[4] Perhaps because of the interpretive difficulties it poses, many of Ralegh's biographers have avoided discussing "Three Things There Be," either making a silent detour around it or dispensing with it as expeditiously as possible.[5] Even Robert Frost, a man rarely at a loss for words, shied away from commenting on it. When Frost lists the contents of a planned verse anthology, "Three Things There Be" is the first poem he mentions, but beyond calling it "the find of this anthology" he says nothing.[6]

Since "Three Things There Be" is a poem in which Ralegh appears to be discovering his emotions in the course of addressing Wat, it is best to approach it by reading it aloud:

> Three thinges there bee that prosper up apace
> And flourish, whilest they growe a sunder farr,
> But on a day, they meet all in one place,
> And when they meet, they one an other marr;
>   And they be theise, the wood, the weede, the wagg,
> The wood is that, which makes the Gallow tree,
> The weed is that, which stringes the Hangmans bagg,
> The wagg my pritty knave betokeneth thee.
>   Marke well deare boy whilest theise assemble not,
> Green springs the tree, hempe growes, the wagg is wilde,
> But when they meet, it makes the timber rott,
> It frets the halter, and it choakes the childe.
>   Then bless thee, and beware, and let us praye
> We part not with the[e] at this meeting day.[7]

Although in its rhyme scheme the poem closely follows the conventions of the Shakespearean sonnet—three cross-rhymed quatrains followed by a rhyming couplet—it is full of surprises. For the first seven lines, the poem seems simple and predictable enough, with the first quatrain introduced by "Three thinges there bee" and the second by "And they be theise"—a riddle posed and then expounded. Appropriately, the lines move with a jaunty, self-pleased swing, fuelled by the alliteration of monosyllables and many repetitions of phrase. We hear the high spirits of a person who poses a riddle and then triumphantly explicates it.

But at line eight—just as the second quatrain is coming to an end—everything changes. To be sure, the line begins predictably with "The wagg," which completes the expected enumeration of "the wood, the weede, the wagg" promised in line five. But the repetition suddenly breaks down. After lines beginning with "The wood is that" and "The weed is that," we don't hear the "The wagg is that" but rather "The wagg my pritty knave betokeneth thee." In place of the expected identification of a third "that," the wag is revealed to be a "thee," a familiar person being addressed as "my pretty knave." As befits the universal application of riddles, the first seven lines vigorously voice a formulation addressed to no one in particular, or to everyone. But the line explicating the identity of the "wagg" directly engages, even accosts, the unsuspecting reader. More specifically, it is calculated to engage and accost one reader in particular: young Wat Ralegh. Though it is wittily unspoken, the name "Wat" silently follows and concludes the monosyllabic, alliterative progression of "wood"—"weed"—"wag."

The reader is invited to imagine the father declaiming the poem to his child, and perhaps Ralegh did deliver it aloud. (Such a performance is suggested by the strongly rhythmical repetitions in its opening lines.) Hearing the poem for the first time, Wat would have been surprised and pleased by his sudden inclusion into the riddle. Both "wag" and "knave" were common parental endearments for mischievous children, and there is warm affection in "*my pritty* knave," which expresses proud kinship with a charming (but naughty) child. In a sense, this kinship has just been acted out, since the father has played a rather waggish trick on his son. But there is a sinister side to the play, since the "Gallow tree" and the vivid detail of the "Hangmans bagg" have immediately preceded the endearments, raising the specter of darker meanings in "knave" and creating an edge of menace. It is as if the father discovers his son's vulnerability in the course of playing a trick on him.

The heavily weighted monosyllables that open line nine quickly shift the speaker's tone again: "Marke well deare boy." The poet Linda Gregerson once remarked that "the unfolding relatedness of speaker and auditor …

may be said to be the poem's real subject," and that changing sense of relatedness is now being conveyed in very few words.[8] While still affectionate, "deare boy" is less intimate than "wagg" and "pritty knave," and no longer teasing. Although Ralegh addresses Wat with an unobtrusive, serious pun on "deare" (meaning both "beloved" and "emotionally costly"), the playfulness has ended, and the poem's jaunty forward motion is arrested, as if to focus the lad's attention on the crucial moral lesson to follow. The father's gravity of feeling suggests that, for him, the gallows and hangman have become all too real.

Of course, "wag" and "knave" are terms of affectionate reproof for boys who are lively mischief makers, not criminals. But Ralegh's imagination is focused on the future rather than the past, which explains why growth and nature are such central concerns throughout the poem, beginning with the evocation of "things" that "prosper up apace / And flourish" in the opening lines. At the nub of Ralegh's ambivalence is the final word in the vigorous tenth line: "Green springs the tree, hempe growes, the wagg is wilde." If this line is removed from its context, being "wilde" appears to be positive, standing as it does in apposition to "springs" and "growes" and suggesting untrammelled, natural life. But since the tree is growing into a gallows and the hemp into a noose, the thought of the wag who is freely flourishing conjures up deep anxieties. Clearly the state of being "wilde" points forward as well as backward in the poem, pivoting from its early sense of vigorous natural growth, the essence of childhood, to distinctly pejorative Elizabethan meanings indicating insubordination and self-will, even lasciviousness.

Ralegh's fearful intimation seems to be that Wat's hitherto attractive rejection of discipline may marshal his way to the frayed, empty noose and gallows that await him. The suggestion is that Wat must deny his natural, boyishly charming wildness in order to avoid the terrible punishment meted out by the state. As Judith Owens deftly puts it, "In the deep logic of the poem, the wildness that fits Wat to the noose is the quality that gives him life."[9] In this sense, the poem is about the death of childhood as well as death on the scaffold—for Ralegh, protecting his son from the noose may involve a form of restraint not utterly unlike choking the child.

The poem's irony is shocking: the wood, the weed, and the wag naturally flourish, but only to be destroyed—when they meet—by the unnatural spectacle of judicial execution. "Wilde," being the last word of the previous line, prefaces the violence that immediately follows and also rhymes with the victim of that violence: "But when they meet, it makes the timber rott, / It frets the halter, and it choakes the childe." These are two of the most powerful lines Ralegh ever wrote, moving matter-of-factly and inexorably through increasingly unnatural phenomena: the decay of wood, a noose worn thin by the dead weight of repeated hangings, a child strangled. In the terrible finality of "choakes the childe," the monosyllabic alliteration (a device that was breezy earlier in the poem) becomes a nightmare onomatopoeia, enacting its sinister work. The poem's earlier references to the gallows and hangman could be characterized, if only barely, as "affectionate teasing," but now the loving poet-father's imagination has carried him to a sudden terror.[10]

Immediately after this steadily mounting crescendo of violence, Ralegh's sonnet concludes with a rhyming couplet that is calmly measured: "Then bless thee, and beware, and let us praye / We part not with the[e] at this meeting day." (To part *with* carries the same meaning as to part *from*, according to the *OED*.[11]) Ralegh speaks in a quiet, quasi-priestly manner, inviting his family to pray with him, invoking blessings upon the boy and urging him to "beware" of the danger that awaits him. The couplet adroitly rounds off the poem when its final phrase ("this meeting day") recalls the ominous line 3 ("on a day, they meet all in one place") but cushions what had been apocalyptic threat by suggesting in its plural pronouns a coming together that is familial and consolatory. As well, there may be hints of a religious union in which body and spirit, or man and God, come together.[12]

One may well feel, however, as one sometimes does at the close of Shakespeare's sonnets, that the rhyming couplet orders and resolves the poem's energies much too tidily, that its very deftness creates an unsatisfactory simplification. Indeed, the consolatory expression seems rather enervated, conjuring up a religious aura but without the force of strong personal belief. Given the terrible vividness of "choakes the childe," which still rings in the reader's ear, the exhortation "Then bless thee, and beware" seems distinctly simplistic, perhaps even evasive and unpleasantly detached. The lack of specific, forceful agency in "bless thee" is telling, and what good can it do to caution a son to "beware" of behavior that is so deeply rooted in the world of nature, including his own nature? As we will see, the other versions of the poem indicate that Ralegh himself seems to have found this consolatory ending unsatisfactory and later deleted it.

Since "Three Things There Be" was not printed in Ralegh's lifetime and since a manuscript text in his handwriting no longer exists, all the evidence for what he wrote is contained in four handwritten copies (transcribed by unknown people) that appear in seventeenth-century manuscripts. These transcripts are precious because without them the poem simply would not exist. There are differences among these four transcripts of the poem, and room for debate about which of them best represents Ralegh's intentions. These four copies can be divided into two groups, one of which comprises a single text. This is the version in sonnet form, which is quoted at the beginning of this chapter and has been referred to throughout, to this point. The other group consists of the remaining three texts, which share a common feature: the absence of the rhyming couplet that identifies the poem as a sonnet.

Among Ralegh's editors, both groups have had their champions and their detractors. In the first scholarly edition of Ralegh's poetry, Agnes Latham printed the sonnet as the best version of the poem, while the more recent edition by Michael Rudick printed a version from the other group.[13] Something can be said for (and against) both. Ralegh was an accomplished sonneteer, and the sonnet version has the obvious virtue of being written in a form he had mastered. Moreover, it would be very odd if a person intent on copying a poem consisting simply of three four-line stanzas would turn it into a sonnet by adding a rhyming couplet. Generally speaking, scribes who are copying a text usually leave out material or simplify the text before them rather than changing it into a more sophisticated form.

But the three slightly different examples of the other version—the ones that do not have the rhyming couplet—possess virtues of their own. Certainly the shorter version, as we will see, is more emotionally expressive than its sonnet counterpart. Also, unlike the sonnet version, which does not have a heading in its manuscript, these three texts without the couplet are all prefaced by headings that identify Ralegh as the author. Two of the three contain the phrase "Sir Walter Ralegh to his sonne," while the third specifies the identity of the son: "his sonne Walter." It is important that these copyists thought they were transcribing a poem by Ralegh, but it does not follow that the sonnet version is inferior (as Rudick suggests) because it does not identify the author.[14]

Both versions of the text are valuable because they may well represent two, or perhaps even three, distinct stages in Ralegh's ongoing composition of the poem. Like many poets, Ralegh returned to earlier poems and revised them; significantly, his most famous revision of a poem of his own involves an important change to its ending, as he appears to have done with "Three Things There Be."[15] There is nothing in the surviving textual evidence that contradicts the hypothesis that initially Ralegh wrote the poem to Wat in the sonnet form printed at the beginning of this chapter. As noted earlier, however, there is something rather anodyne about the final couplet, and it is plausible that at some point Ralegh returned to his sonnet, found the couplet unconvincing, and deleted it. The effect of jettisoning the couplet would be to deconstruct the sonnet form, breaking the larger, more formal structure down into three sets of four-line stanzas, which are represented in the other three texts.

The trio of texts that lack the couplet can be divided into two versions, which appear to reflect two distinct stages of revision. The simpler version is represented by a single text in which the couplet does not appear and nothing is added to take its place.[16] The resulting poem ends with line twelve of the curtailed sonnet: "It frets the halter, and it choaks the childe." This is a closure that not only erases the rather unconsoling consolation of the original sonnet version but swings to the opposite extreme by ending the poem on its most blunt and brutal words. In this text, the poem and Wat's life both end with a sudden jolt, like a rope springing taut.

The two remaining transcripts—one of them printed in Michael Rudick's edition—may well represent a third stage of revision, as they represent Ralegh's dissatisfaction with this twelve-line "choakes the childe" version, perhaps because the truncated ending leaves the poem unbearably devoid of hope.[17] Instead of abandoning the poem—and its speaker—in this emotionally strangled state, this third version fills the silence after "choakes the child" with the poet-father's sudden, desperate cry: "God bless the child." The force of these four monosyllables is clear when we see them on the page:

> Now marke dear boy, whilst these assemble not,
> Green springs the tree, hemp growes, the wag is wilde,
> But when they meet it makes the timber rot,
> It fretts the halter, and it choaks the childe.
> God bless the child.[18]

Standing against the twelve-line body of the poem, this final cry is desperately naked, the poet's attempt to undo or transcend the terrible execution he has just evoked. The rejected final couplet had begun with the words "Then bless thee and beware, and let us praye," a blessing that, in retrospect, sounds a little perfunctory in its rhythmical regularity. In "God bless the child" we may sense a loss, perhaps a rejection, of the sense of control and authority that had carried Ralegh through the poem.[19] There is no more he can say.

If Ralegh's beseeching of the deity tacitly acknowledges the limits of his own power, it also expresses a commitment to his son that cries out with unequivocal and unforgettable force. In these final monosyllables, Ralegh not only truncates the sonnet form that he had manipulated so adroitly, but he also seems to be rejecting art itself, surrendering the specious

Four • Imagining a Son on the Gallows 59

sense of control that crafting iambic pentameter lines in a set form had given him. In the influential interpretation of his life advanced by Stephen Greenblatt, Ralegh suffered from a self-deluding predilection for seeing life as art, but in this remarkable instance the poet's sharp imagining of the loss of his son makes the consolations of art unnecessary and perhaps intolerable.[20] In what seems a modern moment, the poem leaps beyond poetry.

The reader will have noticed that the foregoing discussion of "Three Things There Be" has not placed the poem within the chronological framework of the lives of father and son. Biographical speculation has been avoided out of respect for Ralegh as a poet. Attempting to extract biography from lyric poetry is always an act of diminishment since imaginative suggestion is inevitably reduced to bare fact. By attempting to read Ralegh's fine poem more or less on its own terms, I hope to have opened up its language and emotion, or at least avoided forcing it into a Procrustean bed of biographical speculation. Still, it would be remiss to refrain from speculating about when and why Ralegh wrote this inimitable poem.

"Three Things There Be" is conspicuous for its lack of biographical handholds. Indeed, it makes so little reference to the two Raleghs that, if three of the transcripts had not named Ralegh as the author and Wat as the recipient, there would have been no obvious reason for modern scholars to have connected the poem with either of them. Of course, once the poem is attributed to Ralegh, its references to execution inevitably take on a solemn portentousness, but there is no evidence that he was meditating on the execution to which he had been sentenced on 17 November 1603, much less its delayed fulfillment fifteen years later. It strains credulity severely for a biographer to suggest that Ralegh wrote the poem on the eve of his expected execution in 1603 as he was remembering a falling-down game he used to play with Wat on his knee.[21] After all, it is Wat, not his father, who is threatened with execution in the poem, and public executions were common enough in Elizabethan England to be vividly present in the minds of people who were not facing their own.

If an actual event (recent or imminent) were behind the poem's imagery of execution, it was probably the death of Ralegh's great rival, Robert Devereux, 2nd Earl of Essex. After his failed uprising against the crown, Essex was condemned to death, and as captain of the guard Ralegh played an official role at his beheading in the courtyard of the Tower (20 February 1601). He was blamed by many followers of Essex for showing disrespect at his death, and the charge must have greatly troubled Ralegh. At his own beheading years later he rebutted it: "It is sayd, that (beside that I was prosecutor of my lord of Essex) I stood in a window over against him when he sufferd and pufft Tobacco out in disdayne of him," but in reality "my eyes shed teares for him when he died."[22] In its immediate aftermath, Essex's sorry fate would have reminded Ralegh, if reminder were needed, of the danger an impulsive, undisciplined man might face, since the government had such easy recourse to the gibbet and chopping block.

A plausible year of composition for the poem would be 1602, the year of the portrait of the two Walter Raleghs. At the time Wat was obviously on his father's mind, and similar relationships of father and son are expressed in the painting and poem. The analogy is only partial, of course, since the painting is an outward representation of the two, presumably commissioned by Ralegh, while the poem subjectively explores the interior of the relationship. In their different ways, both works of art suggest tension and ambivalence between father and son. At the risk of turning a lovely painting into a cartoon, one can imagine a thought-bubble above Ralegh's head containing the exclamation, "my pritty knave!" The painting powerfully insists on the similarity of father and son, although Wat radiates an independence that may not bode well for the future of the relationship, while "Three Things There Be" animates for Ralegh's relatively inexpressive face in the painting by voicing a rich mix of parental pride, affection, reprimand, and anxiety.

Not only is it impossible to date with certainty what I take to be Ralegh's original sonnet version of the poem, but it is equally impossible to establish how much time elapsed between his completing it and later returning to it with revision in mind. If only a short time passed, his dissatisfaction with his sonnet may have been largely aesthetic, a rejection of an ending that sounded hollow compared with the preceding lines. If more time had elapsed, however, Wat would have had more opportunity to exercise the knavery that had troubled his father, thus increasing Ralegh's foreboding about the boy's future. If at least a year or two had passed between his original poem and his revisions, Ralegh conceivably could have been revisiting in the Tower a poem he had written in his recent freedom. Having narrowly avoided his own execution, he would have had good reason to fear for the son whom he had encouraged to imitate himself.

• FIVE •

Disinheritance and Corruption of Blood

For many months before the queen's death on March 24, 1603, the prospect of an impending, unpredictable succession destabilized and energized her court. Although Ralegh had always enjoyed an abundance of well-earned enemies—one of whom succinctly characterized him as "the hated man of the world, in court, city and country"—now he found himself in an increasingly weak position.[1] Not only was he blamed by many for the downfall and execution of the popular earl of Essex, but he was also growing apart from his great ally Sir Robert Cecil, who continued to consolidate power at court. The causes of the rift between the former friends are obscure, but its consequences are painfully clear: Cecil gradually withdrew his support and left Ralegh dangling. Sensing his vulnerability, Ralegh sought a place on the privy council, the premier executive body in the land, but Cecil was rapidly becoming its dominant voice, and Ralegh was passed over. While his fellow courtiers jockeyed for position, Ralegh threw himself into service as the new governor of the far-off isle of Jersey, an appointment for which his enemies at court were probably responsible.

Even when he was present at Westminster, Ralegh was clearly out of his depth, still presuming on the good intentions of Robert Cecil, who was busily deploying his own network of spies and collaborators to undermine him and other potential opponents. Ralegh's fate was sealed when Cecil began to collude with the Howards, a family abounding in titles, lands, sons, and venom toward himself. Their (ultimately successful) plan involved paving the way for King James VI of Scotland to assume the throne, and with Cecil's aid they developed a secret correspondence with James. Ralegh's enemies left no slander unspoken in their campaign to poison James's mind against both him and his wife. When, belatedly, Ralegh rode to greet his new monarch and pledge his allegiance, he was met with a quip revealing that libel had done its work: "O my soule, mon, I have heard rawly of thee."[2] After James' coronation, Ralegh underwent a systematic dispossession of the positions and perquisites he had enjoyed, beginning with his appointment as Captain of the Guard. (Before being removed, however, he was allowed to serve in that office at his queen's funeral.) Soon followed other losses, such as his very lucrative monopoly on licensing vintners, a major source of steady income. Particularly demeaning—and intended to be—was the pointedly short notice he was given to vacate his residence at Durham House, which for twenty years he had held on lease from the queen and into which he had poured a large amount of money (against Lady Ralegh's better judgment). The king and his circle were systematically undoing the queen's largesse.

Searching for a counterweight to Cecil and the Howards, Ralegh had become fast friends with one of the most prominent noblemen in England, Henry Brooke, 11th Baron Cobham.[3] Even though Cobham was well-connected—a leading favorite of the queen, brother of Cecil's deceased wife, and married to a Howard—he was not a wise choice for Ralegh. In addition to many shared resentments (Cecil had also frustrated Cobham's hopes for the privy council), the two men possessed common flaws of judgment and character, not the least of which was an explosive temper. Eventually Ralegh and Cobham appear to have entered into a foolish conspiracy, ungrounded and unacted upon, that envisaged nothing less than the landing of a Spanish army in Wales and the deposition of James, who was to be replaced by his cousin, Arabella Stuart. When Cobham's younger brother George was interrogated concerning his involvement in a separate, English Catholic plot against James, he implicated his brother, who was quickly arrested and his own plot brought to light. Under examination in the Tower, Cobham placed the responsibility on Ralegh for their conspiracy. When Ralegh was arrested, damning mutual recriminations followed.

On November 17, 1603, Ralegh stood trial, and a guilty verdict was returned before nightfall. Although he conducted himself with admirable poise while under attack by the crown's attorney as a "monster," a "viper," and "the rankest traitor in all England," the jury reached its morally questionable but perhaps legally inevitable verdict.[4] Ralegh was always brave in the face of danger, and it appears he accepted with equanimity his sentence of death. More troubling for him were the ruinous consequences that he knew his conviction would have on his wife and child, and especially on his cherished plans to provide for his "son and heir apparent," as he usually referred to Wat in legal documents.

Five • Disinheritance and Corruption of Blood

Like Ralegh, Cobham was convicted of treason, and in death as in life he was accorded precedence over his co-conspirator. On December 9, he was led to the scaffold on Tower Green, and after he laid his head on the chopping block the executioner's axe suddenly was stayed. It seems the king had entertained second thoughts about the trial, and certainly he preferred to think of himself—and to be seen as—a compassionate monarch. (It is debatable, of course, how compassionate a reprieve is which delays its lifesaving mercy until the very last possible moment.) Ralegh's execution had been scheduled for a week after Cobham's; he and his family must have hoped for a similar act of royal mercy, but with no certainty. Once again, the ritual of execution was interrupted and Ralegh's life was spared.

Rather, Ralegh's life was spared after a fashion. Pointedly, he was not forgiven his crime of treason, which meant that the penalty of death had not been revoked and so could be enacted at the king's pleasure. In addition to the death sentence, a second grievous punishment for treason remained in force for Ralegh: that of attainder. In effect, attainder was a form of civil death, since the convicted man suffers the extinction of all his titles, offices and rights, including access to the law. Ralegh acknowledged his attainder when (after his conviction) he complained of his inability to recover goods stolen from his estate, bluntly declaring "the law knows me but for dead."[5]

Psychologically, death by attainder extended beyond the forfeit of legal rights. After the king cancelled his execution without annulling his attainder, Ralegh began to perceive himself to be no longer fully alive. In a letter to the king soon after his conviction, he dilated on the extent of his lifelessness:

> The life which I had, most mighty prince, the law hath taken from mee and I am now but the same earth and dust out of which I was made.... Name, bludd, gentillety or estate, I have none; no not so mich as a being; no not so mich as *vita plantae* [vegetable life].[6]

For fifteen years, until his execution was finally carried out, Ralegh was to struggle with his sense of being imprisoned in a shadowy, shameful form of quasi-existence.[7] Not surprisingly, his compromised, strangely provisional identity was soon to unsettle his formerly dominant place in the family.

As Ralegh well knew, the punishment of attainder engulfed the traitor's family and extended into perpetuity. Since treason was considered an offense against the monarch, the estate of an attainted person was deemed to be forfeit to the king or queen, who usually passed it on as booty to his or her favorites. (Lest we think of Ralegh as simply the victim of an unjust system, we should recall that in his glory days he had received attainted properties as a gift from Elizabeth.) Suddenly, Ralegh's great project of leaving a substantial inheritance to his son and heir apparent had come to naught. In one of his life's most devastating ironies, Ralegh himself was responsible—at least legally responsible—for destroying the patrimony that from Wat's infancy he had worked so hard to create and safeguard. The double portrait of the assured father and son, painted just a year earlier, must have seemed mockingly sanguine.

At his trial, Ralegh had spoken a suggestive phrase that reveals the depth and reach of his grief. Inviting the members of the jury to place themselves in his situation, he quickly moves from the threat to his own life to the suffering of his family, especially his offspring. Referring to attainder, he asks the jurors if "you yourselves would like to be hazarded in your lives, *disabled in your posterities*—your lands, goods, and all you have, confiscated—your wives, children and servants left crying to the world..." (italics added).[8] The italicized phrase is powerful because of its suggestion that, in injuring succeeding generations of his progeny, he has also disabled himself.[9] Five years later, Ralegh pleaded (in a losing cause) to retain the ownership of Sherborne because the loss of "the inheritance of my children and nephewes" would mean that "there remaynes nothing with me but the name of life, dispoiled of all ells but the title and sorrow thereof."[10]

Central to being "disabled in your posterities" is an especially repugnant aspect of attainder called "corruption of blood." This legal fiction punishes the descendants of a traitor even beyond disinheritance by attaching the paternal crime to them. Apparently, according to the *Oxford English Dictionary*, the idea of corrupted blood derived from a false etymology, as medieval jurists assumed that "attainder" (originally meaning seizure) marked the presence of an everlasting moral "taint" in the traitor's bloodline. As William Blackstone explained in his history of English law, "By attainder for treason or other felony, the blood of the person attainted is so corrupted, as to be rendered no longer inheritable."[11] Ironically, the only legal aspect of a father's or forefather's status that a traitor's descendants was able to inherit—indeed *had* to inherit—was the stain of being attainted. Although the traitor's descendants did not die a total civil death like his own, they lost all rights of rank and title, and his line did so forever. The only recourse for descendants of a traitor was to be "restored in blood" by an Act of Parliament, a reversal that Wat's younger brother Carew was eventually able to effect, but (with Lady Ralegh's commitment) only after decades of unremitting effort—and at the barely tolerable cost of finally renouncing all claim to the beloved Sherborne.[12] If a malign deity had set about to invent a means of punishing Ralegh, attainder and corruption of blood could not easily have been improved upon.

Five • Disinheritance and Corruption of Blood   65

For the patrilineal Ralegh, the concept of corruption of blood was especially painful because it effectively turned to a curse the proud statement he had made about Wat only a year earlier: that "he is parte of me and I live in him."[13] In the law of attainder, this shared life of father and son—each existing within the other—punishes both figures for their vital connection. Regardless of whether or not the father had committed the crime for which he was attainted, the injustice for sons was absolute; they could scarcely be responsible for the paternal corruption they inherited. And for sons who had fallen out with their fathers, as Wat was beginning to show signs of doing, there could be an additional, ironic twist of injustice: to be punished for bearing the "blood" of a father from whom one is at odds. Even in instances where an exemplary, mutually respectful relationship between father and son existed, it would have been difficult for an attainted son not to blame his father for crippling his prospects.

In Ralegh's defense, it is clear that his failure to provide for Wat did not stem from negligence or lack of sustained effort. As we have seen, his single surviving last will and testament was obsessed with providing for Wat, to the detriment of Lady Ralegh. Much closer to his downfall—only months before Elizabeth's death—he had taken additional steps to ensure that upon his demise Wat would succeed to the ownership of Sherborne and his other properties. In January of 1603, Ralegh had his lawyer draw up a conveyance of his estate to his son. Clearly Ralegh foresaw trouble, but the specific danger he was attempting to avoid is not clear. Since later that same year, he was convicted for treason and suffered attainder, it is tempting to think that he sensed his imminent downfall and sought to prevent the forfeiture of his property by first making it over to Wat. But Ralegh was probably not so prescient—later he claimed he had been negotiating with the trustees for almost two years before the document was signed.[14] His likely concern was that, if he died before Wat came of age—certainly a statistical probability—the boy could be seized as a ward of the crown, leaving his patrimonial estate vulnerable to various forms of legal predation, including meddling in marriage arrangements. (It was this form of legal injustice that Ralegh had sought to pursue with regard to Elizabeth Bassett and her inherited wealth.) If Wat were not of age at his father's death, Sherborne and its beloved grounds would become subject to the creative exploitation of the master of wards, who was none other than the increasingly untrustworthy Robert Cecil.[15]

The indenture that was drawn up between Ralegh and three trustees provides a window into his patrilineal commitment to Wat and future progeny. It is unlike his will and other early documents concerning property in that Lady Ralegh must have been aware of its contents; two of the trustees were related to her, one being her loyal brother, Arthur. But if Ralegh is less devious than before, his focus remains the same. After declaring "the natural Love and affection which the said Sir Walter Ralegh knighte beareth unto Walter Ralegh his sonne and heire apparaunte," the document expresses the dynastic hope that "for so longe tyme as yt shall plese all mightie God" Sherborne and other listed properties shall "remayne, continynewe, be, and discende in the name and bloode of the said Sir Walter Ralegh."[16] The proliferation of verbs of continuance bespeaks an underlying fear of disruption, and Ralegh proceeds to acknowledge the ultimate source of contingency: that his patrimony will endure only "for so longe tyme as yt shall plese all mightie God." A ten-year-old son is very much a hostage to higher powers.

The remainder of the document is taken up with what seems an endless procession of future Raleghs; in a numbingly repeated formulary, various lands are first pledged to Wat and then to the "heirs males lawfully begotten" of his body, a screed applied to entirely hypothetical but carefully enumerated second, third, fourth, and fifth sons. For a reader who knows the Raleghs' story, this language is a poignant mix of mindless bureaucratic redundancy and magical incantation, conjuring up heirs out of thin air. In the Scottish play Shakespeare wrote a few years later, the witches imagined a long line of heirs ("Banquo's issue") stretching into the future, but the playwright's prophesy of King James's ancestors had the considerable benefit of historical hindsight.[17]

Ralegh's prudence in the face of an uncertain future is evident in his cautious retaining (for the duration of his life) of the income from his properties, and in addition he retained the right to revoke the document during his lifetime or by will after his death. Moreover, he acknowledges—given a possible "defaulte" with regard to male offspring—the conceivable necessity of arranging inheritance through daughters, and if they too are in default, he turns (as he had in his will) to his brother Carew and his sons. Lady Ralegh is nowhere mentioned.

Unfortunately, Ralegh's due diligence did not extend to a close reading of the actual document of conveyance to which he put his name. Not long after his conviction, an assiduous government lawyer noticed an unobtrusive yet fatal flaw in the document: that the clerk who copied it from the draft had accidentally deleted a key phrase that conclusively would have removed the ownership from Ralegh. Thus, even though the intent of the document was clear enough, this technicality meant that Ralegh was deemed to be still in possession of Sherborne. As a result, the property would have to be forfeited to the king. In Ralegh's bitterly terse phrase, later repeated by Carew, Wat's inheritance was "lost in law for want of a word."[18] Small wonder that in his *Instructions to His Son* he warned Wat never to trust a lawyer, for "hee will finde an evasion by a syllable, or word, to abuse thee."[19]

After Ralegh's conviction, the idea of patrilineal inheritance no longer remained a magical talisman, and it even began to summon up dark, ironic thoughts. In the winter of 1604–05 (at the end of his first full year in the Tower) he wrote a dispirited letter to Robert Cecil in which Lady Ralegh's imminent childbirth seems to have contributed to his depression. Among other worries, he bitterly expresses his concern for his family—"a wife and a childe and a wife with childe"—who "have nothing elce to inherite then my shame and ther owne misery."[20] He had lived with the intention of becoming an honorably generous ancestor, but his legacy was now worse than nothing. The loss of Sherborne meant that Ralegh could no longer—without shame—continue to define a meaningful patrimony in terms of heritable commodities.

For the first time, Ralegh had reason to see himself not as the heroic antithesis of his father—the man who failed to leave him a patrimony—but rather as a man similar to his father, another Walter Ralegh who failed to provide for his same-named son. However, as Sir Walter would have noticed, there is a crucial difference between the situations of the two of them, a difference that does not redound to his own credit: that while his undistinguished father may have served as a positive stimulus to his son's achievement, Ralegh's ill-fame as a traitor closed doors to his "corrupted" son.

What Ralegh required, for himself and for Wat, was a new understanding of what a father could give his son. In place of his earlier emphasis on the promised patrimony of Sherborne, he would have to think in terms of a patrimony of character and of values to live by. When Ralegh articulated this new understanding to Wat, inevitably he was true to—and perhaps limited by—the qualities he identified in himself. On the assumption that "I live in him and he is parte of me," Ralegh sought to encourage Wat to engage energetically with life, as he had in his own youth. As John Aubrey said of Ralegh, he "was no Slug," being a person "much immerst in action all along, and in fabrication of his owne Fortunes."[21] Ralegh exhorts Wat to fashion a life similar to his own. As Polonius reveals in his admonishment to his son—"to thine own self be true"—when a father encourages a son to be true to himself, the self he has in mind is apt to resemble closely the life he himself has lived.

In a fascinating exhortation that Ralegh wrote for Wat, the second of his addresses to him, we can see his attempt to rally his son's spirits and indirectly perhaps his own. The editors of Ralegh's letters thought he probably intended this 500 word address to serve as an introduction to the *Instructions for His Son*, and tentatively they assigned a date of "?C.1610" to it.[22] We can be relatively certain, however, that he wrote his urgent appeal before the deferral of his execution on 9 December 1603, because he speaks insistently as if his death is an imminent reality.[23] In "Three Things There Be," the imagined death of Wat hung over the poem, but here Ralegh's own death is front and center, the limitation that gives life meaning. Twice he bids "Farewell" to Wat, and he also reassures him that, since there is no "perturbation within mee to depart this world," he is ready to "give place to fresh gamesters." Still more telling is how, after he disavows having "affected promotion" in his career, he solemnly declares (in the language of final testaments) that "the same holy and just ambition I bequeath to thee my deere and wellbeloved sonne." The word "bequeath" indicates that he thinks of this document as the only sort of last will and testament allowed by attainder—one in which only immaterial goods can be transmitted.

Ralegh's desire to create a substitute for Wat's lost patrimony is everywhere apparent though nowhere explicit in the text. Precisely because he knows that Wat cannot receive an estate, Ralegh begins by urging him to "awaken thyself to industrye and rowse upp thy spirits for the world." The next sentence tacitly acknowledges the devastating reality of attainder by making an heroic virtue of economic necessity: "Greate possessions would make thee lazie: I would have thee to be the sonne of thyne owne fortunes aswell as my sonne." Ralegh's phrasing reflects one of the cornerstones of Renaissance humanist thought: the redefinition of nobility in terms of ethics rather than material estate. In the traditional (primarily aristocratic) view, nobility is a function of social rank, and thus it is maintained by patrimonial inheritance. Many humanist thinkers, however, revivified the Roman idea embodied in the tag line *Virtus vera nobilitas est* (true nobility consists in the exercise of virtue).[24]

In another common Renaissance trope, young men who shape their own fortunes are said to be, or claim to be, the father (as in author) of themselves. Thomas Nashe seems to be characterizing himself as well as his innovative prose style when he asserts that "the vein which I have ... is of my own begetting, and calls no man father in England but my self."[25] Much closer to Ralegh's language is a statement made by his friend Gervase Holles in his family history; speaking of different social levels of birth, he says "let it be of never so humble a condition yet it lies in himselfe to

Five • Disinheritance and Corruption of Blood

become the parent of his own nobility as well the sonne of his owne fortune."[26] Ralegh echoes the point by hoping that Wat will be "the sonne of thyne owne fortunes," but he adds "aswell as my sonne." Even when he imagines Wat as fathering himself through self-fashioning, Ralegh insists on his own connection with him. Throughout the exhortation, we can see Ralegh's tacit sense of shared identity with Wat, and we can see his address as not only philosophy but also a remembrance of his own daring youth. What Ralegh seems to be thinking, but not saying, is "We are alike, you and I, and since I lived such a large, brave life, you can do so as well."

Ever the dialectician, Ralegh immediately follows his clarion call to action with a long, vivid evocation of the great perils of the life he has just urged upon Wat. In addition to the timeless truth that "All is vanity and wearynes," Ralegh adduces a particular spiritual danger: that of attempting to make more of ourselves than God's "ordinance and providence" permit. Adopting the imagery of seafaring, always a source of energy in his prose, Ralegh proceeds skeptically to emphasize mankind's inability to control fortune, declaring that "Wee are toyled and hazarded with tempests and stormes that rise abroad.... Publicke affaires are rockes, private conversations are whirlepooles and quicksesandes. Itt is alike perilous to doe well and to doe ill." With his own downfall fresh in his mind, Ralegh seems to be momentarily creating an argument for Wat *not* to venture on the seas of fortune. At the risk of subverting the ethos of ambition with which he opened, he cannot resist stressing the limits of human control: "Oure good or ill depends not simply in oure owne counsels and resolutions but more often upon adventures [chance events] that lye not in oure management."

After this evocation of overwhelming peril, Ralegh returns (perhaps rather cavalierly) to his opening exhortation. Indeed, his opening address ("I would have thee my sonne awaken thyself to industrye") is now echoed by "Nevertheles, my sonne, take harte and courage to thee." It is no coincidence that these two entreaties to action are the only instances in the text in which Ralegh directly addresses Wat as "my sonne." The phrasing points to a thought that is unspoken but clearly on Ralegh's mind: that Wat will be his son to the degree that he undertakes a life of risk commensurate with his own storied life.

At the close, Ralegh breaks out the sea imagery again, now rising to the poetic suggestion that life is an audacious voyage of discovery: "Thy adventure lies in this troublesome barque." Earlier Ralegh had spoken of the "adventures" or chance occurrences that test human resourcefulness, but here he speaks of Wat's life as an "adventure" in the modern sense of the term—an exciting, risky enterprise. He does not minimize the danger, for "troublesome" carries its old meaning of "full of affliction or distress," and a "barque" is a small vessel that would be completely at the mercy of a storm.[27] Perhaps the most one can hope for is to engage in the pursuit with honor and dignity, and Ralegh ends by urging Wat to "Strive if thou canst to make good thy station in the upper decke. Those that live under hatches are ordained to be drudges and slaves." Life may be ordained to be tragic, but one can live with courage and dignity. After bidding Wat "Farewell," Ralegh ends on a religious note that, unlike the final couplet in "Three Things There Be," has a West Country forthrightness: "God only is sure and true evermore to those that are true to him. Noe gospell truer then this in proofe."

The entire address to Wat is powerfully written and deserves a place in future anthologies of Ralegh's best writing. But it may be better prose than advice. Ralegh is still writing from the assumption that he and Wat share a common identity and that his son is an image of himself with a life that could be lived as he had lived his own. After all, was it not Ralegh's unique spirit rather than a filial inheritance that had created his own success? What he had done, perhaps his son (with the help of paternal exhortation) could do. But there may be a flaw in Ralegh's urging a version of his own struggle upon his son—his exhortation does not take into account the very catastrophe that had made the advice necessary. Why would his son's fortunes turn out to be different from his own?

As the years passed, Ralegh's shame at failing to leave Wat a landed patrimony seems to have lost its sharp edge, or at least he spoke of it less frequently. But it was never far from his mind. A full decade after entering prison, Ralegh's lingering bitterness can be detected in one of his many satirical moments in the *History of the World*. Speaking of avaricious men who become fearful for their souls as they near death, Ralegh says they justify their ill-gotten gains by declaring to God that "I shall praejudice my sonne (which I am resolved not to doe) if I make restitution."[28] Ralegh's satire is whetted by his realization that, despite all his efforts, he was not able to accomplish what many truly corrupt men successfully do: leave a valuable estate to their heirs.

• Six •

A Paterfamilias Undone

On December 12, 1603, the day appointed for Ralegh's execution, the king dramatically intervened to cancel the proceedings but declined to rescind the death sentence itself. It was a stroke of mean genius, a demonstration of mercy that was also a show of whimsical power, leaving Ralegh still legally deceased, a dead man pacing in the Tower. The king's grace was especially cruel because Ralegh was prepared for, and in some moods welcomed, his natural death. In his trial, he had done much to restore the good name that was so important to him. For his family, he had done the little that attainder and corruption of blood allowed him to do, seeking every advantage he could think of. Moreover, he still possessed the illusory comfort of believing he had saved Sherborne by having transferred its future ownership to Wat. Certainly Ralegh would have been spared much suffering if the king had not spared his life.

Shortly before his expected execution, Ralegh wrote to his wife a calm, deeply felt letter in which he appears to achieve the acceptance of death for which he had been struggling. With that acceptance came a mitigation of his desire to control his family. Speaking with a rare openness, Ralegh escapes from the prison house of self-regard in tendering to Bess "all the thankes which my heart can conceive or my words can express for your many travailes and care taken for mee...."[1] As in his previous letter to her, he mentions her possible remarriage, but this time with a difference.[2] Instead of trying to define the nature of a future marriage as he had before, he warns her generally of "the pretences of men," adding "I speake not this (God knows) to disswade you from marriage, for it will bee best for you, both in respect of the world and of God." Notably, he no longer attempts to extend his spiritual presence into a new marriage by advancing Wat as a surrogate for himself.

If there is a subtle nudge in the letter, it is not with regard to Lady

Ralegh's remarriage but to her future care of Wat. When Ralegh asks her to "Remember your poore child for his fathers sake, who chose you and loved you in his happiest tymes," he may still feel a twinge of uncertainty about her commitment to their son. While beautifully (and for the only recorded time) recalling their early love, he asks her for his own sake to "remember your poore child," as if her love for Wat alone might not supply sufficient motive for her care. The phrase "*your* poore child" may be a tactful reminder that Wat will be her responsibility in the future. At the close of the letter, however, his customary pronoun reclaims his son: "My deare wife farewell. Blesse my poore boye." Asking Lady Ralegh to bless Wat is a telling gesture, since Elizabethan parents—usually with the father taking the priest-like lead—gave their formal blessing to their children upon parting from them.[3] Poignantly, Ralegh realizes that he will no longer participate in this little domestic ritual—his wife must bless Wat for him.

The delicate equilibrium that Ralegh had achieved within himself and his family was undone by the indefinite postponement of his execution. This eminently proud man, who always had been animated by an awareness of his honor's exigent demands, would struggle to find a new basis for self-respect. Before the king's reprieve, Ralegh felt he had debased his honor by pleading with his domestic enemies (including the king) for his life. Thus, in his farewell letter to his wife before his expected execution, he tasks her with retrieving these shameful pleas:

> Gett those letters (if it bee possible) which I writ to the lords wherein I sued for my life. God is my wittnesse, itt was for you and yours I desired life. But itt is true that I disdaine my selfe for begging itt. For know it (deare wife) that your sonne is the sonne of a true man….[4]

For the patrilineal Ralegh, to be a "true man"—and thus to be a worthy father and respected ancestor—is to live (and die) with indomitable courage and thus with honor. Ralegh is ambivalent about his manhood, as he denies acting out of cowardice ("itt was for you and yours I desired life") but still scorns himself for weakness. When he requests Lady Ralegh to know "that your sonne is the sonne of a true man," perhaps he reveals his own lack of conviction.

After his reprieve, Ralegh found himself continuing to write what he considered demeaning letters in pursuit of freedom for himself and support for his family. Apart from pleading with former friends like Cecil and outright enemies like the king, there was very little that this man given to grandly decisive action could do. As a consequence of his attainder, Ralegh had undergone a civic death, and the sense of having lost his identity (and thus his life) would haunt him for many years. In one of his many dispirited moments, he characterizes himself to Robert Cecil as possessing an existence so tenuous that it "cannot be calde a life but only misery drawn out and spoone [spun] into a long thride."[5]

Ralegh's deep despondency eroded his role as paterfamilias since, his agency having been taken from him by the crown, he no longer felt that he commanded, or even merited, his family's respect. Although he had never attempted to be a domineering patriarch—we have seen his reluctance to command spousal and filial obedience—Ralegh held to the dominant view of his time that a father exercised, or at least *should* exercise, authority over his wife and children. This authority was grounded in the central principle that Ralegh conventionally called "the dominion of Reason over Appetite," which within the family was thought to be manifested in the rule of men over women and children.[6] In theory, the observance of this moral hierarchy creates order within the family, and Ralegh's characterization of this order is simplicity itself: "The rule of the husband over the wife, and of parents over their children, is naturall, and appointed by God himselfe; so that it is alwaies, and simplie, allowable and good." In his own family, however, Ralegh came to understand that this paternal rule was not as "naturall" as he had assumed.

In the Tower years, the Raleghs' family constellation changed markedly. At Sherborne, it had comported in a general way with the age's conventional gender roles in which the spheres appropriate to husband and wife were defined as mutually exclusive. The husband ventured for gain outside the home and the wife remained within it. In the succinct words of an Elizabethan treatise, "The office of the husbande is to go abroad in matters of profite, of the wyfe to tarry at home, and see all be well there."[7] Before his imprisonment, the Raleghs' marriage resembles an exaggerated version of this dichotomy—he trawled through both hemispheres in pursuit of gain and glory, while her primary concern was their Sherborne home and little Wat. That duty required considerable skill in finances and oversight, but it was primarily domestic in nature.

Of course, Lady Ralegh had not been a retiring housewife—she would have appeared at court in an instant if the queen had allowed her to do so—and her personality was not of the retiring kind. She was capable of fury, as her loyal brother Arthur knew when he pointedly referred to her as Morgan le Fay, the legendary figure who attempted on several occasions to kill her brother, King Arthur.[8] And even before her husband's trial and imprisonment, she was perceived by court enemies as a force to be reckoned with. The Raleghs' most virulent opponent was Henry Howard, the earl of Northampton and uncle of the Henry Howard who would marry Wat's intended, Elizabeth Bassett. Northampton's hatred of Ralegh ("the greatest Lucifer") quickly extended to Lady Ralegh, and this venerator of hierarchy and ancient titles declared her to be "as furious as Proserpina," one who "bendes her whole witts and industrie to the disturbance of all motions ... that may disturb the possibility of others' hopes, sinc her owne cannot be securid."[9] In other words, she had the temerity to cross his lordship.

Clearly Lady Ralegh had never been as silent and docile as the ideal wife proposed by clergymen, and was becoming markedly less so, but the shape of the Raleghs' marriage had been essentially traditional. After Ralegh's arrest, however, the familiar apportioning of roles was suddenly inverted. His imprisonment in the Tower became a caricature of the figurative bondage to the home that preachers often associated with wifely duty, while his wife ventured into the world of politics to acquire the means for her family to survive. With intrepid energy, she rallied friends and placed maximum pressure—often involving guilt—on the men who were determining the fate of the three of them. As he was losing his familiar self in this inversion of roles, she found a voice and a calling. Ralegh must have had his wife as well as his late queen in mind when he later took issue with an early Father of the church: "Cyril affirmeth, 'That the souls of women are very womanish; hard, and slow

At the height of the family's prosperity, Lady Ralegh is depicted wearing her finest attire. Unknown artist, *Portrait of Lady Ralegh* (née Elizabeth Throckmorton) England, 17th century (1565–1647), 1603 (courtesy the National Gallery of Ireland).

to understand hard things.' But, by his leave, some women, even in this, have been able to match the greatest men."[10]

Ralegh's patrilineal cast of mind is clear when, before his trial, he pleaded with his principal accusers to restrain themselves and not "carlessly to distroy the father and the fatherlesse."[11] His assumption that the destruction of the father entails that of the son is based on a sober understanding of the law of attainder, but it ignores the agency of the mother. Lady Ralegh's interventions, however, would prove to be crucial. During Ralegh's long incarceration, two fellow prisoners—Lord Cobham and Lord Grey—suffered total financial ruin, and his own family's avoidance of that fate can be attributed largely to the intrepid efforts of his wife.[12]

One of the earliest indications of Lady Ralegh's newfound agency was her decision—soon after the countermanded execution—to leave Sherborne in order to take up lodgings (along with Wat) in Ralegh's quarters in the Tower of London. Her desire to live with her husband in prison was highly unconventional, even startling. (The king must have approved, however, since the Tower was formally a royal palace as well as a prison, and all decisions about the living situation of its inhabitants were his to make.) We can be sure that Lady Kildare and Dorothy Percy—the wives of Ralegh's fellow prisoners, the Lord Cobham and Henry Percy, earl of Northumberland—harbored no wish to abandon their manors and join their husbands. (Percy purchased a lodging in the Tower adjacent to his own so his six-year-old son and the boy's servant could visit for extended stays, but Lady Percy did not join him and was presumably not invited.[13]) Lady Ralegh's act was certainly brave and devoted, but more was involved than a desire to live in supportive proximity to her husband. By joining him, she was removing herself from the periphery of action and placing herself as close as possible to the center of decision-making concerning her family.

While there is no reason to think he was consulted, it is likely that Wat would have been delighted by the prospect of moving to London. Beautiful as it was, Sherborne was not a very stimulating environment for a boy who had lived there all his life, and the thought of living in the Tower with both his father and his mother must have been comforting. Presumably London would not have been entirely new to Wat, for before his father's downfall he and his mother must have visited him at his center of operations at Durham House on the Strand. Though the splendid rooms were only leased, not granted, by the queen, Ralegh poured money into them, covering the walls with tapestries that after his downfall he would be forced to sell for a song. We can imagine the attraction for Wat of his

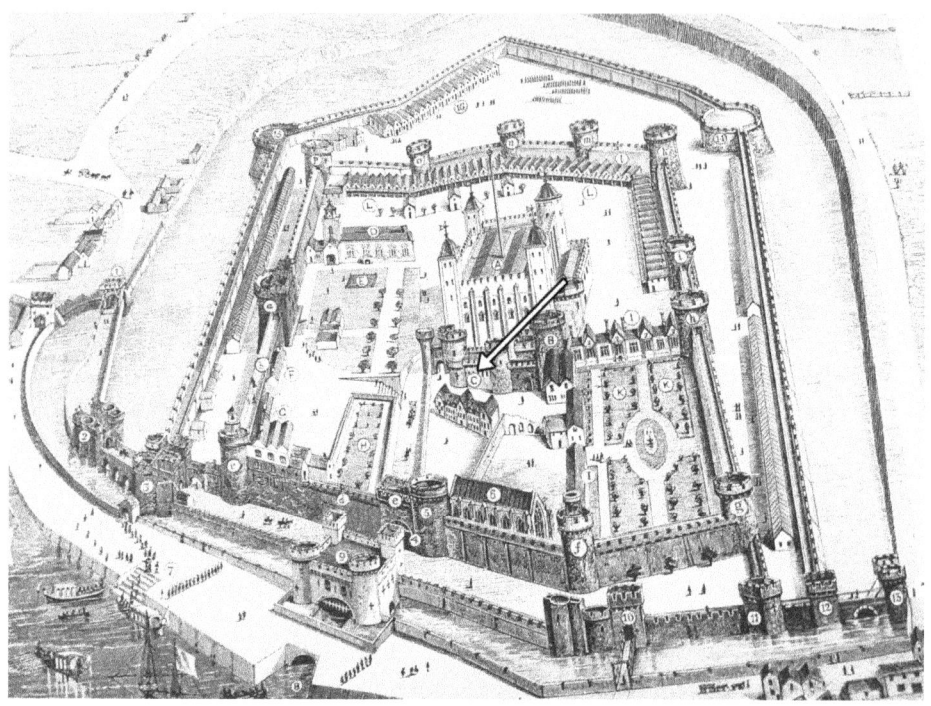

The Tower of London was Ralegh's home for thirteen years. His quarters (white arrow) are over the gateway at the inner wall (from William Hepworth Dixon, *Her Majesty's Tower*, 6th ed. vol. 1 [1870]).

father's collection of maps and abstruse navigational devices, to say nothing of the trophies (including some natives) brought back from many expeditions.

But the Tower of London must have been incomparably thrilling for a boy of ten who may have heard tales from his parents of their own imprisonments. It was the dark embodiment of England's long history of political violence, its places of death notable and numerous. In fact, his father's chambers were connected to the so-called bloody tower, the scene of Richard of Gloucester's often retold and always fiendish murder of the two young princes. Of course the tower green, site of so many judicial beheadings throughout the years and perhaps graced with a permanent chopping block, was an ominous presence, especially since Wat's father had only recently and narrowly escaped becoming another victim. But the Tower was full of life as well, and his father's chambers above the tower gate provided a fine site for observing the stream of comings and goings. Within the Tower, there were many attractions untouched by the macabre history of the place, such as the royal menagerie, which had become a major attraction after its celebrated resident lions produced a litter of "whelps" that were closely monitored by the king and many others—Wat would often have been present at feeding time.[14]

As Wat was discovering a new world, his parents must have been recovering a lost dimension of intimacy in the two chambers allotted to Ralegh (and to two servants).[15] In the fall of 1604 Lady Ralegh discovered she was pregnant. Although the Tower provided amenities (at a cost) for its prisoners, who were in a sense guests of the king, it was certainly not a safe environment for childbirth and babies. In late 1604, when Lady Ralegh was well along in her pregnancy, Ralegh complained to Cecil of "my poore child having lien this 14 dayes next to a wooman with a running plaug [plague] sore and but a paper wall betwen, and whose childe is also this Thursday dead of the plauge."[16] Lady Ralegh and her son must have found new London lodgings very soon after this dreadful incident because—forgetting about the mortal danger to Wat that he had just stressed—in his next line Ralegh complains to Cecil that "now my wife and child and others in whom I had cumfort have abandoned me, and in what fearfull estate the Lord knows." He was not to be outdone in victimhood.

Lady Ralegh took a nearby house on Tower Hill, close to the parish church of All Hallows Barking, an area she would live in for more than a decade.[17] The Raleghs' child was born—probably in Lady Ralegh's lodgings—in early February of 1605, and on the 15th he was christened in the Tower in the aptly named chapel of St. Peter ad Vincula ("St. Peter in Chains") as Carew Ralegh. Perhaps his name points to a shifting of weight within the marriage, since (unlike those of his brothers) it reflects the family of Lady Ralegh as well as that of her husband; in addition to being the first name of Ralegh's trusted older brother, "Carew" was the maiden surname of Lady Ralegh's mother.[18] Perhaps because he did not think that Carew would be his heir and rarely was in his company, Ralegh seems never to have developed strong feelings for this child, who proved to be a far more dutiful son than his older, more intractable brother. In the decades to follow, Carew would labor with his mother (unsuccessfully) to regain Sherborne and (successfully) to restore the blood and good name of the family through an act of parliament.

The Raleghs' divided household resulted in a good deal of coming and going on Wat's part, noted in a communiqué to Robert Cecil by Sir William Waad, the newly appointed Lieutenant of the Tower. Waad, who had served as one of the king's commissioners at Ralegh's trial and was no friend, complained to his patron Cecil that Ralegh "challenges his keeper [himself] that the lords gave him more liberty for his son to go abroad, and his physician to resort to him, which I assure he uses only to justify himself."[19] What is this "liberty for his son to go abroad" that Ralegh claims Waad reneged on? It has been interpreted as "permission for Wat to travel on the Continent" or "the freedom to go to Oxford," but these glosses are highly implausible given that Wat was only twelve and the family finances strained.[20] An important textual detail indicates that Ralegh is challenging his keeper to give Wat comparatively "*more* freedom" to go abroad, a qualification that makes no sense regarding putative travel to the Continent or Oxford.

The difficulties evaporate if "abroad" is taken in its now archaic meaning of "out of one's house or abode." Ralegh's charge that "the lords gave him more liberty for his son to go abroad" means that the keeper is not allowing Wat to come and go from the Tower as often as the privy council had promised. (Ralegh's accusation is supported by a document—sent to Waad some months earlier—in which the lords list Ralegh's "Lady and his son and her waiting maid" as persons allowed free access to him.[21]) Wat's freedom to come and go was important to his father, for reasons beyond the pleasure of tweaking Waad's nose.[22] At this time (December 1605), Wat must have been essential as a messenger to Lady Ralegh, who had little mobility since she was organizing her new dwelling and preparing for childbirth. It is easy to imagine the curious lad deriving great satisfaction from being of service to his parents and in the process discovering his freedom. As London neighborhoods went, Tower Hill was relatively sedate, with large residences and open streets—they lived on Broad Street—but for the boy from Sherborne any degree of urban bustle and busyness would have been stimulating and enjoyable.

Wat's time at the Tower, however, was to have a less entertaining side, as an ominous entry in the list of visitors allowed to Ralegh suggests: "Talbot, a Schoolmaster."[23] Being now in sustained contact with Wat—perhaps for the first time—and with a mind to prepare him for Oxford, Ralegh decided to institute a serious educational regimen to make up for lost time. Given his own background and his plans for Wat, it was a foregone conclusion that his son's tutor would be an Oxford man, and John Talbot fit the bill. Soon after receiving his B.A. at Magdalen Hall (1596), Talbot became a fellow of Merton College, taking his M.A. in 1600.[24] (He may have come to Ralegh's notice through Bess, who had social connections with several women in the extended Talbot family.[25]) John Talbot's tutoring must have pleased his employer (if not his student), for he moved into Ralegh's quarters in the Tower, becoming his secretary and remaining with him for the long remainder of his imprisonment and beyond. As well as being Wat's tutor, Talbot may have brought a companion for him—a list of persons allowed by the lords to remain in the Tower with Ralegh includes (along with Talbot and a servant) "John Talbot, a boy."[26]

Ralegh would not have entrusted Wat's education to a person whom he did not respect, and years later, in a letter from Guiana, he praised Talbot as "an excellent general scholar and as faithful true man as lived."[27] No evidence of Talbot's interactions with Wat survives, but we can be sure that an emphasis on reading and writing Latin—the *sine qua non* for admission to university—was a central focus of the boy's studies. Inevitably, there would have been plenty of memorization as well as making English translations from and then back into Latin. Although discipline must have been insisted on, Talbot was no bloodless pedant.

Clearly Ralegh trusted both Talbot's learning and sound values, and a little-known episode tells us a good deal about Talbot's forthright character. When Ralegh's old friend, Henry Percy, earl of Northumberland, was being tried in Star Chamber for his supposed participation in the Gunpowder plot, a young man was heard questioning vociferously (and dangerously) the justice of the government's proceedings. The outspoken man was drawn into conversation by a timeserving bystander, who identified him as Talbot and promptly denounced him to Robert Cecil. Fortunately for Talbot, when Cecil received the informer's documents he did not initiate an action but rather circumspectly filed them away in his family's enormous archives.[28] Given the force of his loyalty, it comes as no surprise that Talbot sailed with Ralegh and Wat on their perilous voyage to Guiana.

For Ralegh, it was natural to feel gratitude for his servant's loyalty through the years, but his feelings toward his equally loyal wife were complicated by the fact that he was becoming uncomfortably beholden to her. Her vigorous interventions on behalf of her husband and children threatened his sense of honor and manhood, and he was sensitive to a common opinion articulated by his friend Henry Percy: that always "when the woman governs, the man grew straight into contempt."[29] Even before the birth of Carew, Lady Ralegh was successfully engaged in advancing the family's fortunes. Lady Ralegh's early interventions with Cecil and the king helped to account for a crucial anomaly: that, unlike those of his convicted conspirators, Grey and Cobham, Ralegh's attainder did not immediately strip him of his lands.[30] Moreover, Lady Ralegh cajoled from her old friend Cecil the crucial promise that Sherborne—by far the family's most valuable asset—would be placed in trust for her and Wat, which was soon done (but later undone by subsequent legal rulings).[31]

In part, Lady Ralegh's campaign prospered because of ambiguities in the law of treason, a subject in which her family was extremely well-versed. (Her father, Sir Nicholas Throckmorton, was one of the rare men who underwent trial for treason and was not convicted.) This legal uncertainty was especially exploitable for the wives of convicted traitors. The patrilineal punishment of attainder stressed male "blood" in a way that could leave wives in a relatively better financial situation than their supposedly corrupted children. Customarily, the condemned man's wife lost her right to the usual widow's dower at her husband's death (usually one-third of his lands), but this was not inevitable. Moreover, in some circumstances "she could retain lands she possessed in her own right apart from dower," and there was a possibility (depending on the monarch's whim) that she could be granted her husband's goods and movables.[32] Lady Ralegh had room to maneuver, and she took full advantage of it.

English law considered treason a personal attack upon the monarch, to whom the traitor's forfeitures always went, so the reigning king or queen had a largely free hand in creating the terms with which the traitor's family was treated. Since James was new to the English throne and not bound by rulings of his own, his hand was uncommonly free, thus offering additional opportunities for Lady Ralegh. Of course, it was to her advantage that James saw himself—and wished to be seen—as a forgiving and loving monarch, an image that his trial and imprisonment of Ralegh had not burnished. Since she had been a good friend of Robert Cecil's lamented wife, Lady Ralegh had access to a king and his right-hand man who were guilt-prone with regard to Ralegh's family, if not to Ralegh himself.

Unlike his wife's, Ralegh's attempts to aid his family were perforce confined to letter-writing, and even his letters suffered from a form of confinement. His internalization of the role of rational (male) authority persisted, constraining the language in which he sought redress for his precious family. Lady Ralegh felt no such constraint. In their letters to Cecil, both the Raleghs placed a good deal of emphasis on little Wat, who had no enemies and could not be blamed for his parents' actions. But in parallel pleas, they did so in very different ways.

Though we cannot doubt his deep concern, Ralegh's pleas for his family are usually couched in the logical, emotionally reserved terms deemed appropriate for statesmanlike discourse. Thus, in a plea to Cecil on behalf of his family, he sounds slightly grudging as he speaks of how his wife and son, "who are altogether healpless, and who dayly wound my sowle with the memory of their miseries, force mee in despight of all resolvedness both to bewayle them and labor for them."[33] He sounds unwillingly put upon, as his dependents "force" him to lament them and to work on their behalf, and he seems to justify his ensuing distress by claiming to have marshalled "all resolvedness" to resist grieving for them. Although this letter does not provide evidence for questioning Ralegh's familial love and loyalty, it certainly shows how difficult it was for him to acknowledge those emotions to his superior.

Unlike her pointedly detached husband, Lady Ralegh takes a direct, personal approach to Cecil in an attempt to evoke his pity and guilt. In a letter contemporary with her husband's, she implores him to "Pitti the name of your ancient frind on his poor littell cretuer [creature], wich may leve [live] to honnar you; that wee all may lift up our handes and hartes in prayeur for you and youres."[34] To refer to Ralegh as Cecil's "ancient frind" succinctly recalls their long relationship, but her main emphasis is on Wat. It is with a deft patrilineal touch that she asks Cecil not simply to pity Wat but rather to "Pitti the name of your ancient frind on his poor little cretuer" so that he may live to "honnar you." Still more deft is her ending with a promise of prayer for "you and youres." Her final word is carefully weighed, for "youres" refers primarily to Cecil's heir and only son, William, the boy whom the Raleghs had taken in and comforted when his father was engaged in matters of state.

Lady Ralegh lost little time in securing what was left of her husband's goods and chattels, which the king's favorites—most notably the avaricious Henry Howard—were attempting to seize. Though her intervention with Cecil was crucial, Lady Ralegh did not receive these goods in her own name. Through letters patent, the king granted "all and singular the goods and chattels as well as personal moveable and immoveable" to John Shelbury and Robert Smyth (the former being Ralegh's solicitor and the latter a friend), who implicitly are to act as trustees for Lady Ralegh.[35] To be sure, the king's generosity was perhaps not all that great since Ralegh's considerable debts were to be paid from his goods and movables, but the victory put the wind in Lady Ralegh's sails, and she determined to fight for every available advantage. As her interventions increased, so did her husband's uneasiness. Every step of progress she made was a reminder of his own inadequacy, and his discomfort at his wife's success can be heard. Thus, after he acknowledged to Cecil that "It pleased the Kinge to promis my wife her goods and chatells," Ralegh rather ungallantly took the credit for her actions by claiming that "I have willed her to sew [sue] for them."[36] The confident Ralegh of old would have thought it unseemly and unnecessary to have claimed his agency.

Probably through Lady Ralegh's efforts, the royal attainder (forced forfeiture) of their lands was not immediately enacted, so in the early years of Sir Walter's imprisonment his wife was able to pursue schemes for retaining as much as possible. In letters and in physical appearances, Lady Ralegh increasingly directed her attention to the king. As useful as Cecil had been, he was not endlessly patient—after Edward Wingfield's wife lengthily had solicited him on her husband's behalf, Cecil frostily warned her that any further efforts would "do him harm rather than good."[37] Besides, it was the king whose discretion—and mercy—really mattered. We can see Lady Ralegh's effective rhetorical approach to James in an attempt to retain a "fee farm" in Dorset that was in danger of reverting to the crown. In a letter, she beseeches his "abundant goodness" to relinquish his right to the property and (biblically) to "suffer those poore harmless children to injoy the same."[38] Rather adroitly, she urges this monarch, who saw himself as God's representative on earth, to act "in imitation of the most just and mercifull God, who though Hee punished the fathers, yet Hee gave the land to the guileless and innocent children." It is not clear if James acceded to this tacit denial of contagion of blood.

She did, however, make considerable headway. In July of 1604 the king granted to two loyal friends of the Raleghs as trustees "the Sherborne Estate for 60 years or so long as Sir Walter Raleigh should live, for the benefit of Lady Raleigh and the eldest son Walter."[39] This grant was significant, as it staved off forfeiture for the immediate future, but of course the king could determine how long "Sir Walter Raleigh should live" since he was still under the sentence of death. Still more promising was an extraordinary draft that James later sent to Robert Cecil, instructing him to draw up a grant concerning Ralegh's lands in which all the royal "title and interest may be past [passed] over unto his wife and children, that We be no more troubled with their pittifull cries and complaints for that busines." This unqualified grant of Sherborne to Lady Ralegh and her sons was too good to come true, and it did not—either Cecil decided to forget about it or James changed his mind.

With regard to Lady Ralegh's means of persuasion, one comment in the king's unfulfilled grant is particularly important. The reason James gives for making it is not a desire to imitate God but rather sheer irritation: "that We be no more troubled with their pittifull cries and complaints for that busines." It looks as if Lady Ralegh and her children may have worn the king down by repeatedly troubling him with outbursts that are full of pathos and accusation, cries and complaints. Unlike her husband, who was reluctant to humble himself even in his letters, Lady Ralegh decided to flaunt her family's abjection by staging it publicly before the king. Since

James would not give her the private audiences she desired, she and her sons would waylay him in a blend of guerrilla warfare and street theater, confronting him with the spectacle of an aggressively prostrate family who were in desperate need of help and also of justice.

In Ralegh's first year of imprisonment, we get a glimpse (rarely mentioned by biographers) of Lady Ralegh's modus operandi. In a letter of court news, Philip Gawdy informed his brother Bassingbourne that "I stoode this last Sonday harde by an olde Mrs [mistress] of yors My La. Rawly, who withe her sonne wer petitioners to his Majesty, but he wolde no way respecte them, nor so muche as looke towards them."[40] Many years earlier, when she was still Elizabeth Throckmorton, Lady Ralegh had declined a marriage proposal from Bassingbourne, and the pleasure his brother takes in describing her humiliation is palpable.[41] It is significant that Gawdy specifies that Lady Ralegh was a petitioner "withe her sonne," making Wat an actor in the scene. Despite the snub to his mother and himself, Wat may have felt a certain satisfaction in confronting the king, a step on his way to the contempt for social formalities that would mark his future development. Although James had affected not to listen, he and his mother had made themselves heard.

Having survived Queen Elizabeth's mortal wrath, Lady Ralegh was certainly not undone by the king's portly hauteur, and indeed she resolved on a still more confrontational strategy. In situations when their presence was not expected, she and her children would block the king's path, dramatizing their submission in a manner calculated to embarrass. In the years to come, this tactic of waylaying James became something of a habit for her (and a royal pain for him). In September of 1606, she re-enacted the primal scene—presumably accompanied by Wat and perhaps by Carew as well—by prostrating herself at court before him. Once again, we are told, the king "simply sidestepped the obstacle, walking by without a word."[42] Even though she did not engage the king in conversation, much less change his mind, her tactic of publicly confronting a reclusive monarch who liked to think himself a model of forgiveness was to pay dividends.

In the extremely eventful chronicle of the Raleghs' attempts to retain Sherborne—it is said to have "changed hands at least eight times from 1604 to 1616"—a key moment was the court's formal ruling (in 1608) that the earlier conveyance through which Ralegh had attempted to transfer the ownership to Wat was flawed.[43] This meant that, finally, the king could seize the estate as a forfeiture. Though the surrender of Sherborne was inevitable—James was eager to bestow it on his reigning favorite, Sir Robert Carr—Lady Ralegh concentrated on winning the best possible terms for herself and her sons. Throughout the court's festivities in the winter of 1608–1609, she mounted her final, desperate campaign; as an observer remarked, she was "an importunate suitor all these holy-dayes in her husbands behalfe, yet yt is past recall…."[44] The key moment in the drama is captured in an account probably written by Carew decades later: "The Lady Ralegh with her children humbly and earnestly petitioning the king for compassion on her and her's, could obtain no other answer from him, but that he *mun have the land, he mun have it for Car*."[45]

If the king's words sound apologetic or even guilty, it is because Lady Ralegh's long campaign was capped by a rather harrowing performance (as described by Carew):

> She being a woman of a very high spirit, and noble birth and breeding, fell down upon her knees, with her hands heaved up to heaven, and in the bitterness of her spirit beseeched God Almighty to look upon the justness of her cause, and punish those who had so wrongfully exposed her and her poor children to ruin and beggary.

In the end, Lady Ralegh's role as suffering mother and avenging angel proved to be successful: the final legal transfer of Sherborne occurred early in 1610, accompanied by a settlement in which the sum of £8,000 went to trustees acting for the Raleghs, with an annuity of £400 going to Lady Ralegh and Wat for as long as either should live. In the long run, however, Sir Walter proved to be the prime beneficiary of the settlement, for most of it went into financing his disastrous second voyage to Guiana.

Had Wat been in a reflective mood when watching his mother berate the king at court—and there is no reason to think he was—he may have remembered a similar scene that occurred three years earlier, a disturbing scene in which his mother similarly had used himself and the infant Carew as evidence of the oppression suffered by the family. In this earlier incident, however, Lady Ralegh acted as plaintiff against injustice that she charged was committed not by the king but by Ralegh himself.

We know of the incident through a letter Ralegh sent to Cecil, stressing his great suffering in prison. He cites two causes of his "torments," the first being his terror at recurrent visits of physical paralysis: "I am every second or third night in danger ether of suddayne death, or of the loss of my lymes [limbs] and sense, being sumetyme two howres without feeling or motion of my hand and whole arm."[46] He follows this appalling medical report with the second cause, which is very different but apparently no less troubling: he fears the suffering Lady Ralegh may inflict on him when she returns from a visit to Dorset. He worries that "I shalbe made more then [than] weary of my life by her criing and bewayling … when shee heares of your lordships departure and nothing don." His emphasis on her "criing and bewayling" reveals his fear of a passionately vocal outburst similar to those she would later unleash against the king.

Ralegh's next sentence reveals that his great anxiety about being confronted by his wife derives from a recent domestic conflict that was obviously disturbing:

> She hath alreddy brought her eldest sonn in one hand and her sutting [nursing] child in another, criing out of her and their destruction, charging me with unnaturall negligence and that, having provided for myne own life, I am without sense and compassion of theirs.

To be sure, Ralegh is attempting to enlist Cecil's (male) sympathy, and his acute self-concern is apparent throughout the letter, but in this recollection he expresses real pain at his distraught wife's outburst. (We can already see his vulnerability to Lady Ralegh's anger—and her reason to feel it—if we recall his much earlier concealment of his arrangements for Sherborne from her lest she "exclaim" against him.) Plaintively, he says he is "receiving nothing but torments and outcries wher I should look for sume comfort." Clearly he is disturbed by a powerful doubleness in his wife's affect, as she is "criing and bewayling" her family's miserable lot but also (prophet-like) "crying out" against him for being oblivious to her and her sons' suffering while looking out for himself. One suspects that some of Ralegh's acute discomfort stemmed from his perception of truth in her charge. Her appearance with her children in arms created performative evidence of her protection of her family and of his detachment from it.

In their different ways all four of the Raleghs may have been disturbed by this confrontation. The most complicated response was surely that of the twelve-year-old Wat, who most likely felt a sharply divided allegiance. He had been living in two worlds, residing with his mother (and infant brother) on Broad Street but also regularly visiting his father in the Tower for lessons and talk. At home, he would have heard, and to some degree sympathized with, his mother's grievances against his father for "unnatural negligence" toward his family. But his early sense of identification with his same-named father would not have been forgotten or totally rejected. It is likely that Wat had never seen his father on the receiving end of such a tongue-lashing from his mother. He had participated as a living prop in his mother's diatribe, but he may have felt some sympathy for the diminished man who in better times had commanded everyone's respect.

There is no record of the family engaging in another scene like this, and perhaps it was not repeated because it was regretted by all of them. It appears not to have created an irreparable rift in the marriage, for Lady Ralegh continued to visit Sir Walter in the Tower, and (against her better judgment) she would invest most of her own financial resources in the Guiana voyage that he was to lead many years later. But the subsequent relations between the Raleghs appear to show a cooling of affection that is due less to this single episode than to his increasing marginalization and her growing centrality. One indication of this change is Ralegh's rather lukewarm response to the king's decision to prohibit Lady Ralegh from taking up temporary lodging in the Tower when it suited her. James instructed the privy council to inform her that she "must understand his Majisties express will and commandment that she resort to her house on Tower Hill … and not to lodg hereafter within the Tower."[47]

Ralegh's response amounted to considerably less than a thundering rebuttal. In a letter attempting to convince a sympathetic official to lift the ban, he betrays a certain embarrassment as if he fears his request is somehow unbecoming or insufficiently manly. The sole reason he gives for his self-consciously "miserable sute" is feeble: that "to my great impoverishing I am driven to keip to [two] howses."[48] (Since there is no reason to think that Lady Ralegh ever wished to take up permanent residence in the Tower, the family required a second house, regardless of whether or how often she visited.) It may be that Ralegh is actually concealing his need for his wife's company under the guise of invoking financial necessity, but his lack of frankness seems to point to irresolution on his part, as does his closing comment that "the matter is of no great importance (though a cruell destinie hath made it so to me) to desire that my wife may live with me in this unsavery place."

With regard to property and income, there is no question but that Ralegh came to feel irrelevant and disempowered. As he complains in a letter concerning Sherborne to Sir Henry Hobart, the king's attorney general, the king's grants "both of the land and leases are to the use of my wife and for the present releife of my children, and not to me."[49] He goes on to emphasize his consequent dependency on his family, noting that they have still more leases "in their owne names in which I have no other interest but as a father during the infancie of my childe and as a husband during my wives life."

From these facts he draws a conclusion about the shift of "power" and "strenght" within the family:

> And therefore as ther is left in me no other powre then my perswasion only, who am but a dead husband to theone and a dead father to the other (your sute in law agaynst us having made them know mich of their owne strenght) it will not now be easy for me to order them concerning their whole livelehode and estates, who … can never more harme them by my mislike nor healp them by my indevor.

Ralegh's view of himself as a "dead husband" to his wife and a "dead father" to his children conveys his sense of utter irrelevance to and impotence within the family. More darkly, Ralegh's regret that he can no longer "harme" nor "healp" his family (with the impulse to harm coming first) reveals a self-pitying embitterment. Like King Lear on the heath, he has lost the "power" to order the lives of his family, and with this power his formerly unquestioned authority over them has also vanished. Ralegh senses that just one form of agency is left to him: "my perswasion only." In his former life, his enemies had feared the power of his persuasiveness, but in the Tower and within his family his words ring insubstantial and empty.

There is wistfulness, perhaps even fatality, in Ralegh's final sentence, and certainly a sense of withdrawal:

> These things I leve to your honorable consideration, hoping yow will rather chang the cries and sorrowes of my wife and children into their prayers for yow then that yow will ether increase them or continew them.

In these lines Ralegh is displacing his responsibilities onto Attorney General Hobart, as he leaves to him the issues of income and ownership that need to be resolved. Moreover, he hopes that by aiding his family Hobart will transform into quiet prayer "the cries and sorrowes of my wife and children," a phrase that calls to mind his own painful experience of his wife's outcries. In the years to come, Ralegh's wounded reluctance to exercise authority and to assume responsibility becomes a central feature of his family relationships, figuring silently in the *Instructions for His Son* that he was writing.

• SEVEN •

Instructing and Neglecting a Son

Over the years, many readers have lamented that the Ralegh whom they admire is not the father they encounter in the *Instructions to His Son*. For readers interested in the relationship of the two Walter Raleghs, a particular disappointment attaches to this tract. After Ralegh's previous addresses to Wat—the fascinating poem "Three Things There Be" and the prose exhortation to live life as if it were a tragic voyage of discovery—one is likely to find the *Instructions to His Son* to be diminished in emotional range and imaginative energy.[1] This disappointment has taken too many forms to catalogue, but the most common is a negative reaction to the perceived small-mindedness of Ralegh's advice, especially its emphasis on self-protection in friendship and love. In an attempt to account for this diminishment, the author of the significantly titled *Sir Walter Ralegh: The Last Elizabethan* declared that "We can suppose only that the *Instructions* were written in some 'black night of the soul,' when his sick mind and body fell back to acceptance of the smug narrow doctrine of men comfortable and padded in their lives."[2] What limits the scope of the *Instructions*, however, is not Ralegh's relapse into smugness but just the opposite: a renewal of his constricting pain. Instead of helping to fashion his son's future, his admonitions open wounds from his own past.

Rather than deriving the *Instructions* from some mythical black night of his soul, we will be on firmer ground if we begin with the conventional literary form in which Ralegh was writing, the father's advice to his son. It should be said at the outset that this genre is not a likely vehicle for literary excellence. From the middle of the sixteenth century to the middle of the seventeenth, the instruction of one's heir was widely perceived to be a duty of the paterfamilias.[3] To be sure, mothers sometimes took it upon themselves to advise their children, in person and in print, but they usually characterized their words as an uncontrollable outpouring of their love rather than the fulfillment of a weighty duty to instruct. For fathers, the dominant concern is usually the preservation of the family estate. This overarching patrilineal focus is evidenced by the fact that, with very few exceptions, a father addresses only one child: his eldest son, the heir to his patrimony.[4] (The impulse of mothers is more inclusive; being concerned with the souls of their children, they usually address all of their offspring.) Often written in a voice of authoritative impersonality, paternal admonishments voice a commitment to the continuity of male ownership. Above all, the instructive paterfamilias perceives the prime duty of himself—and his properly instructed heir—to be the preservation and transmission of the patrimonial inheritance. Not surprisingly, these directives rarely venture far from their central commitment to the prudent management of finances and families.[5]

Ralegh makes his allegiance to this patrilineal view explicit in a blunt instruction to Wat: "Amongst all other things of the world, take care of thy estate"—which appears to mean his son should care for his estate *above* all other interests.[6] But we should note from the outset that, despite this comment and some subsequent conventional remarks about the danger of indebtedness and the unreliability of servants, the concern with maintaining an estate is not central to the *Instructions*. (It is revealing that Ralegh's instruction to "take care of thy estate" does not appear until more than halfway through his tract and is not part of a consistent argument.) This diminishment of emphasis is not surprising if we recall that by the time he wrote his advice Ralegh had already lost his estate—and Wat's. He mentions the importance of estate almost as a reflex, since it had long been his dream for Wat, but his concern is less pressing and certainly less detailed than that of fellow advice-writers such as Lord Burghley and Henry Percy, who were passing on very substantial holdings of land and buildings.

Although Ralegh places less emphasis on estate than do many other fathers, he shares their defensive, even paranoid orientation toward the world. In this view, the world is primarily a treacherous place, and thus in his final section Ralegh counsels Wat to "stand upon thine owne guard against all that tempt thee ... into its practises" (X, 97). Successful self-preservation requires strategies of secrecy and self-control. In what may seem a paradox, wealthy, privileged fathers caution their heirs to live in fear. They assume, and conjure up, a world in which servants are to be suspected, friends to be distrusted, and wives to be controlled (from beyond the grave, if possible). For great lords and jousting courtiers, the world is a treacherous theater in which, as Ralegh remarked at the end of his first section, "the fancies of men change, and hee that loves today, hateth tomorrow" (I, 11).

Since the *Instructions* shares these not very edifying emphases with the advices of other fathers, one could argue that Ralegh was simply writing as a man of his time. But the attempt to interpret the *Instructions* as conventional expression can never be very convincing because Ralegh himself was scarcely a typical product of his time. Rightly or wrongly, we expect more of him. Ultimately, like so much else in his life, the *Instructions* is sui generis—an uneven, flawed creation to be understood not simply as an expression of a patrilineal culture but also as *his* response to the pressures and challenges of experience. Moreover, and this is a more complex issue, his tract is an index to his relationship with the son for whom it was written. But, as we will see, the *Instructions* tells us far less about its addressee than its author.

The giving of advice and admonishment—Ralegh's is more the latter than the former—always involves issues of identity. Inevitably, our primary understanding of the world is rooted in our own experience; any life-counsel we may communicate is likely to be predicated on our subjective experience. Of course, we can speak in empty platitudes, and in Elizabethan England well-worn commonplaces were a staple of paternal discourse, but Ralegh's powerful sense of his own importance always saved him from relying heavily on accepted formulations.

Implicitly, our advice is apt to say as much about ourselves as it does about the world we purport to describe. With regard to our children, the bond of family identity may especially incline us to assume that what happened to us might, if not warned against, happen to the child we are cautioning. When, as in Elizabethan England, the admonishment is being proffered from a paterfamilias to a son who will be his replacement in the next generation, this sense of shared identity is likely to be heightened. In the case of a father who has long dwelt on the idea that his same-named heir "is parte of me," the risk is still greater that the advice will be self-reflective. Ralegh appears to be unaware of the danger of imposing himself on his son, perhaps because he does not acknowledge the possibility of difference. On the whole, the *Instructions* is at risk of losing its imaginative engagement with Wat and becoming son-blind.

Whatever its source, there is a striking lack of direct engagement with Wat throughout the *Instructions*. Although we deduce that Ralegh is addressing him, he rarely engages with Wat in a way that brings his son's identity or even presence to the forefront. The contrast with the intimacy of Ralegh's endearments to Wat ("wagg," "pritty knave," "dear boy") in "Three Things There Be" is shocking. It is remarkable that in the entire *Instructions* he never once calls his son by name. (A single, well-placed naming of "Wat" would have made the tone of the entire work more intimate.) Still more oddly, Wat is never addressed as "son" in the document, and in the *Instructions* the word never appears apart from its title. By the same token, Ralegh identifies himself as "thy father" only once, and then not until some three-quarters of the way through (V, 67). Ralegh's only personal memory of his unnamed son is with regard to Wat's infant behavior toward his nurses, which is strangely adduced as evidence of the transitory nature of sexual love.[7] Although a calculated impersonality pervades the literature of paternal instruction, rarely has a father been so silent about his relationship with his son, and about the subject of fathers and sons in general. Tellingly, Ralegh provides no advice on how Wat should raise *his* sons.

An indication of how rarely and impersonally Ralegh addresses Wat is the fact that biographers have sometimes identified the recipient of the *Instructions* as his much younger brother, Carew. This error seems to have been made by the first publisher of the *Instructions*, perhaps because Carew was alive and active, Wat having died fifteen years earlier. It has been repeated by some modern commentators.[8] Given the almost universal preference of early modern fathers to address their eldest sons, and given that Carew was not born until 1605, Agnes Latham is surely right to insist that Ralegh must have written the *Instructions* for an adolescent Wat rather than an infant Carew.[9] However, apart from observing that Wat was a "wild, irreverent scamp" or that he had "a reputation for filthy horseplay," the biographers who have identified him as the subject of the advice have done little to connect his life with his father's admonishments.[10] The nature of Ralegh's approach makes this a difficult, perhaps impossible, task.

The problem of linking the *Instructions* to Wat's life would be greatly alleviated if the tract had contained even a brief prefatory address to him. But there is no introduction, not even the "Dear Son" address that opens most letters of advice. Unlike Ralegh, fathers often begin by acknowledging, or at least hinting at, the occasion that has prompted the lesson that follows. In the most widely circulated of early modern instructions, Lord Burghley prefaces his "Ten Precepts" for his son (Robert Cecil) by committing to provide "rules for the squaring of thy life as are gained rather by much experience than long reading" so that his son will be ready for "entering into this exorbitant age" and be "the better prepared to shun those cautelous [treacherous] courses whereinto this world and thy lack of experience may easily draw thee."[11] Abstract as Burghley's language is, we gather that the bookish Robert Cecil is on the verge of entering public service and is reckoned by his supremely politic father to be in need of a large dose of reality therapy.[12]

In contrast, the absence of an introductory statement from Ralegh leaves his intention unclear. As the *Instructions* was not published until fourteen years after his death, it is possible he had written an introduction that was lost, and his rousing exhortation for Wat to live life fully and dangerously (discussed in Chapter Five) has been identified by some commentators—mistakenly, I think—to be the missing introduction to the *Instructions*.[13] But even if this highly rhetorical letter had been intended to serve that function, it is so thematically disconnected from the tract as to cast no light on why Ralegh wrote this little treatise for Wat.

In addition to the absence of an introduction, there is another, more fundamental structural problem that makes it difficult to deduce Ralegh's intention: the apparently haphazard organization of the *Instructions*. Like Burghley's "precepts" for Robert Cecil, and perhaps following its example, Ralegh's advice is divided into ten numbered sections. Such an unimaginative and unadventurous organization suggests the absence of a deeper, more organic structure; an author is easily tempted to rely on the numbered progression of discrete points without creating logical or narrative links between them. To be sure, this unpromising structure can be shaped by industry. In his "Ten Precepts" for Robert Cecil, Burghley lays out many of his discrete sections in an implicit chronological progression, beginning with marriage, moving to children and family governance, and then addressing the preservation of the family's estate. Moreover, Burghley makes a perhaps ill-considered attempt to justify the number ten by reminding Robert that these precepts should be memorized "next unto Moses' tables."[14]

With the *Instructions*, however, the numbered sections have no such discernable coherence. When an astute student of Ralegh's prose noted that "the overall principle of organization is problematic," he was being charitable.[15] The looseness of Ralegh's organization is apparent when his first three sections are contrasted with Burghley's. Ralegh begins with a section on choosing friends, moves to the grounds for choosing a wife, and then jumps to the terrible dangers of flattery, without explicit links to connect them. There is at least a vague parallel between choosing friends and a wife (one should think of the long run), and one might see an unstated link with the danger to rational judgment that flattery poses. But as the *Instructions* unspools, its organization becomes increasingly arbitrary. For instance, the seventh section consists of a single sentence warning about the folly of purchasing "gay garments"—Ralegh had plentiful experience—while the eighth calls for attention to be paid to the poor, and the ninth inveighs at considerable length against the dangers of wine, quoting many authorities in Latin and also in English translation. The *Instructions* concludes with a section that, rather abruptly, exhorts Wat to "Serve God."

It would be natural enough, but almost certainly mistaken, to read the *Instructions* as pointing to various propensities of his son that Ralegh is attempting to correct or forestall. Such an approach would rest on the assumption that Ralegh's tract is based on his objective assessment of his son's character and predilections. But that assumption is contradicted by the fact that Ralegh makes so little reference to Wat throughout his tract that we never receive anything like a clear picture of him, or even a sense that Ralegh is paying much attention to him. Moreover, as we have seen, the organization of the *Instructions* does not point to a coherent set of risks that a specific kind of person might face, nor does Ralegh reprimand Wat a single time for engaging in the behavior that he criticizes. In a word, the relevance of Ralegh's directives to his son is not clear or compelling.

But what reason would Ralegh have to admonish Wat if he is not addressing perceived weaknesses in his son's character? Clearly he must think that his advice will prove to be useful to his son. Otherwise, why bother? Ralegh's unspoken assumption seems to be that the dangers he himself has faced will threaten Wat in the future. Indeed, the *Instructions* is full of usually unacknowledged references to Ralegh's own experience, and especially to events immediately before and after his great downfall. The connection between the father's past and the son's future, a connection never made explicit in the tract, is Ralegh's assumption that Wat is a part of himself and that his own hard-earned experience will therefore serve as a relevant, even necessary warning to him.

It comes as no surprise, and is certainly no coincidence, that Ralegh's prose in the *Instructions* is most alive and most passionate when it concerns situations that are painfully familiar from his own past.[16] One of the most astute critical comments on the *Instructions* is the remark by Philip Edwards that Ralegh's advice often seems "to bear the stamp of a man who has just been stung by a disappointment or a piece of treachery."[17] Ralegh's most charged passages occur primarily in the early chapters, which provide much of the work's impetus and perhaps its inspiration as well. On the whole, Ralegh's admonitions lose focus and emphasis as he moves forward, which suggests a flagging interest on his part, as if the propulsive energy of the tract is largely spent and he is now laboring to complete the ten sections to which he appears to have committed himself.

Ralegh's engagement is clear in the first section of the *Instructions*, the nominal subject of which is a common topic in paternal advice: that of friendship. Ralegh's treatment, however, is unprecedented in its bitterness, especially when he recalls how "great men forget such as have done them service, when they have obtained what they would, and will rather hate thee for saying, thou hast beene a meane of their advancement, then [than] acknowledge it" (I, 9–10). Following this mordant blast, he slips into the first person—a rare occurrence—declaring that "I could give thee a thousand examples, and I my selfe know it, and have tasted it in all the course of my life" (I, 10). We can hear the idea becoming increasingly present and disturbing for Ralegh, as he moves from the subjunctive "I could give thee a thousand examples," to the declaration of immediate knowledge in "I my selfe know it," and then to the intense subjectivity of having "tasted it in all the course of my life." One senses that Ralegh is releasing a very personal, pent-up grievance that grows in the very act of being articulated. As a passage—not included in the print versions but appearing in a manuscript copy of the *Instructions*—shows, Ralegh was thinking about the earl of Essex's cruel betrayal of his loyal followers.[18] But he also had a grievance of his own against Lord Cobham, another "great man" whose betrayal of a friend (Ralegh himself) led to a conviction for treason.

Although Ralegh does not explicitly refer to his conviction and his subsequent imprisonment—delicate topics that could jeopardize any hopes he had for clemency from the king—his wounds from these tragedies are everywhere apparent in the *Instructions*. The closest he comes to being explicitly personal—with regard to acknowledging both Wat and his own experience—is in Chapter V, following his exhortation to him to "take care of thy estate." After warning Wat against standing surety for another man's debt, a traditional concern in paternal advice, Ralegh declares that paying other men's debts means "thou wilt be a begger" (V, 66–67). Suddenly, the word beggar releases an impassioned and eloquent outpouring about the evil effects of poverty:

> beleeve thy father in this, and print it in thy thought, that what vertue soever thou hast, bee it never so manifold, if thou be poore withal, thou, and thy qualities shall be despised. Besides, poverty is ofttimes sent as a curse of God; it is a shame amongst men, an imprisonment of the mind, a vexation of everie worthy spirit ... [V, 67–68].

Ralegh's instruction for Wat to "beleeve thy father in this, and print it in thy thought" is the most forceful and personal of all his remarks to Wat, and the only passage in which he refers to himself as "thy father." Even after this powerful declaration, he requires still another nineteen lines of embitterment before he can disclose all of the shame that impoverishment has brought upon him.

Of particular biographical interest are some remarks that Ralegh makes late in this remarkably sustained and eloquent litany of poverty's destructiveness: "thou shalt bee driven basely to begge, and depend on others, to flatter unworthy men, to make dishonest shifts; and to conclude, poverty provokes a man to doe infamous and detested deedes." The most cursory reading of Ralegh's letters after his imprisonment provides many examples of the terrible dependency and self-abasement that are so freshly evoked in this passage. Even if one were not aware of Ralegh's sudden decline into poverty following the attainder of his possessions, one would know that the speaker of this diatribe has painfully experienced what he describes. Given his deep depression in the Tower, Ralegh's characterization of poverty as "a shame amongst men" and "an imprisonment of the mind" is especially moving.

The shifting focus of this pained discourse reveals, in microcosm, the unevenness of the undertaking as a whole. Although the chapter begins in a conventional way, with references to protecting estates and to the perils of standing surety, it quickly becomes a very personal statement. Despite his request for Wat to "beleeve thy father in this, and print it in thy thought," Ralegh's awareness of his son's presence is quickly eclipsed by the vividness with which he pours out the humiliations he has suffered—and clearly still suffers. Of course, the entire passage is nominally directed to Wat, and surely Ralegh's (unspoken) worry that his son may follow him into poverty contributes to its energy. As well, later in the chapter Wat seems to return to Ralegh's mind when he praises the many advantages of wealth, including its patrilineal provision of "meanes to thy posterity to live, and defend themselves, and thine own fame" (V, 70–71). But these allusions to Wat's well-being do not conceal the fact that the primary source of Ralegh's eloquence remains a painful personal truth: his own experience of humiliating impoverishment. No reader who has responded to this or similar passages in the *Instructions* can liken Ralegh, as some have, to Shakespeare's Polonius.

Ralegh first spoke of Wat as "parte of me"—one who shared the same "kinde"—in a discussion of his son's future relationship with his (widowed) mother. It should come as no surprise, then, that wives figure largely in his identification with Wat in the *Instructions*. When advising their sons about women, Elizabethan fathers often let their mask of anonymity slip, but even so Ralegh's warnings are uncommonly vivid and outspoken. For the most part, the tract's attitude is severe, even resentful, toward women and marriage. What is especially interesting is that in these sometimes misogynistic comments Ralegh seems to be unaware that he is speaking to the son of his wife. Although he does not make explicitly negative comments about Lady Ralegh, he seems not to notice (or perhaps to care) that his strong opinions may be raising questions in his son's mind about the nature of the union that created him.

Ralegh's acerbic tone is clear in the wildly categorical insistence of his remarkable opening statement about women: that the "only danger" in choosing a wife "is beauty, by which all men in all ages, wise and foolish, have been betrayed" (II, 20). Is his implication that he was somehow betrayed by Wat's mother, or, conversely, is he saying she was loyal but not beautiful? In his next paragraph, his distrust of the "witchery" of beauty returns, as he declares that "I never yet knew a poor woman exceeding fair that was not made dishonest" by the desire for wealth or social honor, and he proceeds to instruct Wat to "evermore [take] care that thou be beloved of thy wife rather than thyself besotted on her…" (II, 21). Ralegh is not advising Wat to forgo love for a future wife, but his counsel to avoid becoming "besotted" would instill excessive caution in the heart.

Certainly Ralegh's emphasis is on the dangers rather than the satisfactions of love and marriage—he is counselling marriage without giving Wat a reason to want to be married. His only two positive criteria for choosing a wife are narrowly self-centered: that "she have care of thy estate" and that "she study to please thee." He makes no reference to his own commitment to his wife, which must have been substantial as well as long-standing, and one wonders why love as a value does not arise. Since Ralegh's general account of marriage does not take explicit account of his own, one wonders if he wishes for a different relationship for the son who is part of himself.

Lady Ralegh had played—and was continuing to play—a central role in Wat's upbringing, and so it is particularly interesting that a wife's role in the bearing and raising of children is not deemed worthy of mention. With regard to wives and children, Ralegh's single observation stresses the analogy between human reproduction and animal breeding. Above all other concerns, he says, Wat should "have care thou dost not marry an uncomely woman," for "if thou have care for thy races of Horses, and other beasts, value the shape, and comelinesse of thy children…" (II, 18–19). A knowing wife will "value" this comeliness of her children since in the marriage market beauty is riches. Perhaps Ralegh has the handsome Wat's situation in mind, since his own attainder severely wounded his son's prospects, but whatever thoughts he may have on this score are not expressed.

In his discussion of marriage, Ralegh's most striking conflation of his identity with Wat's is in regard to his (Wat's) death and his future wife's widowhood. It seems a curious concern, considering Wat's youthfulness, for Ralegh to be instructing him about preventing the ills his wife could bring about after his death, but perhaps in paternal advice estate planning (i.e., assuring patrilineal transfer) cannot begin too early. He counsels Wat to write a will that would limit his wife's control of the estate, a not uncommon strategy (as we have seen in his own case) in a patrilineal society. Without saying as much, he advises Wat to adopt the strategy that he had used, namely to "leave thy estate to thy House and Children in which thou livest upon earth whilst it lasteth" (II, 26). As Judith Owens observed, "Ralegh's own will left virtually everything to Wat, and, in recommending the course of action that he does here in his Advice, Ralegh is essentially instructing Wat to disengage his affections from his mother."[19]

What is surprising is the passion and detail with which Ralegh imagines the effect of Wat's widow remarrying. He counsels Wat to remember that what he bequeaths to his wife after his death will be a gift to the man who will supplant him, a second husband who "will despise thee, thy memory, and thine ... enjoy thy love, and spend with joy and ease what thou hast spared, and gotten with care and travel [travail]" (II, 23–24). As Ralegh continues, he projects onto Wat a very explicit sexual envy of his widow and her second husband, their pleasure imaged as a kind of castration:

> for if she love again, let her not enjoy her second love in the same bed wherein shee loved thee, nor flye to future pleasures with those feathers which death hath pulled from thy wings; but leave thy estate to thy house and children in which thou livest upon earth whilst it lasteth [II, 26].

This passage seems to have a subterranean connection to the farewell letter that Ralegh wrote to Lady Ralegh in July of 1603. This is the letter in which he said (in regard to a future second husband becoming a sexual partner), "let my sonne be thy beloved for he is parte of me and I live in him...."[20] In the *Instructions*, Ralegh is imagining his son as a replication of himself and Wat's hypothetical wife (and yet more hypothetical second husband) as a reincarnation of Lady Ralegh, a woman whom he fears will forget Wat in the pleasure of another man. In particular, Ralegh's enjoining Wat to "let her not enjoy her second love in the same bed wherein shee loved thee" seems inappropriately graphic and much too emotionally engaged for a possibility so distant in young Wat's future.

It would appear that, in addition to Ralegh's perceived betrayal and his devastating impoverishment, there is an important domestic context: his displacement from his position of authority within the family. Though scholars have not agreed on a date of composition for the *Instructions* (there is virtually no determinative evidence), a reasonable agreement prevails that Ralegh must have written it in the Tower.[21] Placed in this context, Ralegh's *Instructions* appear to be an attempt to reclaim, at least in his own mind, the role that he had enjoyed in the boy's younger days. Such an impulse would help to explain the tract's rather blithe assumption that Wat would be able to enjoy an estate of his own, much as Ralegh had always planned. And if he wrote it after the unsettling domestic imbroglio discussed in Chapter Six, it may be that there is an element of denial in his refusal to name Lady Ralegh, much less acknowledge her crucial contribution to the family.

The sense of authority conveyed in the *Instructions* is at best beleaguered. He was simply not writing with the easy, explicit emphasis on his own experience that more established and authoritative fathers expressed. When Thomas Howard, fourth Duke of Norfolk and one of the greatest noblemen in the realm, was awaiting execution for treason in 1572, he sent a bluntly forthright letter to his children, addressing each of them in turn. Howard's command to Philip, his son and heir, could not have been more confident and direct: "I charge you as a father may do, to follow my direction … my experience can better tell what is fit for you, than yet your young years can judge."[22] His directions involve a forthright criticism of his son as well as a demand for radical improvement: "Beware of pride, stubbornness, lechery, taunting, and sullenness (which vices nature doth somewhat kindle in you), and therefore you must with reason and discretion make a new nature in yourself." Because he is unsure of himself and unwilling to differentiate Wat from himself, Ralegh makes no such criticism of his son, no demand for him to change.

Significantly, it is in the final two sections of the *Instructions* that Ralegh's diffidence concerning his authority is most apparent. (In its opening chapters, we recall, he was writing from such a deep sense of personal grievance that his authority for speaking as he did was simply not an issue.) The ninth section is a very long and repetitive diatribe on the "bewitching and infectious vice" of drunkenness (83–84), consisting largely of a rag bag of quotations from classical authors (divine and secular). These sometimes lengthy passages are translated into English but are also quoted in their original Latin for good measure. One cannot help but feel that Ralegh is marshalling all of these authorities (probably from one of many Renaissance collections of commonplaces) because he is not sure of what he really has to say and perhaps does not even care very much. The glint of autobiographical experience seems to be entirely missing. It is conceivable that

Seven • *Instructing and Neglecting a Son* 99

Ralegh is addressing a serious problem of Wat's, who may have been a bibulous student at Oxford when the *Instructions* were composed. But there is no evidence that Wat's bad behavior at university involved drinking, and if Ralegh were responding to a problem directly threatening Wat, one might expect an effort that is more engaged and certainly less cut-and-paste. If he wished to end his admonitions to his son on an extremely forceful note, he was not successful.

The paragraph that constitutes Ralegh's final section is clearly intended to have a summary function, beginning as it does with the temptations of "the world" and suddenly turning to an admonishment to "Serve God" (X, 97–98). This invocation of God (with, as usual, no mention of Christ) is artfully phrased so as to suggest the common authority of fatherhood shared by himself and the deity.[23] (It is now Ralegh and God who share a common kind.) In the first of two parallel "Let" constructions, Ralegh entreats Wat to "let him [God] be the Author of all thy actions, commend all thy endevours to him," a plea that appears to acknowledge his own inability to be the efficacious "author" of Wat's instruction. Then he ends the *Instructions* with a parallel expression that brings the efforts of himself and God together: "let my experienced advice and fatherly instructions sink deep into thy heart, So God direct thee in al his wayes and fill thy heart with his grace." If Wat allows the *Instructions* to do its work, then God will direct and grace him. This formulation sounds rather like the (ultimately rejected) final couplet of "Three Things There Be," a resolution of differences that is altogether too tidy.

There is no record of Wat's response to the *Instructions*—or even of his having read it—but in lieu of such evidence we can turn to Ralegh himself for a possible assessment of its efficacy. His *History of the World* is rich in oblique comments on his son and heir, and one of these may allude to Wat's disappointing response to the *Instructions* or perhaps another example of what Ralegh called his "experienced advice and fatherly instructions." In his discussion "Of the beginning and establishing of Governement," Ralegh noted that in the earliest governments "the Fathers of Nations were then as Kings, and the eldest of families as Princes," but this orderly rule by primogeniture collapsed when obedience, which he calls "the fruit of natural reverence" was overwhelmed by pride and withered away.[24] Of particular interest is Ralegh's analysis of the collapse: "the soft weapons of paternall perswasions ... became in all over-weake, either to resist the first inclination of evil, or after (when it became habituall) to constraine it." Ralegh's inclusion of this detail about the inadequacy of the "soft weapons of paternall perswasions" sounds like his personal addition to a traditional myth about government. Perhaps it glances at his own failure to have prevented an inclination toward violence on Wat's part that—at the time of the *History of the World*'s publication in 1614—was showing signs of becoming "habituall."

While his deep engagement with Wat never diminished, Ralegh found it increasingly difficult to invest his energy into plans for shaping a son whose intransigence prevented instruction. In his probing essay "Of the affection of fathers for their children," Montaigne makes an observation that is very relevant to Ralegh's ongoing relationship with Wat. The great skeptic says that the "simple reason" men love their children is because they have begotten them—"wherefore we call them our other selves"—but he adds that this identification fails to remain deeply satisfying for fathers. A truer expression of paternal identity is to be found, he says, in "what we engender by the soul, the children of our mind, of our heart and our ability, [which] are produced by a nobler part than the body and are more our own. We are father and mother both in this generation."[25] Unfortunately for father and son, as Wat grew older, each had less reason to find happiness in the other. It would be simplistic, but not altogether wrong, to say that Wat grew up to be his own person and that Ralegh created a more satisfying expression of himself in the *History of the World*.

It is misleading, however, to suggest that Ralegh's magnum opus was an alternative to offering instructions to sons. He hoped that the *History of the World* would help to educate a newly acquired surrogate son: no other than Henry Stuart, Prince of Wales and heir to King James. Prince Henry was the same age as Wat, and in him Ralegh discovered the son he wished to have, a son not only vigorously masculine like Wat but also (unlike him) possessing political and military ambitions. For Ralegh, Prince Henry had the great virtue of being a son who welcomed his advice, and the thought of winning a contest with James for the young man's respect would have been deeply gratifying. Before undertaking the *History of the World* Ralegh penned a number of tracts on political and naval topics for the prince, who became the audience and muse of a reborn writing career.[26] Behind the writing, always, was Ralegh's hope that someday Henry would unlock the gate of the Tower.

Although they probably never met, Prince Henry and Wat had a good deal in common. Both were high-spirited sons who were alienated from fathers for whom they were losing respect. As we have seen, Ralegh's humiliating incarceration in the Tower diminished Wat's regard for him, and King James's self-appointed role of *rex pacificus* and friend to Spain left his militantly Protestant son cold. That James had locked away such a distinguished anti–Catholic warrior as Ralegh was for Henry proof of his father's disrespect for heroism, and the prince is reputed to have declared that "None but my father would keep such a bird in a cage."[27] As well, Henry tried to save Sherborne for the Raleghs by forcing Sir Robert Carr to surrender it to him, so that he could return the estate to them after he ascended the throne. Prince Henry's ravaging illness and sudden death in early November of 1612 dashed the hopes of many, but none more than the Raleghs. Two years after Henry's death, the first volume of the *History of the World* appeared. At its close, Ralegh wrote that he would not undertake the second and third volumes he had planned since "it hath pleased God to take that glorious *Prince* out of the world, to whom they were directed."[28] Such hopes as remained for Ralegh returned to the difficult son who was his own.

• Eight •

Escape to Oxford

At Wat's birth, it was a foregone conclusion—as soon as his gender could be ascertained—that he would attend university. In post-reformation England, the universities of Oxford and Cambridge expanded greatly, ceasing to be dedicated exclusively to preparing men for careers in the church. Study at university (but not necessarily the acquisition of a degree) was deemed a valuable accomplishment, especially for scions of the propertied classes. As many humanist educators declared—and humanism was at heart an educational movement—true nobility was not simply an accident of birth but also the mark of a mind informed by liberal studies, especially the classics. Predictably, families of high standing sought to guarantee their sons' status by providing for them a university education to supplement the nobility into which they were born. As a modern historian observed, "Never before or since … has the social elite been so determined to give their children a truly academic education before they went out into the world to take up their hereditary responsibilities."[1]

For the Raleghs, as for many families of the gentry, sending a son to university was evidence of their—and his—gentility and good breeding.[2] An uncertain status had always been a problem for Ralegh, since he was merely the fourth son of a not-wealthy country gentleman. (Had he been of higher birth, he certainly would not have been so widely reviled for damnable pride.) Following his father's conviction for treason and his subsequent attainder, Wat's claim to gentle status was further complicated by what had become a divided social heritage: his father's corrupted blood and his mother's still-elevated social standing. For his parents, the education of Wat offered a means of maintaining the dignity of the family line.

Ralegh's attitude to education included but also transcended its importance as a signifier of social status. His humanist belief in the intrinsic moral value of a sound education is apparent in a striking comment he makes in his *Instructions to His Son*, which he may have written late in Wat's university career. In a section of the treatise dealing with marriage, Ralegh unexpectedly raises the issue of educating one's children. One reason he gives for instructing Wat to marry before reaching the age of thirty is that he may live to educate his children:

> if thou stay [i.e., postpone marriage] long, thou shalt hardly see the education of thy Children, which being left to strangers, are in effect lost, and better were it to bee unborne than ill bred; for thereby thy posterity shall either perish, or remain a shame to thy name and family.[3]

It is remarkable—and unprecedented in the paternal advice of the time—for Ralegh to warn Wat that his son's children will be "in effect lost" if he is not present to "see" (and oversee) their education. (Having himself married at thirty-nine, Ralegh must have worried about living long enough to see Wat enter university, and certainly he lost no time in dispatching him to Oxford.) Rather than expressing confidence in Wat's aptness for learning—his career at Oxford was in fact turning out badly—Ralegh is stressing the crucial value of education. He clearly assumes that sound education is necessary for the continued physical and moral health of the family. Without it, his posterity may suffer shame and even death.

One might not guess from his praise of education that Ralegh's own university experience had been minimal. In 1572—between his French campaign and his first attempt to catch on at court—he was registered at Oriel College (Oxford) as a "gentleman commoner"; the hint of oxymoron in the title is relevant to his ambiguous status, but it means that he enjoyed privileges not available to ordinary students paying for room and board at the college. He seems to have remained only a term or two, but the brevity of his attendance should not be taken to indicate a lack of interest in learning. Though Ralegh was not destitute, John Aubrey describes him as being "under streights for want of money" and reduced to borrowing a gown from a college-mate that "he never restored, nor money for it."[4] Drawn from Oxford by ambition and (relative) penury, Ralegh remained a lifelong autodidact with a deep thirst for learning, and on his sea voyages he was said always to have brought with him a trunk of books. Perhaps he saw in his young son an opportunity to re-engage vicariously with the formal studies he had abandoned for action and plunder. If so, he was surely disappointed. In education, as in much else, Wat failed, or refused, to become the son Ralegh imagined.

But what were Wat's expectations for university? For him, as for so many students throughout the centuries, a major attraction of the university environment would have been the absence of parents. Stimulating as London was when he and his mother first arrived from Sherborne, his life on Tower Hill must have come to feel insular and constraining, whether being schooled in his father's dim quarters or living in his mother's nearby house. His university experience created distance: the sixty miles between Oxford and Tower Hill being also the distance between his father's large presence and a personal freedom that did not include books. Despite his father's best efforts to the contrary, at Oxford Wat seized the opportunity—for the first time in his life—to make decisions for himself.

Wat Ralegh was matriculated at Corpus Christi College (Oxford) on 30 October 1607, a week or two after his fourteenth birthday.[5] This age seems highly unusual today, but at the time it was not remarkable. Will Cecil, Robert Cecil's son and Wat's former playmate at Sherborne, was matriculated at St. John's College (Cambridge) at only eleven, and at Wat's time roughly twenty-five percent of Oxford matriculants were fifteen or younger.[6] It seems likely that Wat was eager to escape to university, and his parents would not have thought they were sending him away precipitately. Arthur Throckmorton, Lady Ralegh's older brother, had gone up to Oxford (Magdalen College) at fourteen, and at the same age Ralegh had left home for a bloody education in the French civil wars. (An extremely early age of matriculation, like Will Cecil's, revealed more about a boy's wealth than his intellectual precocity since it declared that his family had the means to have provided sound tutoring before Oxford as well as extra help after he had gone up.) For many privileged boys, family tradition rather than academic preparedness determined when they left home; when Sir William Wentworth advised Thomas, his son and heir, that "All your sonnes would goe to the university at xiiii yeares old … and staie thear two or three yeares," he did not consider possible differences of training or intelligence among his grandchildren.[7]

Ralegh's choice of university for Wat is predictable enough, given his own attendance at Oxford, but if the same university, why not the same college? Why did he choose Corpus Christi rather than Oriel, the college he had briefly attended? Presumably Ralegh had no deep attachment to Oriel, and there was much to recommend Corpus Christi. Founded in the second decade of the 1500s and dedicated to the humanist pedagogy of Erasmus and his circle, the college was known for its renowned library of the classics, which Erasmus himself had praised. But religious learning was not overlooked. Under President John Rainolds, Corpus was central to the great scholarly project of creating the King James Bible, which was published in 1611, the year after Wat's graduation. Better yet (for Wat), Corpus was a college that fostered collegiality, being one of Oxford's smallest, most wealthy, and most attractive.

Eight • *Escape to Oxford*

But for Ralegh the primary attraction of Corpus must have been the men who would assume responsibility *in loco parentis* for the teenager who was growing increasingly wayward. From the Tower, he frequently sent directives to Wat's tutors and monitored various aspects of his schooling—including his competence on the viol—but his world was far removed from his son's. Given his own distance and beleaguered authority, Ralegh required strong surrogates on the scene. It goes without saying that he would seek them among scholars who hailed from the West Country. The colleges with the strongest regional affiliation with the West were Exeter and Corpus, and since Ralegh's deepest personal connections at Oxford were with fellow countrymen at Corpus, it won the day.[8]

As early as 1605, his second full year in the Tower, Ralegh had his eye on Corpus Christi for his twelve-year-old son. In that year, the Privy Council sent to Sir William Waad, the new Keeper of the Tower, a list of persons who were allowed to visit its aristocratic prisoners "at convenient [appropriate] time," and Ralegh's visitors included "Gilbert Hawthorn, a preacher."[9] Hawthorne, who was in his early thirties and a fellow at Corpus, had received all of his degrees at the college: BA, MA, and on 16 May 1605 the BD (with license to preach).[10] He had the additional virtues of being a West Country (Somerset) man and no friend of Puritans. It is likely that (among other duties) Hawthorne oversaw the preparatory tutoring for Corpus that John Talbot would administer to Wat in the Tower. Admission to Oxford was through the applicant's intended college, and a supportive fellow or two on the inside would have been useful. After Wat took up residence at Corpus, Hawthorne served as Ralegh's main connection with his son, probably sending him regular reports and occasionally visiting him in the Tower. After his service with Ralegh had ended, and doubtless with his support, Hawthorne became vicar of a parish in Somerset (1614) and rector of Caundle Bishop in the Ralegh country of Dorset (1618), where he served until his death sixteen years later.[11] He appears not to have left any stories about his life behind him.

Historically, the West Country representation at Corpus included its most famous alumnus, Richard Hooker, the author *Of the Laws of Ecclesiastical Polity*, a foundational defense of the Anglican faith and its church-government. Richard Hooker was the nephew of a figure whom we have already met, John Hooker, the Exeter historian who had praised Ralegh in the Preface to the enlarged edition of Holinshed's *Chronicles*. A supporter of the reformed religion, John had attended Corpus for a short while before he fled to Germany to escape Queen Mary's attention, and after his return to a safely Protestant England he sent three of his sons to the college, one of whom was chosen by Ralegh to be Wat's tutor.

The chosen son was Peter Hooker, who had matriculated at Corpus a year before Gilbert Hawthorne and, like him, was a fellow who had taken his BA, MA, and BD at the college.[12] Not much is known of his life beyond Corpus, but we can be certain he was (like his student's father) a man with a temper and a willingness to speak his mind. In 1614, an acrimonious debate broke out concerning the President of Corpus, and Hooker wrote a letter attacking the incumbent in such colorful terms that the college's historian remarks with a touch of *pudeur* that "Some portions of this letter do not admit of reproduction...."[13] The historian does, however, quote the letter's clenched-jaw closing: "Yours as you use me, Peter Hooker." Ralegh may have found Hooker's forthrightness attractive, but in the end it did not serve him (or Wat) well.

In Wat's time, Oxford was enjoying an unprecedented growth in student numbers and had become primarily an undergraduate university. In an attempt to monitor the burgeoning numbers of young students, the colleges assigned to every undergraduate a tutor, who played a central role in overseeing his charge's finances, moral discipline, and health, to say nothing of his studies. Depending on the student's level of discipline and docility, tutorship could be a very taxing duty, and Wat Ralegh proved to be intractable. Tutors often turned to less senior (and of course lower-paid) staff to act as readers for recalcitrant students, and with Ralegh's approval Hooker enlisted Daniel Featley, a fellow of Corpus who matriculated seven years after him, to serve as Wat's reader.[14] The duties of the reader varied, depending on the tasks the tutor wished to delegate, but usually included weekly meetings in which classical texts were read aloud and their meaning expounded.

From the outset Hooker and Featley quarreled about their responsibilities, which Ralegh may not have laid out clearly enough.[15] The arrogant Hooker and the thin-skinned Featley proved to be perfectly ill-matched. Featley came by his sensitivity honestly, being the son of a cook at Magdalen College and also an uncommonly short man. In the rank-obsessed world of Oxford he could claim only the respect deriving from recognition of his intellectual accomplishments. Featley took his work with Wat seriously and was offended when—as he complained to Ralegh—"Mr Hooker told me from you that he was *Absolute* tutour and I but a subaltern under him," adding that Hooker "seemed to mistak the subject of his auctority, supposing himself my tutor not Wats."[16] No doubt Wat was amused to see his learned tutors so engaged in squabbling with each other and did his best to sow discord between them.

Far removed from Oxford, Ralegh worried about Wat and monitored his academic progress, or lack of it, as closely as he could. In addition to receiving information from Hawthorne, he corresponded (separately) with Hooker and Featley, urging them to stricter oversight of Wat. Ralegh was not the only father who—fairly or unfairly—faulted university tutors for failing to correct a haughty and headstrong son. Sir Robert Cecil maintained a considerable correspondence with the tutor of his underachieving son Will, and he expected a report from Cambridge at least once a fortnight.[17] Cecil's advice, like Ralegh's, failed to have the desired effect, and in a fit of exasperation he declared to the tutor that Will "cannot speak six words in Latin."

None of Ralegh's letters to the Oxford tutors is extant, but his intrusive monitoring of Wat's education is clear from a fascinating manuscript in the Bodleian Library. The manuscript is Daniel Featley's assemblage of his own early writings, which contains his revised drafts for three letters (no longer extant) that he would send to Ralegh.[18] Featley did not date his drafts, but various references point to the second half of 1608, by which time Ralegh was clearly alarmed by his son's lack of progress.[19] Since Featley is expressly writing in response to paternal missives, Ralegh is always front of mind, and in some ways the father is more present than the son who is the nominal subject. The young, improvident tutor's eagerness to please and praise his employer—"I find your judgment of him [Wat] in every part to be most true"—suggests that his comments about his pupil never deviate greatly from the paternal assessments he received (54b).

Early in his first letter, Featley expresses his eager acceptance of a twofold role that Ralegh has instructed him to play: "to oversee his [Wat's] cariage and instruct him in learning, in both which you required my care, and gave me very good directions in your letter" (54b). While this division of a tutor's responsibility into oversight of learning and behavior is conventional, it is notable that in Wat's case the parental concern with "cariage" comes first. The focus of Ralegh's attention is apparent in the now archaic word that Featley uses to characterize it. In Elizabethan England a person's "carriage" usually denotes his demeanor or social deportment—how he carries himself—rather than his ethical or religious values.[20] It is likely that the "cariage" Ralegh had in mind was that of the gentleman: a gracious, controlled presentation of self that promoted respectful interactions with others. As Wat's future conduct would reveal, Ralegh's concern was prescient and Featley's supplemental overseeing would prove to be ineffectual.

Immediately after genuflecting before this emphasis on carriage and learning, Featley articulates in rather cryptic terms the gist of what Ralegh has shown him. He says that, by dint of giving him these "very good directions," Ralegh was discovering unto me two of the most dangerous evills, one unto [Wat's] mind, "the other unto his body, unto which he is subject: straunge company and violent exercises." Since Featley is repeating to Ralegh the gist of the instructions Ralegh has given him, we can be sure that, whatever sense we make of them, "straunge company and violent exercises" are words calculated to assure the father of the tutor's attentiveness, perhaps being the father's exact expression. Given the fact that these are "two of the most dangerous evills" to which Wat was subject— how many did he have?—some interpretation is called for. A useful starting place is provided by Featley's comment that the first poses a danger to Wat's mind and the second to his body.

When dealing with Wat, a generally wise procedure is to foreground his physicality, and so it is preferable to begin with the evil of "violent exercises." The phrase derives from Galenic medicine and denotes motions that are both strong and rapid, such as (in Galen's example) throwing weighted spears while moving quickly in heavy armor.[21] Such exercise was thought to inflame the blood and thus to be particularly dangerous for the young, who were already more than sufficiently hot-blooded. Not surprisingly, the advice of early modern fathers to their sons often includes the directive to avoid pernicious exercise. In a letter to his son, Sir William Wentworth proscribes a useful list of "violent exercyses": "Use no violent exercyses as foteball, piching heavy barrs, leapinge, running leape, dauncing above grond highe, vauting [vaulting], or anie such lyke ... that maie straine yow in anie parte of your body."[22] While activities like tennis and hunting hares could be described as "violent exercises," Featley's use of the phrase probably points to some intense gymnastic work with weights, a likelihood supported by the impressive strength that Wat will display in future years.[23]

The other evil, more mysterious and insidious, is the one that threatens Wat's mind: "straunge company." In broad cultural terms, Ralegh's warning against keeping bad company, like his concern with a son exercising violently, was a commonplace of Elizabethan parental anxiety. Fathers in privileged circumstances worried that their sons at university—removed from paternal oversight for the first time—might be drawn to a fellowship beneath their social status, thus endangering the family's standing.[24] When the young George Manners arrived at the Inns of Court, he attempted to reassure his father by regurgitating to him the precepts with which he had been sent to school: "Your chiefest precept[s] were these, vide, to applie my booke, to use good company and flie the contrary, to wright, and to give myself to honest and lawfull exercises for my boodie."25 This advice was self-evidently true for fathers and thus familiar to their sons.

But Ralegh's anxiety about the company that Wat keeps—which is after all an "evill"—seems more than a conventional concern. At its root was his own social status, which had always been at best ambiguous, cloven by the pervasive discrepancy between his abundant hauteur and his lack of familial nobility. Following Ralegh's condemnation for treason, as we have seen, the family's social standing and honor underwent a profound decline. Being now the son of a traitor, Wat (like his father) legally lost the rights associated with the possession of a civil identity and suffered a kind of death. In his prison letters, Ralegh repeatedly expressed his sense of having lost an identity that connected him to society, and it is possible that he harbored a fantasy of restoration: the hope that his son—the Oxford student—could exhibit behavior so strikingly honorable and noble that it would remind onlookers of his father's and family's intrinsic worthiness. Such a pipe-dream necessitated an appropriate "company" with whom Wat could be identified. But, as his father discovered, the company that Wat found was on the dark side of Oxford.

In early usage, the single word that Featley uses to define Wat's dangerous choice of company—"straunge"—often denoted something foreign or alien, something introduced from beyond what is known.26 It is tempting to imagine Wat enjoying the company of students from abroad, but this is most unlikely since virtually all of Oxford's students hailed from England or Wales. The likelihood is that "straunge company" were foreign in the sense of living outside the ambit and good will of the university, and perhaps of the law as well. The most obvious candidates would be the unsavory characters who preyed on ingenuous, moneyed students living away from home for the first time. But Wat was scarcely an innocent, and the indolence of dice and the alehouse leaves little room for the exercise of vigorous force that he enjoyed.

For a student with Wat's interests, the most likely place to encounter various kinds of "straunge company" would have been in Oxford's so called "schools" of dancing and fencing.27 In the early seventeenth century these were fairly dodgy establishments, attractive to the young because they existed outside the boundary of the university and were frowned upon by authorities. Since students at Oxford and Cambridge had long been forbidden to bear weapons, the instruction in fencing was especially on the shady side of the law. In a sense, these schools commodified a fashionable foreignness by offering instruction in activities that were Continental and hence exotic. As would remain true for fencing masters for at least a century, an instructor's necessary cachet was to have been foreign born and trained.

Because these establishments were at best quasi-legal, disappointingly little documentation about their operations and offerings survives. Unfortunately, no lists of the students attending these shadowy, vanished schools survive, and it is impossible to establish that Wat actually attended one. They are, however, certainly congruent with what we know of his interests, especially when one thinks of them as gymnasia rather than the polite finishing schools that "dancing and fencing school" might call to mind. After all, what dancing and fencing had in common was nimble, highly disciplined footwork, and various forms of rigorous training would have been available. Certainly a range of apparatus for sophisticated vaulting, including the "great horse," was available.[28] One offering that Wat may have found particularly attractive was the fencing itself, since in his eight years of life after graduation in 1610, he engaged in many duels and violent altercations, invariably emerging as the victor. It may be that the environs of the university provided the rudiments of this skill as well as contributed to the foundation of his strength.

Presumably it did not take Ralegh long to discover that, notwithstanding Featley's honesty and decency, the tutor was no match for his strong-willed son and namesake. Certainly Featley realized that Wat was more than he could handle, though he could hardly say as much to Ralegh. (There is a disquieting possibility that Wat treated Featley with a contempt that the needy tutor could not acknowledge to his employer.) But his sensitivity to Wat's forcefulness certainly manifests itself. In one of his most striking phrases, Featley employs the imagery of Ptolemaic astronomy to characterize Wat's impulsive, wayward behavior as "his planetary and irregular motions," thus suggesting its scarcely controllable dimension (57).

Given his own difficulties, Featley must have felt some sympathy for Wat's hapless music teacher, whom Ralegh had criticized for failing to force his son to practice on the lute as often as required. In the "planetary and irregular motions" letter, Featley reports to Ralegh the music instructor's simple, honest response: that Wat "would never tak any care of his play, and he had no power to enforce him...." (57). For his part, Featley expresses a (lukewarm) willingness to further Wat's music. If the instructor helps with notations, Featley will take out his orpharion (a stringed, lutelike instrument) and sit down to play some duets with Wat. As Featley must have surmised, his fantasy was in no danger of coming true. There is no evidence of any form of harmony ever emanating from these two men.

Eight • Escape to Oxford

With mutual ill-feeling, the frustrated relationship of Daniel Featley and Sir Walter soon came to an (undocumented) end. In their different but perhaps equally humiliating ways, the two Walter Raleghs had contributed significantly to the disrespect and exploitation that Featley was feeling at Corpus Christi, and doubtless his experience with the father and son contributed to the life-changing decision that he was soon to make. He complained in a letter—not to Ralegh—that a group of insiders "have scattered speeches in the colledg very false and injurious against me."[29] Ominously, in his final draft letter to Ralegh he likened himself to Claudia, the chaste Roman maiden who committed suicide after suffering public calumny (56v).

In 1610 (the year of his former student's graduation), Featley abandoned Oxford to take up religious orders, becoming chaplain to the English ambassador in Paris. The former obsequious, disgruntled Fellow who had signed his letters to Ralegh with his old, uncouth Yorkshire name (Daniel Fayreclough) was on his way to becoming the passionate and celebrated Protestant controversialist, Daniel Featley. But his unhappy past did not remain in England for long. All too soon, Ben Jonson would arrive in Paris to provide an official record of a debate between Featley and a Catholic theologian, and Jonson would bring with him the young man on whose dime he was travelling, Wat Ralegh.

It is frustrating to puzzle out exactly what Featley's diplomatic comments to Ralegh really say about his son, but fortunately another, much more direct, account exists of Wat's doings at Oxford. This account is vividly, even brutally forthright, and it comes not from a deferential tutor but from a fellow student. In his useful and entertaining account of Ralegh in his *Brief Lives*, John Aubrey quotes a description of Wat given to him by his cousin James Whitney, who matriculated at Oxford in 1611, only a year after Wat's graduation (when stories about him were still very fresh). According to Whitney's succinct account, Wat

> was a handsome lusty stout fellow, very bold, and apt to affront. Spake Latin very fluently; and was a notable disputent and courser, and would never be out of countenance nor baffeled; fight lustily; and, one time of coursing, putt a turd in the box, and besmeared it about his antagonist's face.[30]

This vivid, unfiltered view is fascinating, and while it casts no obvious light on the "straunge company" that Wat kept, it is certainly consistent with the young man Featley said was drawn to "violent exercises." Virtually every word relates to conflict, with the brusque opening sentence that evokes his "lusty stout" physique—he was not working out for nothing—and suggests a combative personality, "very bold, and apt to affront." Even Wat's surprising aptitude for disputation in good Latin is put to, and perhaps driven by, the end of winning in verbal combat. When Aubrey relates the comment that Wat could "fight lustily," it is not clear if the conflict is verbal, physical, or some combination of the two.

Clearly, Aubrey's cousin was very impressed by Wat's skill as a "notable disputent and courser." (Fortunately for the fluent Wat, at Oxford the rhetorical tradition was alive and well, and academic disputations loomed large in the assessment of students, being a central requirement for receiving the BA degree.) The word "courser" requires a gloss, for the activity of coursing does not, as one might think, derive from "discoursing" but rather is a hunting term for pursuing small game with fast dogs (*OED*, 2). It says a good deal about the violent, helter-skelter nature of Oxford debates that the term became attached to "the opposing and challenging of a thesis" (*OED*, 3). At the end of the seventeenth century, Anthony Wood supplies a very relevant description: "Coursing in the time of Lent, that is the endeavour of one party to run down and confute another in disputations, did commonly end in blows."[31] Even in the context of these pugilistic outcomes, Wat's behavior is shocking, which is presumably why Aubrey's nephew thought to include the incident in his account. On Wat's part we see not only a combative instinct but also a nasty plan to humiliate the overwhelmed opponent. It goes without saying that this episode of coursing turned out to be an uncommonly violent exercise.

Aubrey's characterization of Wat is especially suggestive if we think of his similarities to and differences from his father. Featley, we recall, assured Ralegh that Wat was "bearing the image not onely of your body but mind too." But Featley's assurance needs to be taken with a grain of salt, since he was hardly qualified to understand Ralegh's complex mind and may never have seen him. A much more knowledgeable judge of father-son similarities was Lady Ralegh, as is clear in her response upon hearing how Wat—several years after graduating from Oxford—had contrived to make his chaperone Ben Jonson drunk and then displayed him on the streets of Paris on a cart. Lady Ralegh, as we will see in the next chapter, was delighted with the story, declaring that "his father young was so inclined," while Ralegh is said to have "abhorred it." The story is a reminder that—in a reversal of the fatherly pride expressed in the double portrait—there were now more similarities between father and son than Ralegh wished to acknowledge.

Though Aubrey is not comparing father and son, his characterization of Wat suggests some parallels to "his father young." Some of these similarities were positive, such as the quickness of wit and the self-possession that allowed Wat never to be put "out of countenance or baffled." (Ralegh's enviable gift for answering a challenge is especially noteworthy in the transcripts of his trial for treason, where he stood quite alone.) There are, however, less attractive similarities, as is apparent in Aubrey's account of Wat's feculent attack on his opponent. Though Aubrey does not draw the connection, there is a suggestive parallel between a story he tells about Ralegh's younger days and his nephew's story about Wat's besmearing of the turd. The story concerns Ralegh's encounter with Charles Chester, who according to Aubrey was a "bold, impertinent fellowe … a perpetuall talker, and made a noyse like a drumme in a roome." Ralegh must have grown tired of Chester's noise, because "one time at a tavern, Sir W.R. beates him and seales up his mouth, i.e. his upper and neather beard, with hard wax."[32] In both instances, we see the father and the son demonstrating their physical prowess for the benefit of onlookers and at the expense of the hapless opponents who have triggered their ire. And in both instances we see a violent humiliation at work. To be sure, there are differences of degree. Certainly the father's hot wax is less disgusting than the son's application of excrement, and Wat's mockery is clearly the more deeply transgressive of the two. But the actions are so similar that one wonders if Wat had heard the story of his father's tavern exploit (perhaps from his mother?) and decided to improve on it.

On balance, it would appear that—contrary to educational theory—Wat's time at Oxford did not serve to mold him into a gentleman scholar, the goal of the arts faculty. Since he received the B.A. degree, we assume that he made his way successfully through the rather old-fashioned statutory curriculum, with its emphasis on training in logic and rhetoric.[33] Fortunately for Wat, the authorities looked upon the B.A. as a lower degree, and there were few set requirements. In addition to attending lectures and engaging in various disputative exercises, the primary requirement was four years (sixteen terms) in residence. Wat did not meet the letter of this requirement since he matriculated in October of 1607 and received his degree in June of 1610, but various dispensations were available, and he duly graduated.[34] Certainly he had no intention of pursuing a higher degree, and perhaps he had an understanding with his parents: that he would persevere to obtain his B.A. if that were the end of his schooling.

Despite his undistinguished academic record, it would be a mistake to characterize Wat's Oxford years as wasted time. To be sure, he did not accomplish the successes that the university publicists of today tout, such as the discovery of a field of study resulting in a profitable career or the acquisition of a lifelong network of devoted (and useful) friends. But he was not in search of such accomplishment. What he sought was experience in the world, and especially a culture in which he could test himself by confronting others. And of course he did dramatically increase his interactions with a wide range of his contemporaries. Most important, he discovered that he could live apart from, and in defiance of, his father, and perhaps his mother as well.

A silent but telling indication of Wat's independence is the signature he affixed to an important document that his parents had already signed (in December of 1609) in the Tower. Wat must not have been present at that occasion, for his signature required a witness different from the two family retainers who vouched for those of his parents. Wat's witness was Gilbert Hawthorne, the fellow of Corpus Christi who was overseeing his progress for his father, and the likelihood is that Wat signed when he was in residence at Oxford. His signature was essential, for the document laid out the terms of settlement by which the family would (finally) surrender the ownership of Sherborne and the rest of Ralegh's properties to the crown.[35] The value of Sherborne to the Raleghs was altered in subsequent negotiations, being finally set in the Court of Chancery at £8,000, with the amount of an additional annuity to Lady Ralegh and Wat remaining the same as the letter had proposed: £400 for the two of them, with "the longest liver of them" receiving the full amount for the remainder of his or her life.

On the document surrendering the Sherborne estate, Wat's signature, underneath those of his parents on the right, is surprisingly firm and controlled (the Woburn Abbey Collection, courtesy His Grace, the Duke of Bedford).

Wat's signature—perhaps the only one of his that survives—stands out on the page. At the brink of his adult life (and clearly proud of his student status), he records his inevitably derivative name but sets himself apart from his father by identifying himself in Latin: "Waltherus Ralegh filius." (A more sophisticated, or more pretentious, Latinist would have preferred "Gualterus.") He writes in notably firm strokes, in a carefully shaped italic hand with precise spacing and perfectly level lettering—quite distinct from the cramped, spidery signature of his father and the spindly linearity of his mother. The insistence of Wat's forcefully concentrated signature belies its physical placement at the bottom of the traditional family hierarchy of father, mother, and child. This tension calls to mind the earlier portrait of him and his father, where Ralegh looms over a son whose assertive attitude seems to challenge his dependent place in the composition. In signing the document, Wat is surrendering his patrimony, but he is also claiming a place for himself.

• NINE •

Continental Drifting with Ben Jonson

The obvious question to have asked Wat Ralegh, seventeen years old and a newly minted graduate of Oxford, was *Quo vadis?* But perhaps the question was not asked. No one in the family had thought of Oxford as a stepping-stone for him, and there was no obvious path for him to take after he finished his studies. Having added his name to the family's surrender of Sherborne, Wat could no longer indulge the fantasy of becoming master of the estate. An eldest son and gentleman with nothing to inherit, he faced the challenge of many a younger son who (like his father) had to carve out his own future, perhaps as an adventurer on the high seas or a soldier in the Low Countries. But Wat had been raised with the expectation of entitlement, and it seems that for an extended period of time he did nothing at all. For almost two full years—from graduation in June of 1610 until the spring of 1612, when he set off for the Continent with Ben Jonson—there is no evidence of Wat's whereabouts, with a single exception.

Unfortunately, this exception does not tell us much. It is an entry for 27 May 1611 in the diary of his mother's brother, Sir Arthur Throckmorton, which tersely records that "Sir Hatton Fermor brought Walter Ralegh here and supped here."[1] (Since his father was still in the Tower, "Walter Ralegh" must refer to Wat.) "Here" is Paulerspury, Throckmorton's Northamptonshire estate, an easy ride from the Fermor estate of Easton Neston. Throckmorton's phrasing—Fermor "brought Walter Ralegh here"—suggests that Wat was not visiting the county on his uncle's invitation, and the reference to him as simply "Walter Ralegh" does not register pleasure. This is the only reference to the Raleghs in this volume of the diary, suggesting Throckmorton had little connection with his sister or her family at the time.[2] More to the point, it is not clear what Wat's connection was with

116

Hatton Fermor, who had no discernable link with the Raleghs and was more than a decade older than his companion. One senses a desultory existence on Wat's part, as his primary residence probably remained with his mother and young brother on Tower Hill, an arrangement that would have provided little challenge to and engagement of his energies. It would appear that his father's concerns were elsewhere—Sir Walter was fully engaged in writing *The History of the World* and discreetly wooing the patronage of Prince Henry.

It is not clear how the plan to send Wat on a continental tour came about, or indeed whose decision it was. There was little to hold him in England, and Europe beckoned. Given Ralegh's disappointment in Wat and his withdrawal from family affairs, Lady Ralegh's biographer is probably right to say that "Bess planned for him [Wat] to complete his gentlemanly education with a tour of Europe, along the lines taken by her brother Arthur decades earlier."[3] But times had changed. Wat's tour was quite different from his uncle's, which had been characterized by a Tudor earnestness being conceived primarily in educational terms and featuring significant purchases of books in many languages.[4] Given Wat's lackluster academic record at Oxford, it is perhaps not surprising that intellectual ambition, or even curiosity, appears to have been quite absent. For Wat, as for many young gentlemen in his cohort, a European tour was looked upon less as an educational opportunity than as a status-marker, a chance to acquire a patina of social sophistication deemed to exceed what England could offer.

In one crucial regard, however, Wat's time abroad was to be different from that of most gentlemen—it had to be conducted on a modest allowance. In continental travel, honorable display was much more important and extravagant than it had been at Oxford, where Wat could enjoy a gentleman's lifestyle for an outlay of no more than £100 per annum.[5] But even the economy version of a European tour would easily cost at least twice as much.[6] At the high end, young English aristocrats easily incurred expenses of £1,000 a year, or more.[7] Before his death in 1612, Robert Cecil had squandered vast sums on his son Will, culminating in two tours so elaborate as to resemble minor invasions. Not only was Will chaperoned by two full-time tutors, but according to a witness he travelled in good company, with "some 30 gentlemen and servants in his train."[8] The best the Raleghs could afford would be but a small party: only Wat himself, accompanied by a tutor or governor, with perhaps a servant each. His tour would not be grand.

Although Ralegh was probably not the prime mover of the tour idea, the choice of a mature companion for Wat would have been his to make, as it had been at Oxford. This time he opted for the learned poet and playwright Ben Jonson, a man with no West Country or Oxford connections. On the face of it, Jonson was an odd person for Ralegh to choose, even though the renowned historian William Camden may have recommended him.[9] To be sure, Jonson was an excellent Latinist—thanks to his study as a boy with Camden—and possessed a deep understanding of Roman history, which he had plumbed in two recent tragedies. Ralegh must have respected his scholarship since he apparently inserted a narrative by Jonson about the Punic Wars into his *History of the World*.[10] But Jonson had some very obvious drawbacks as a travelling tutor. Despite his great facility in Latin, he seems to have had no competence in the French language (unlike the fluent Sir Walter), apparently the result of a lack of interest in French culture. In praising an English translation of French verse, Jonson had described his own poetry as "the child of ignorance / And utter stranger to all air of France," which was after all Wat's prime destination.[11]

A different cause for parental worry would have been provided by the nature of the single visit across the Channel that Jonson had made. According to his own account, as a young man Jonson had entered military service in the Low Countries, where "he had, in the face of both the camps, killed an enemy and taken *opima spolia* from him."[12] But his violence was not confined to the continent. After his return to England he entered a theatrical world in which a slashing mode of satire prevailed, leading to bitter rivalries between individuals and wars between acting companies. In a nighttime affray with Gabriel Spencer, an actor with whom he had fallen out, Jonson killed him with a rapier thrust. Jonson's later claims—that his opponent had the benefit of a much longer sword and that the conflict was a duel—do little to conceal the sordid violence.

But Ralegh may have known of these episodes and been impressed by Jonson's manly willingness to stand his ground. In his poetry, Jonson was fond of depicting himself as a centered, stoical figure, a plainspoken man who defended virtue and was unafraid to reprimand vice. In a contemporary portrait, Jonson is a vivid, imposing presence. Though his beard is beginning to go grey, we see a robust, energetic man who is accustomed to making his words listened to. (Unlike his fellow playwrights, Jonson had become noted for insulting public audiences that did not appreciate the learned craft of his plays—courtiers were another matter.) His eyes, however, betray a sensitivity, perhaps an uncertainty, that is at odds with the dominant impression of self-confidence. Hailing from humble beginnings and dependent on patronage, Jonson must have felt the stress of performing for the requisite approbation of the court—not that he was incapable of delivering home truths on the nature of true (that is, inward) nobility.

Like many other seventeenth-century fathers with fractious sons, Ralegh was in search of a learned tutor who could also be a forceful governor, and Jonson fit the bill. Wat's father was not the first person to think Jonson could combine these two opposed roles. In the previous year Robert, Lord Lisle, the younger brother of the late Sir Philip Sidney, had chosen Jonson to oversee the studies of his difficult son and heir. The troubled William Sidney was in desperate need of tutelage because he had stabbed his previous tutor with a knife, resulting in the dismissal of the tutor, of course.[13] Late in 1612, William died of smallpox, leaving Jonson free to act as governor and tutor for another intransigent scion. From Wat's recent Oxford experience, Ralegh had developed a healthy respect for his son's ability to manipulate his minders, and the thought of him living in Paris with only an academic milquetoast for governance would have been alarming.

Portrait of Ben Jonson by Abraham van Blyenberch (c. 1617). Forceful but with an uncertain gaze, the poet Ben Jonson is depicted in plain dress, several years after his dubious service as Wat's governor abroad (courtesy National Portrait Gallery, London).

With Jonson as governor, Ralegh did not have to worry about the fate that befell another tutor during a sojourn in France. The unfortunate tutor of the young Earl of Derby was said to have been "a gentleman of parts, virtue and prudence, but of too mild a nature to manage his pupil," and the wild Derby encouraged "some young French rakes" to beat him and toss him in a blanket.[14] For Jonson, the blanket was certainly no threat, since only a troop of exceptionally muscular rakes could have lifted, much less tossed, a torso that was on its way to weighing some fourteen stone (280 pounds). Perhaps Ralegh did not pay adequate attention to the gargantuan appetites that produced what Jonson proudly called "my mountain belly and my rocky face."[15] In the event it was as if Shakespeare's King Henry IV had hired Falstaff to govern the wayward Prince Hal.

For students of English literature, the question is not why Ralegh chose Jonson but rather why the author of many excellent lyrics, court masques, and plays—culminating in his darkly comic masterpieces *Volpone* (1606) and *The Alchemist* (1610)—would agree to take more than a year out of his productive writing career in an attempt to govern Wat Ralegh. What was in it for Jonson? After all, he was largely a creature of patronage, and the Ralegh family was scarcely likely to be a reliable source of future support, given the death sentence still hanging over Sir Walter, to say nothing of the family's limited financial resources. Perhaps Jonson had hopes of ingratiating himself with Prince Henry by dint of earning the gratitude of the man who seemed to be in the process of becoming the prince's mentor, but a year's service seems a rather large investment for a middle-aged man to make.[16] Given his future misbehavior in France, however, one has to suspect that Jonson's motive was simpler: the desire for an extended holiday from England.

For Wat, as for most young Englishmen, the visit began in Paris, but his time abroad turned out to be less a tour of the Continent than an extended stay in that city, with a trip through the Low Countries providing a substantial flourish at the close. He and Jonson remained in Paris for the better part of twelve months (March or April 1612 to March 1613), punctuated by visits to places of interest beyond the city. One such expedition was the increasingly popular trip along the Loire to Lyon; years later, Charles Baron Stanhope noted in his copy of Jonson's *Works* that "I kneaw Ben Jhonson at Lyons hee travelld with yoonge Watt Wrawleigh."[17] In a common itinerary, their stay in Paris was followed by three or four months in the Low Countries, with stops at Brussels, Antwerp, and Leiden. Interestingly, they did not set foot in any of the German or Italian territories that were mandatory destinations for statesmen's sons preparing for diplomatic service to the crown.

The focus on Paris suggests that Wat's plans involved gaining knowledge only in the social sense of acquiring a gentleman's skills. A certain class status attached to one's having attended Oxford, but to be seen as a true gentleman required the finishing touches that only academies in France or Italy could provide. Though expertise in music and dance, along with competence on the tennis court, were much sought after, it was primarily the Siren call of training in horsemanship and fencing that drew ambitious young Englishmen to the academies of Paris. Making a familiar point, an

English guide to travel in France stressed the acquisition of equestrian and fencing skills for those who "will returne ably qualified for his countries service in warre, and his own defence in private quarrel."[18] (In *Hamlet*, Shakespeare indicates the conventional nature of Laertes' stay in Paris by alluding to his studies with a dashing instructor of fencing and horsemanship, the ominously named Lamord.[19]) For wealthy scions of the English nobility, the first choice was the equestrian academy of M. Antoine de Pluvinal, whose pupils included the flower of England's noble youth, among them Will Cecil, Sir Thomas Puckering, and Henry Clifford, the twenty-year-old fifth earl of Cumberland.[20] Though horsemanship was de Pluvinal's drawing card, fencing was also mandatory in his curriculum.

Wat had never shown an interest in horsemanship, an inordinately expensive undertaking, so it is not surprising that there is no evidence to indicate that he attended de Pluvinal's academy or any other. It is unthinkable, however, that a young, athletic English gentleman like Wat would have remained in Paris for a year without taking steps to improve his skills in the art of fencing, probably with a private instructor. In the early seventeenth century, the art of fencing could not be separated from its evil sibling, the duel, which in France was enjoying a lethal popularity. In his long stay in France, Edward Lord Herbert engaged in many duels, blaming what he called "the Inclination of the French at that tyme": that there was "scarce any man thought worthy the looking on that had not killed some other in a duel...."[21] Since Herbert was himself pathologically proud, his observation should be taken with a large grain of salt, but there is no doubting that many died, rapier in hand, proving their noble manhood.

For Wat, anything he may have learned at Oxford about the rapier would have seemed in retrospect pathetically provincial. In France, more rigidly than in England, the right to bear a sword was limited to gentlemen, and fencing was by definition a noble art. It offered an arena for self-display in which one's courage and control allowed one to enact one's nobility for all to see, and Wat's straitened circumstances meant that the only nobility available to him was performative. Also, the gladiatorial aspect of a match, in which there is a clear winner and loser, must have engaged the highly competitive young man who had enjoyed turning rhetorical disputation at Oxford into open combat.

Wat's predilection for victorious, self-aggrandizing performance is at the center of a wonderful story that Ben Jonson told of their time in Paris. Even though his story is essentially a joke at his own expense, Jonson must have been fond of telling it, since several contemporaneous versions were recorded. The most detailed version was recorded by the Scottish poet

William Drummond of Hawthornden not long after Jonson visited him on his epic walk from London to Scotland in 1619, the year after the two Raleghs' deaths. In Edinburgh, Jonson spent his visit regaling Drummond with pungent opinions and recollections, which his reverent auditor carefully recorded. Here is Jonson's story in full:

> S[ir] W. Raulegh sent him governor with his son, anno 1613, to France. This youth, being knavishly inclined, among other pastimes (as the setting of the favour of damsels on a cod-piece), caused him [Jonson] to be drunken and dead drunk, so that he knew not where he was; thereafter laid him on a car which he made to be drawn by pioneers [workmen] through the streets, at every corner showing his governor stretched out, and telling them that was a more lively image of the crucifix than any they had; at which sport young Ralegh's mother delighted much, saying, his father young was so inclined; though the father abhorred it.[22]

Jonson's detail about Wat's being "knavishly inclined" resonates with Ralegh's address to the lad in his early poem as "my pritty knave," and we can think of the Paris incident as the sort of trouble for which he feared his son was headed.[23]

When Jonson refers to the incident of Wat's orchestration of his drunkenness as merely one "among other pastimes," the mind boggles, and one wishes for more stories. Certainly the parenthetical line about Wat's "setting of the favour of damsels on a codpiece" (presumably his own) is suggestive. In the chivalric and Petrarchan love rituals of the time, men wore love-tokens from their lady to symbolize their amorous devotion, and Wat's unprecedented insistence on adorning his codpiece with ladies' (note the plural) favors mocks the display of love-service. Or perhaps his use of this location implies that—in a neat reversal of convention—by his sexual potency he has won the devotion of the ladies. Clearly, this is the action of a young man who wants to draw the attention of others and to do so offensively—not only mocking social custom but also mocking the women with whom he has been involved.

In the main incident that Jonson relates, Wat's mockery cuts much deeper, raising concerns about his daringness and providing stronger evidence for his father's early anxieties. At one level, the point of the "sport" is the scorning of paternal authority, which is why his father's surrogate is twice referred to as Wat's "governor." It is interesting that in various retellings the story's point is the comeuppance that Wat ministers to Jonson, and, through him, to his father. In a version that descended through the secretary of Jonson's patron, the Earl of Pembroke, Wat is described as "a gay young spark who could not brook Ben's rigorous Treatment" and used Jonson's weakness for drink to "throw off the Yoak of his Government."

This version takes place in England, and its punchline is Wat's sending men to carry the drunken Ben back to his father, announcing to him that "their young Master had sent home his Tutor."[24] In another, very short notation of the story, the display of the drunken tutor is all that remains of the anecdote. The clergyman who recorded it simply noted that "B Johnson was with yong Wat Rawleigh in France & would there be drunk—See you my governor said hee—."[25]

The gusto with which Jonson told the story to Drummond, and presumably to others, is on its face odd, since he is himself its comic butt. Apparently, Jonson saw in Wat's mockery of himself a parable about the limits of self-righteous authority, which explains why he included a fictionalized version of the incident in his last great play for the public theatre, *Bartholomew Fair*. Jonson wrote this comedy in the year after his return to England, and in it he glances at his own experience in the figure of Humphrey Wasp, the short-tempered, pompous governor of a foolish lad called Bartholomew Cokes. (Jonson's editors note that "the adventures of a tutor with an ill-conditioned youth are very feelingly described."[26]) Cokes happens to be nineteen years old—Wat's age in Paris—but he is a childish innocent and a willing victim of the fair's numerous predators, the exact opposite of the mocking, rebellious Wat. At the end of the play, however, the episode in Paris clearly colors the relationship of the arrogant governor and his feckless charge.

After Wasp and Cokes have become separated, the irascible governor is caught up in the fair's quarreling and drinking, rendered incoherent, and clapped into the public stocks for all to see. Observing his mentor's humiliation, the hitherto docile Cokes understands Wasp's hypocrisy and admirably refuses to accept chastisement from him. In response, Wasp speaks for the first time with sober self-knowledge, sounding a good deal like his chastened author when he concedes that "the date of my authority is out; I must think no longer to reign, my government is at an end. He that will correct another must want fault in himself."[27] Jonson's transformation of the Paris incident into theatre—coupled with his subsequent willingness to tell the unflattering story to friends—indicates he may have learned from the incident, and certainly it was a tonic for his art. But Wat was no wide-eyed Cokes, and Jonson's fictional transformation concealed how disturbing and dangerous the event must have been.

According to the account Jonson told Drummond, Wat said something far more dangerous than "see you my governor." He announced to the Parisian crowd that the large (apparently unidentified) drunken man splayed out on the cart was "a more lively image of the crucifix than any they had." As if his words were not blasphemous enough, Wat compounded his insult by his manner of presentation. It is significant that Jonson is described as being wheeled "through the streets," with Wat formally presenting him to the crowd "at every corner." This procession through the streets, with periodic stops to uncover and display a precious object, is a carnivalesque parody of religious processions, and in particular it mocks the festival of Corpus Christi, in which symbols of Christ's presence are carried through the streets to re-enact the mystery of his divine spirit entering into the society that is his body.

As Jonson's biographers have noted, Wat's mockery was exceedingly dangerous. Only two years earlier, King Henri IV had been assassinated by a religious fanatic, and violence was in the air. Even before Henri's murder, crowds were alert to the dangers of blasphemy, and an English traveler had noted that if someone "forbear[s] to worship the sacrament as they do, perhaps he may be presently stabbed or otherwise most shamefully abused, if there should be notice taken of him."[28] Wat saw to it that notice was taken of himself.

Fortunately, Wat was not so foolish as to disrupt an actual Corpus Christi festival, and it is possible that he staged his provocation under the cover of carnival. David Riggs astutely notes that in 1613, the Mardi Gras celebration (a promising occasion for getting Jonson "drunk and dead drunk") fell on 26 February and that "Jonson and Raleigh departed from Paris as soon as the carnival was over."[29] Only two weeks later, the secretary to the English ambassador in Paris sent to William Trumbull, the resident at Brussels, a letter of introduction for Jonson, saying that after "having spent some twelve months travele in this Country, in Mr. Raughley's companie," he "hath now taken a resolution to pass by Sedan into your partes."[30] After some extravagant praise of Jonson—including reference to the "testimonie of his extraordinarie and rare parts of knowledge and understanding, which make his conversation to be honored and beloved in all companies"—the letter ends with the suggestion that the poet be offered "the best cupp of claret that Brussels shall affoord."

But the secretary quickly revised his praise of Jonson, for several days later he folds into an unrelated business letter a private slip indicating that he had written the earlier recommendation "at Mr Johnsons entreatie."[31] One senses the force of Jonson's personality in the disingenuous caution with which the secretary characterizes the poet's motive: "I suppose he was desirous to have to prevent the rumour of some cross busyness wherein he hath been interested [implicated] here." (After the word "some," he had first written the word "ill" and then marked it out and substituted the less pejorative "cross," meaning "contrary to one's desire or liking.") Even when he is acknowledging his earlier failure to mention the poet's bad behavior, the secretary is still careful to employ euphemisms. It is very likely that the drunken episode with Wat was the "ill" or "cross busyness" that precipitated the pair's immediate departure. If yet another (apparently undocumented) escapade were the source of Jonson's embarrassment, then his career as Wat's governor was yet more checkered—and the behavior of his charge perhaps even more obstreperous.

From a Protestant perspective, Wat's blasphemy was a commendable attack on the Catholic doctrine of the Real Presence of Christ's body in the sanctified wafer taken at the Eucharist. This was a frequently and hotly debated point of theology. Indeed, a few months earlier the Reverend Daniel Featley, Wat's former tutor at Corpus Christi College and now a renowned controversialist, had represented the Church of England in a Paris debate with an English Catholic about the transubstantiation of Christ's body in the Host.[32] We know of the event because one of the invited spectators was Ben Jonson, who later was asked to vet an official (Protestant) summary of the event. It is not known whether Wat attended, but if he did not he certainly would have been given an account by his governor.

It seems unlikely, however, that Wat's dangerous provocation had the force of religious belief behind it. If he had heard of the event, the reverend Daniel Featley probably would not have welcomed Wat as a fellow warrior for the Word. Indeed, Wat's mockery could as easily be construed as blasphemously anti–Christian as it could be seen as doctrinally anti–Catholic.[33] Of course, neither alternative would have invited affection from the Parisians, and perhaps Wat became so caught up in his sport that he failed to realize how dangerously offensive it had become. What is certain is that Wat and Jonson left Paris soon after the incident, and not a moment too soon.

From the outset, Jonson had intended for the tour to include the Low Countries, and the Paris incident may have served as a useful reminder that it was time to socialize with some sober scholars. (Jonson's desire "to prevent the rumour" of his bad behavior from prejudicing the learned community before his arrival was prudent.) For his part, Wat cannot have been eager to meet scholars, however distinguished, and it may be that—with his good reputation in mind—Jonson was equally unwilling for his scoffing charge to be present. That this leg of the tour did not generate any stories involving Wat suggests that his governor kept a close eye on him, and perhaps both were on their best behavior.

Like France and unlike Spain (as well as much of Italy), Flanders was a Catholic land that did not pose dangers for respectful Protestant visitors. For Englishmen on tour, Brussels and Antwerp were common destinations throughout the seventeenth century. Then, as now, Brussels was a center of diplomatic activity, being the residence of the Archduke's court, and on his visit Jonson would have had the opportunity to engage with many learned men. William Trumbull, the English resident at Brussels, was a career diplomatic official who was also a lover of literature, and we can be sure that (perhaps warily) he shared his best claret with Ben.

Wat and Jonson must not have spent more than two weeks in Brussels, for on 3 April 1613, an English agent in Antwerp sent a message to Trumbull in Brussels, saying the pair had arrived and were desperately short of money. The agent notes that he is enclosing "Mr. Rawleghe and Mr. Jnosons [*sic*] bills: who Importuned me soe earnestly for £10 more, that I could not refuse them. I have entered £20li uppon your accompt."[34] Bills of exchange were the bank drafts of the day, a good way to avoid carrying too much cash—highwaymen were common—and for fathers to limit the amount of money available to their sons at any given time. The travelers carried a bill of exchange for £10, which the agent honored, and they convincingly pleaded that they required another ten. Whether the shortfall indicates poor planning, high living, or some combination of both, it is impossible to know.

After spending less than a month in Antwerp, Wat and Ben set out for the United Provinces and especially for Leiden, some 80 miles to the north, where they arrived in March. For its stalwart support in the war with Spain, the city had been rewarded by the Prince of Orange with the gift of a new university (1575), which by the early seventeenth century had already become one of the most prestigious Protestant universities on the Continent, drawing many English students and scholars.[35] In particular, Jonson wished to confer with the great humanist and poet Daniel Heinsius, who taught at the university and was being wooed to come to the English court.[36] Apparently, Jonson successfully met with Heinsius, receiving from him documents which an English friend required for editing Martial's epigrams, and in his own critical writing Jonson was to plunder several of Heinsius's important treatises.

Jonson's biographers agree that he and Wat must have returned to London before 29 June 1613, when the Globe Theatre burned in a conflagration that, in a poem written ten years later, Ben says "I saw."[37] But the biographers cannot be right because an overlooked document indicates that Wat—with or without Jonson—was still in Leiden when the Globe burned. The document is a matriculation register for the University of Leiden, which contains the following entry: "*1613 Juliis 31 GUALTERUS RAELE, Anglus, 21, studiosus litterarum. D. Nereus.*"[38]

Since this entry is dated a month after the burning of the Globe, Wat presumably remained in Leiden until this time. If Jonson returned without Wat (or without obtaining permission for leaving him behind) Ralegh surely would have felt that Wat's governor had acted irresponsibly in Leiden, as he had earlier in Paris. Upon Jonson's return, as we will see, there was no love lost between father and governor.

Brief as it is, the matriculation entry contains a good deal of information. Wat's correct name, nationality, and age confirm that the entry could refer only to him. (To be sure, he had not reached his 21st birthday, but perhaps he thought it useful to present himself as no longer a minor.) The reference to "D. Nereus" records Wat's place of residence in Leiden. "D" is short for the honorific "Dominus" (Sir), and "Nereus" is the name of his distinguished landlord, Richard Jean de Nerée, latinized as Richardus Janus Nereus. De Nerée was an Arminian minister in the Dutch Reformed Church who "had acquired a reputation as being a respectable pedagogue or loco parentis for students throughout Europe. In their large double house on Leiden's prestigious Rapenburg canal, De Nerée and his wife supplemented their income by renting rooms to students ... many [of whom] were the sons of nobility."[39] Certainly Wat's residence in a well-established, religiously observant household would have been useful in assuring his parents he was in good hands.

At the University of Leiden, matriculation was not necessarily a sign of academic commitment, being inexpensive and providing valuable benefits such as a university court that granted legal protection for foreigners.[40] Nor does the description of Wat as "studiosus litterarum" (a student in the faculty of arts) bespeak academic ambition. According to Dr. Martine Zoeteman, it was "a quite common term for beginning students, who could visit any class they desired, and there was no supervision at all." In other words, Wat's matriculation indicates his intent to coast on the work he had already done at Oxford. At Leiden the spectrum of English students ranged from those with Calvinist connections—who usually completed degree programs (often in divinity)—to gentlemen who were essentially pleasure-seeking visitors to Leiden, usually remaining at the university for less than three months.[41] Wat Ralegh definitely belonged to the latter contingent.

What pleasures did Wat pursue? In the first place, there would have been the felicity of being free of Ben Jonson and indeed of all active adult governance. As the title of a recent study of youth culture in the Low

Countries might suggest—*Sex and Drugs* Before *Rock 'n' Roll*—there were plenty of pleasures for young men in this prosperous, if Calvinist, land, and we need not be too specific in identifying Wat's pastimes. Perhaps it is best not to think of him as a wild hedonist—after all, it was not Wat who was lying "drunk and dead drunk" in that cart in Paris. As seems to have been the case at Oxford, it is likely that his lusty excesses took the form of "violent exercises," and the University of Leiden would have been an excellent place for him to develop the skills he had acquired in Paris, especially the art of fencing.

Unlike the University of Oxford, where the absence of fencing from the curriculum necessitated a master be found in town, the University of Leiden established a prestigious fencing school of its own for gentlemen, or would-be gentlemen. (Among European institutions the competition for well-heeled international students was intense.) Unlike Oxford and Cambridge, where fencing was frowned upon because students were forbidden to bear arms, there was a long tradition at Dutch universities of noble students being allowed to carry lethal weapons (pistols as well as swords).[42] As well, the incorporation of the Leiden fencing school into the University gave the fencing masters an unparalleled academic cachet. A strain of mathematics was typified by Ludolph van Ceulen, who opened a fencing school in Leiden in 1594 and six years later was appointed the first professor of mathematics at the University, where he eventually worked out π to 35 places as his tombstone records. Certainly, the engraving of the Leiden fencing school in 1610—not long before Wat's stay—intends to convey a mathematical rigor. In addition to the loosely circular placement of the pairs of students, the sense of abstruse geometric design is especially insistent in the fascinating floor design in which a circle is inscribed inside a square and bisected by many diameters. A sense of powerful self-control is vividly bodied forth in the gentleman on the great horse who extends himself in a perfectly horizontal plane with the support of only a single hand.

In the early seventeenth century, the fencing school at Leiden was regarded as the best in Protestant Europe, and it is likely that Wat matriculated at the University so that he could attend it. If this is so, a new dimension of Wat's character—one quite different from the knavish impetuosity that Jonson described and perhaps also provoked—comes into view. As we can see from the illustration of the Leiden fencing school, the successful practice of the art required great discipline, to say nothing of cold calculation. In Leiden, where he lived in the residence of the august minister and his wife, Wat appears to be treading on a relatively straight and narrow

Nine • *Continental Drifting with Ben Jonson* 129

A depiction of the Fencing School at the University of Leiden (1610) stresses the geometry of self-control in the midst of potentially lethal action (courtesy Erfgoed Leiden en Omstreken).

path after the dangerous excesses of Paris. There is, however, no documentary evidence that Wat attended the Leiden fencing school—very little information about the school survives, and no lists of its students are extant—so his study of fencing at Leiden is not a proven fact.[43] But Wat's immediate future provides a good deal of evidence to indicate that somewhere he had learned valuable skills with a rapier.

Although Wat's Continental tour may well have improved his fencing skills, it appears to have soured his relations with both Jonson and his father, who wound up at loggerheads themselves. It is not surprising, given Wat's mockery of Jonson, that governor and pupil fell out. Although Jonson ultimately transformed the Paris incident into a comic parable of self-knowledge, he could not have been pleased, and it is revealing that in the account to Drummond he specified in a self-exculpatory comment that Wat "*caused him* to be drunken and dead drunk." Certainly whatever good feelings Wat and Ben may have entertained for each other at the outset were deeply abraded by the end. Izaak Walton's understated recollection of the simmering discord between the two sounds as if it came from Jonson himself: "Within a short time after their returne, they parted (I think not in cole [cool] bloud) and with a love sutuble to what they had in their travills (not to be comended)."[44]

After the tour ended, Sir Walter Ralegh and Ben Jonson broke off relations completely. Ralegh had considerably more reason than Wat to be unhappy with Jonson. According to Drummond, Jonson reported that when the Raleghs heard the story of his inebriation and Wat's mockery in Paris, they responded very differently: "young Ralegh's mother delighted much, saying, his father young was so inclined; though the father abhorred it."[45] Perhaps intensified by his wife's expression of pleasure, Ralegh's abhorrence is a revealing reaction; it bespeaks a disgust directed at both Wat and Ben—at Wat for mocking his authority by scorning his surrogate and at Jonson for disrespectfully finding mirth in his own dereliction of duty.

For his part, Jonson made comments about Ralegh that—soon after his execution—were, to put it mildly, ungenerous. Complaining to Drummond of Ralegh's appropriation of his history of the Punic War, Jonson declared that "the best wits of England were employed for making of his History," suggesting that *The History of the World* was only an epic cut-and-paste job.[46] Less unfairly, he criticized Ralegh as one who "esteemed more of fame than conscience." Perhaps the latter comment indirectly acknowledges and rebuts the widespread praise that—only two months earlier—Ralegh's courageous death on the scaffold had won, but Jonson would have none of it.

But perhaps the most eloquent evidence of the falling out of Ralegh and Jonson is a mutual silence. Before Jonson had left England with Wat, he wrote a substantial poem in which he explicated the allegorical, elaborately engraved frontispiece that would be the title page for Ralegh's *History of the World*. Two years later, following the travelers' return, the *History* was printed, with Jonson's poem (titled "The Minde of The Front") facing the title page which it was written to elucidate. But Ralegh does not acknowledge its authorship; indeed, he emphasizes his displeasure at Jonson by failing to include even the poet's initials. Jonson responded in kind. Two years later, in the massive folio edition of his own collected *Works*, he responded with a de-authoring slight of his own, making his poem effectively self-contained by giving it a curious new title: "The Mind of the Frontispiece to *a* Book" (italics added).[47] He refused to be complicit in Ralegh's fame.

Notwithstanding the alienation of Jonson, the greatest damage caused by Wat's continental tour was inflicted on the relationship of the father and son. Unfortunately, the absence of written correspondence between the two means we have to surmise how they felt toward each other, but we can be sure that Ralegh's modest expectations for his son were disappointed. Upon his return, Wat was no closer to finding a place for himself, or perhaps even desiring a place for himself, than he had been before leaving. Worse yet, Ralegh may have sensed that Wat's gentlemanly training in Paris—and especially his schooling in arms—had the ill effect of confirming in him an awareness of his high honor and of the demands it placed on him to defend it. Certainly Ralegh did not have long to wait before his suspicion was confirmed.

As his future would attest, Wat had good reason to think he was the match of anyone he confronted in personal combat. In the two tumultuous years following his return, virtually everything we know about him is related to the numerous duels and affrays into which he threw himself. From this point onward, the primary connection between father and son would be less personal than legal: Ralegh's repeated interventions with legal authorities on Wat's behalf. Although one cannot question the father's deep concern for his son's well-being, there is no reason to think these (for the most part successful) interventions served to endear Sir Walter Ralegh to his namesake. Wat's future commitment to the rapier is foreshadowed by the fact that the earliest evidence for determining the date of his return to England comes from the correspondence of authorities attempting to prevent an illegal duel that he was planning.

• Ten •

A Son in Arms

The final years of Wat Ralegh's short life are marked—in several senses—by his ardent engagement in violent conflict. With the exception of the clash that ended his life, this violence was entirely private and personal. For many young Englishmen touring the Continent, the ongoing war between the Protestant Netherlands and Catholic Spain was a central attraction since it offered a taste of military engagement not available at home.[1] But in his journey with Jonson through Flanders and into the Dutch republic, Wat showed no apparent interest in the conflict and made no attempt to channel his aggressive energy into it. To be sure, within a year of his return to England, he was back in the Low Countries again with armed conflict on his mind, but his intent was to fight a duel with a fellow Englishman. At home and abroad, Wat would engage in an accelerating series of duels and violent affrays, but apparently never on political or religious grounds. Unlike his father, whose antipathy to the Spanish empire was shared by many, he found enemies of his own.

As Lady Ralegh reminded her husband after they heard of their son's mischief in Paris, he had once been young, too. In those days he too had eagerly taken up weapons on his own behalf. Her point is well taken, for if Ralegh had died at twenty-five, as Wat did, his life may not have appeared much more promising, or less violent, than his son's. Certainly a pugnacious strain ran through the family line. John Aubrey says of Sir Walter's grandsons, with whom he went to school in Dorset, that although they possessed "excellent tuneable voices" they were "all proud and quarrelsome."[2] Certainly the early double portrait of father and son—emphasizing Wat's studied imitation of Ralegh—suggests that the origin of Wat's recourse to arms is to be located in the man standing proudly beside him. Although Ralegh eventually regretted the passion with which Wat took up the sword, every gentleman wished his son capable of deploying effectively the weapon which it was his prerogative to wear and duty to wield for his family's honor.

A quick glance at Ralegh's earliest days at court (before he had attracted the queen's attention) reveals that he was on the verge of falling into a series of violent personal quarrels similar to his son's some thirty-five years later. (Wat moved from one altercation to another with such alacrity that historians have had trouble keeping his opponents straight.) Within only a month, the elder Ralegh was involved in two violent conflicts in the court's environs, both of which resulted in the imprisonment of him and his adversary. Although modern commentators often have characterized these incidents as duels, the clerks of the privy council refer to each as a "fray"—their term for an armed brawl—and there is no reason to think the clashes were as premeditated and procedural as a duel. The mayhem of frays brought before the council often involved a lord's armed retainers, such as the two servants of the earl of Oxford who were "committed to the Marshalsea for committing of disorders and frayes appon the gentlemen of the Innes of the Courte," or the servant who was killed fighting alongside his master Sir John Parker in an "affray."[3]

Ralegh's first altercation occurred shortly before 17 March 1580, when "Sir Thomas Parrot, knight, and Walter Rawley, gentleman" were "called before their Lordships [of the privy council] for a fraye made betwixt them."[4] Perrott and Ralegh were nearly the same age, and Ralegh may have been galled by the fact that his opponent had been knighted only a few months earlier, a reward for having served in an (unsuccessful) pirate-chasing expedition led by his father.[5] It is easy to imagine Ralegh—close to being a down-at-heels gentleman without visible prospects—feeling a combination of scorn and envy toward his (improperly) honored contemporary. Since Thomas was the eldest son of the wealthy and powerful Sir John Perrot, an illegitimate son of Henry VIII and an honored favorite of Elizabeth, the altercation reveals that Ralegh was unafraid to clash with a person considerably more powerful than himself. Regardless of their difference in status, the two men were punished equally, both being committed to the Fleet prison. A week later, they were released after having provided sureties that they would keep the peace towards each other, "and in the mean season to demean them selfes quietly."[6]

Ralegh's quiet demeanor did not last long. Only a month later, he reappears in the privy council records in a frustratingly laconic notation: "Walter Ralley and _____ Wingfield, committed to the Marshalsea for a fray besides the Tennis Courte in Westminster."[7] The location is suggestive, as tennis courts were common sites of fractious behavior among young men; it was at a tennis court that Sir Philip Sidney and the earl of Oxford famously quarreled, forcing the privy council and queen to intercede to prevent a duel.[8] This time, Ralegh's opponent was Edward Wingfield, the eldest son in a branch of a large family distinguished by its military service.[9] (The clerk may have left his first name blank because there were so many Wingfields to choose from.) At the time, Ralegh was moving away from his (dependent) association with the unstable earl of Oxford, and several lords who had become bitter enemies of the earl later charged that Wingfield had been suborned by Oxford to waylay and murder Ralegh.[10] Given the exaggerations these same lords were given to—they also charged that Oxford planned to have Sir Philip Sidney murdered in bed by twelve gunmen—we cannot be sure that Wingfield actually attempted to assassinate Ralegh, but the fight must have been real (and dangerous) enough.

Whatever the cause of the "fray," the privy council would not have been amused by Ralegh's prompt flaunting of their command for quiet demeanor. It is not clear how long he was held in the Marshalsea, as the privy council does not record his release, but it was a much rougher prison than the Fleet, and council's displeasure would have been very clear.[11] After he was freed, Ralegh wisely decided— perhaps with a push from the lords of the council—to remove himself from the courtly cycle of ambition and resentment by taking up a commission to lead a troop of a hundred soldiers to Ireland. In the theatre of war, he could vent his hostility on the battlefield, and soon he displayed a good deal of both bravery and brutality.

It is fair to say that Wat inherited his father's aggressiveness, but the environment in which he exercised it was very different from Elizabethan England. By Wat's time, a new culture of genteel, even punctilious violence was flourishing in England, and the rapier was its weapon of choice. With an edge for slashing and a sharp point for sudden thrusts, the long, light rapier was altogether more elegant and lethal than the traditional, rather unwieldy English broadsword, which it replaced in the 1570s and 1580s.[12] (Even at the best of times and in the best-trained hands, the rapier was a difficult weapon to control, and many a student as well as some instructors lost an eye in training.) To be sure, the broadsword retained its military primacy, and it enjoyed a certain nativist repute for advantaging sheer strength and hearty English manliness. But despite incidents in which broadsword-wielding Englishmen—named Austen Bramble, Bartholomew Bagger, and Cheese—taunted and grievously wounded Italian fencing masters, among gentlemen the rapier won the day.[13]

The rapier was a sophisticated weapon that had to be *learned*, and for preservation of life as well as social cachet, the fencing school became a fashionable venue in which gentlemen could master the art. Having become a respected courtier who had left tennis court frays behind him, Ralegh was attracted to the lure of fencing and became a patron of London's most genteel school. The fencing master Rocco Bonetti had come to London in the late 1560s or early 1570s and founded a school in Blackfriars, the hub of modish entertainment. Never short of pride, Bonetti disdained to refer to his establishment as a "Fence-schoole" and preferred to call it "his Colledge."[14] The sumptuous interior of the building—in which the coats of arms of noble students hung above their weapons—suggested an integral connection between high birth and the art of fencing. Unfortunately, Bonetti's appeal to aristocratic taste proved to be inordinately expensive for a property that was, after all, only rented, and his debts mounted alarmingly. Being an admirer of Bonetti and perhaps also a student at his College, Ralegh took it upon himself to plead with the landlord to extend the fencing-master's lease, but with unknown success.[15]

There was a darkly pragmatic side to the age's fascination with fencing, for beneath the nobility and complex geometry of swordplay was a brutal reality: that a gentleman's handling of his rapier could spell the difference between life and death. The practice of fencing was inseparable from—and ultimately dependent on—the duel. Although "fence" derived from "defence," the point (so to speak) was to learn how to kill.[16] Needless to say, those who had developed superior skills were more likely to engage in duels than their less talented or more pacifist peers. Fencing offered an opportunity to display quasi-aristocratic virtues such as courage and self-possession because mortal danger was always present.

In late Elizabethan and Stuart England, as on the Continent, the duel was predicated on the assertion of one's honor, and the accidental or deliberate violation of rituals of precedence caused many conflicts. For instance, a duel was narrowly prevented in 1621, when the newly elevated earl of Berkshire was "committed close prisoner to the Fleet from the Higher House [House of Lords] for brabbling with the Lord Scrope that carelessly and unawares stepped in at the door before him."[17] Worse could have happened, and often did. At the end of a military campaign, Sir John Burgh and Sir William Drury fell out over a question of who should take precedence in a parade before the French king. In the duel that ensued, Burgh gave Drury a slash to the hand that turned gangrenous, leading to amputation of the arm and his death soon after.[18] Several years later, Burgh led an unsuccessful expedition to the West Indies and, perceiving an insult from Sir John Gilbert II (Ralegh's nephew), challenged him to a duel.

Gilbert killed him with a rapier thrust. In a letter to his nephew some time later, Ralegh took credit for arranging his pardon and discharge from prison.[19]

Anyone who was a gentleman and carried a sword could be provoked into fighting a duel, for "readiness to fight was a peremptory duty."[20] The code of honor held that anyone who declined a challenge would face ridicule and worse, but the pressure to fight was especially coercive for men of uncertain or marginal status, men with something to prove.[21] Thanks in good part to his father, Wat Ralegh had a good deal to prove. For him, as for most young men, it was crucial to establish from the outset a reputation for pugnacity; a failure to respond to a challenge was sure to bring on more challenges. But the onus on Wat was particularly great, as he carried the name of a man noted for his courage. A still more important factor in Wat's willingness, even compulsion, to fight can be laid entirely at the doorstep of his father: the ambiguity of his status as a gentleman. As we have seen, Ralegh's conviction for treason and consequent attainder created many problems for the rest of his family, and especially for Wat. His father's legal loss of social identity drew into question the nature of Wat's status, making provocative questions inevitable. How could he, the son of a traitor, really be a gentleman? Indeed, how could he not be tainted by the corrupted blood that engendered his father's treason? Finally, there was a question that he had to ask himself: What could he do to restore his own honor, if not that of his father? These were all fighting words.

For Wat Ralegh and other aspiring duelists, the dangers inherent to rapier swordplay were compounded by a new dimension of threat: a concerted legal challenge to the duel, led by King James himself. James had never approved of bloodshed, either in public or in private conflict, and the early 1610s saw a rash of lethal duels (many involving at least one Scot) that appalled him.[22] Finally, a terrible duel in which two of his friends made simultaneous, fatal thrusts triggered a barrage of royal proclamations and legal reforms (some spelled out in a volume by the new attorney-general, Francis Bacon) that were calculated to punish men who participated in duels or even attempted to engage in them by sending or accepting challenges.[23]

The king's prohibition of dueling gained support from what must have seemed to Wat Ralegh an unexpected quarter, his father. In the final book of his soon to be published *History of the World*, Ralegh inserted "*A digression, concerning duels.*"[24] This essay begins in a dry historical mode, classifying types of personal combat throughout the ages, but it comes alive when Ralegh arrives at a contemporary phenomenon, "the challenge of combat" leading to duels "founded upon mere private anger; yea, or upon matter seeming worthy of anger in the opinion of the duellists." Ralegh derives this "fashion" from "French gentlemen" and sardonically observes that it has "grown to be a custom, whence we have derived a kind of art and philosophy of quarrel with certain grounds and rules...." He scorns especially the punctilio of "giving of the lie"—the public challenge of a person for lying, thus compelling a duel—which "is become the most fruitful root of deadly quarrels." Although Ralegh concedes that being publically accused of lying is a serious insult, he does not think it justifies a duel and dryly observes that "all that is rude ought not to be civilized with death."

There is no doubt that Ralegh was writing this essay for the king's eyes, as the conspicuous similarity of his arguments to those of King James and Lord Bacon indicates. Moreover, he directly praises James for having "done a most kingly and Christian-like deed in Scotland," which was to outlaw "that hereditary prosecution of malice, called the *deadly feud...*" (465). Having lost the hope of release by Prince Henry, Ralegh was evidently seeking favor with his father; since there is sharp criticism of absolute regal authority earlier in the *History*, perhaps the interpolated essay on the duel was Ralegh's attempt to assure the king of his support. Ralegh's hope becomes clumsily apparent at the essay's end, when he tells the story of a loyal French admiral who was betrayed by his king and condemned after an unjust public trial, only to be saved when "the king's justice, surmounting all other his passions, gave back unto him his honour, his offices, his liberty, and his estate" (468). Needless to say, the immediate effect of the *History of the World* was not what Ralegh hoped—James denounced its censure of kingship and instructed his officers to purchase and destroy any unsold volumes.

In addition to the king, Ralegh had another individual in mind when he was writing his essay against duels—his older son. There is no evidence that Wat had participated in a duel before the *History of the World* was published (29 March 1614), but Ralegh must have feared that his truculent son would put his considerable fencing skills into bloody practice, as so many other young gentlemen were doing.[25] Indeed, in May Wat was apprehended for attempting to arrange a duel in the Low Countries. Conceivably, Ralegh may have had Wat in mind when he praised the king for preventing the threat posed by "the audacious, common, and brave, yet outrageous vanity of duellists" (465). Certainly Wat's many forthcoming fights not only manifest his passion for dueling but also serve to thumb his nose at the two male authorities who sought to restrain him: his king and his father.

Wat's first (intended) duel proved to be amazingly ill-timed, so ill-timed as to seem calculated to provoke the animus of the king and perhaps of his father as well. Not long after the publication of *The History of the World* and also the king's *Proclamation against Private Challenges and Combats*, Wat Ralegh and Robert Knollys quarreled in England and, like many before them, they agreed to meet in the Low Countries to resolve their differences with rapiers.[26] (The Continent was a popular destination for duels because it was traditionally beyond the reach of English law.) Nothing is known of the grounds of their quarrel, but there had been bad blood between their families since—in an act perceived by the Raleghs as betrayal—Robert Knollys's uncle Henry had unilaterally withdrawn his ships from an expedition commanded by Sir Humphrey Gilbert, whose younger stepbrothers Walter and Carew Ralegh also captained vessels.[27]

In Robert Knollys, Wat found a formidable opponent—his elder by three years, heir to a prominent Berkshire gentleman with many family connections, and recently elected to sit in the so-called Addled Parliament.[28] More to the point, Robert had military service under his belt. After graduation from Oxford, Knollys had visited the Continent, but (unlike Wat) he was drawn to the wars and served with the English troops who aided the Dutch in their successful siege of Juliers in 1610. At the time, duels were common between members of two English regiments whose leaders were quarreling. Knollys's service was presumably satisfactory and satisfying because in the 1620s he would return to the struggle in the Low Countries as a commander.

Fortunately for both principals, the duel between Wat and Knollys never came about. Someone had alerted Sir Ralph Winwood, the Principal Secretary of the Privy Council and—a rarity among James's senior officials—a person sympathetic to Ralegh, that a duel in Flanders was afoot. Winwood was able to detain Knollys before he could board ship, but Wat had already sailed. Winwood's recourse was to instruct the Lieutenant Governor of Flushing, Sir John Throckmorton, to locate his young kinsman and return him to England.[29] Interestingly, when he sends Wat to the governor under armed guard, Throckmorton says nothing about an intended (and illegal) duel and makes no mention of Robert Knollys. In his despatch accompanying Wat, Throckmorton emphasizes to the governor the speed with which he followed Winwood's instructions and "within a very fewe [h]owres" apprehended "Mr. Walter Raleygh." Clearly the informant who had alerted Winwood knew exactly where Wat was to be found. It is conceivable that this information came from Knollys after his apprehension, or perhaps from a person who had agreed to be a second for one of the disputants. Alternatively, the informant may have been someone who knew Wat and his plans well, perhaps even Ralegh himself, who would have trusted Winwood to handle the matter discreetly.

Eleven days after his report to the governor, Throckmorton mentioned the episode again—this time in a letter to his colleague William Trumbull, the English resident at Brussels. (It was Trumbull who, two years earlier, had been asked to provide his best claret to welcome Ben Jonson and his charge to Brussels.) Though brief, this second account is franker than Throckmorton's previous, more official one; he observes to Trumbull that "The occasion of my sending back Mr. Ralegh was by reason of a quarrel which in England fell out between him and one Mr. Knowles, the heir of that house."[30] His final sentence indicates why he has taken Trumbull into his confidence: "You may not have heard of this, and then you will take it uncertainly what you find written of him [Wat] in my letter." Presumably Throckmorton is referring to a no longer extant letter to Trumbull asking for help in returning Wat to England but not spelling out the circumstances of his arrest, and he wishes Trumbull to know the whole story. In the months to come, this humane bureaucrat in Brussels would prove to be a key figure in smoothing the troubled young man's path and would earn his father's gratitude.

Between Wat's return to England in the last week of May and his arraignment (with Knollys) before the Star Chamber on November 26th, we can be sure the Raleghs were doing everything that their own straitened circumstances allowed to aid their scapegrace son. We would expect them to have approached Lady Ralegh's brother, Sir Arthur Throckmorton, for help, and there is a tantalizing clue to indicate they did so. On the 2nd of June—only a week or two after Wat was returned from Flushing—the Privy Council sent a letter to the Lieutenant of the Tower stating that Sir Arthur Throckmorton had asked for and should be granted permission "to repair unto the sayd Sir Walter Raleighe, at seasonable and convenient tymes, as his occasions shall require."[31] The unspecified "occasions" requiring Throckmorton's frequent visits to his brother-in-law must have concerned Wat. It may be that Wat had been released to the recognizance of his uncle at his Mile End residence, which would have allowed easy access to him for his mother and little brother. In any event, Wat apparently made it through the entire summer without mishap.

Even though Wat and Robert Knollys had not crossed swords, they had planned to do so and thus were in violation of laws against dueling that James had recently promulgated. On the theory that duels could not exist without challenges, the king issued "A Proclamation against private

Challenges and Combats" (February 1614) in which he declared that "no man shall presume ... either to send or accept of Challenges."³² On the advice of Sir Francis Bacon, the attorney general, cases involving dueling were determined in Star Chamber, where the king's will could be easily imposed since the privy council sat as judges, supplemented by compliant chief justices from the king's courts. Though King James could observe any Star Chamber proceeding that he wished, he rarely attended unless a duel was involved. In "a case of challenge" between Inns of Court students named Bellingham and Christmas (February 1617) James delivered an eloquent speech against duels after the two were fined and sentenced to the Tower.³³ But the fine and imprisonment (and perhaps the speech, as well) were mainly for show, and a month later the punishments were remitted.

A precedent of sorts for Wat's case occurred in January of 1614 and was published in a pamphlet by Bacon soon afterwards. The accused were William Priest and Richard Wright, men who were, significantly, of low birth and no political consequence. The charge was that Priest had written a letter of challenge (along with "a stick which should bee the length of the weapon"), which Wright as his second had carried to the challenged party, who declined to fight and ungallantly reported his opponents to the authorities.³⁴ Priest and Wright were, of course, found guilty and committed to the Fleet, with the former being fined five hundred pounds and the latter a third less, five hundred marks. Given the abundant killing of one noble by another in duels that were never brought to court, it was a mockery of justice that these wannabe gentlemen were punished so grievously for brandishing their pathetic paper and stick. Favored because of his high status and many connections, Knollys would have been treated more leniently than these men whom Bacon had disparaged as "meane persons," and presumably this treatment would have been extended to Wat as well.

Interestingly, what appears to be the single contemporary reference to the legal proceedings against Wat and Knollys also mentions Priest, Wright, and Bacon's little book. In a letter to Sir Edward Herbert in Paris dated 26 November 1614, John Danvers notes (with shaky grammar and spelling) the recent publication of Ralegh's *History of the World*, adding "his Sonn Mr. Walter Rawley having quarreld with Mr. Robert Knowles that was att Juliers are by the Kings attorney brought to answer in the Stare Chamber after the example of the Boucher [Butcher] and Barber who were there finde [fined], of which there is a booke in Print...."³⁵

As Danvers says, Bacon arraigned Wat and Robert Knollys before the Star Chamber, but as Knollys's biographer notes, "all trace of any proceedings against them has been lost."³⁶ Since the case was heard in Star Chamber, the conviction of the two young men was probably a foregone conclusion. Most likely, as with Priest and Wright before them and Bellingham and Christmas after them, they were each fined a substantial amount of money and imprisoned for a short time. (A fine of £500 would have cut deeply into the Raleghs' ready money.) The Knollys family was very well represented on the privy council, since Robert's uncle, William, was not only a lord of Council but also basked in the especial favor of the king, having been created Baron Knollys (May 1613) and named master of the king's wards (October 1614). Given the status of Wat and Robert Knollys as essentially co-defendants, perhaps the royal favor towards the Knollys family served to shield rather than disadvantage Wat; even in Star Chamber, it would have been patently unjust to have punished Wat alone for the duel, especially since it never happened.

If Wat were indeed imprisoned, his confinement could not have lasted for more than a month or two because early in 1615 he was involved in a violent London quarrel in which his opponent was "dangerously hurt." Had the king attended Wat's Star Chamber arraignment and delivered one of his anti-dueling speeches, not much of a royal impression was made on the young man, and even if James were not present, it is remarkable that—so soon after what was intended to be a minatory reprimand in Star Chamber—Wat became involved in another violent altercation. Of course, there was a precedent for Wat's prompt recidivism in the youth of his father, who was haled before the Privy Council only a month after it had ordered him to demean himself quietly. But, as always, there is a difference. Upon his second infraction, Ralegh changed the direction of his life, but his son forged ahead with unabated fervor. Indeed, Wat was engaging in so many nearly simultaneous fights that it is extremely difficult to create a lucid, linear narrative.

In Wat's new altercation—"with one Jaye"—the Low Countries once again feature as a destination, and yet again we learn of the planned duel through exchanges within the English diplomatic corps. This time, the letters are written by Sir Henry Wotton, the English resident at The Hague, and they are addressed to the same two men with whom Sir John Throckmorton had communicated concerning Wat and Knollys. In a letter (6 May 1615) to Robert Trumbull at Brussels, Wotton concludes a long discussion of diplomatic business with a note on Wat:

> Sir Walter Rawleys sonne ... is come over hether this weeke to fight with one Jaye. The rendezvous was Utrecht, but myself havinge gotten some knowledge of it have by his Excellencies auctoritie intercepted that purpose and cawsed the said Rawley to be fetched hether [to The Hague] this daye from Leyden.[37]

With regard to Wat's fights, what's past is sadly prologue. As he had hoped to do with Robert Knollys, Wat intended to fight a duel with Jay in the Low Countries, and once again the authorities learned of the plan and prevented the duel. Wat did get one step closer to a duel than before, since this time both opponents had found their way to the Low Countries before they were apprehended. (The authorities were not fooled by their attempt to feign friendship by eating together in Leiden, perhaps at an establishment that Wat and Ben Jonson had frequented.) When Trumbull read this letter he must have taken a deep breath and poured himself a glass of his best claret. First Knollys, now Jay. Would young Wat Ralegh never learn?

Two weeks later, Wotton writes a second letter about the Jay incident, this time in a report to his London superior, Secretary Winwood. After repeating the essence of what he had told Trumbull (the planned duel with Jay, the arrest of Wat in Leiden, and the transfer of him to The Hague), Wotton proceeds to supply information about the origin of the intended duel. He says that Ralegh's arrest

> will rather defer than prevent this evil [a duel], for the difference between them is irreconcilable, Jaye having some four or five months since been dangerously hurt by the other in a private chamber, and Rawley being so far from avoiding the challenge, that (as it is thought) he hath only gotten leave to travel for this purpose.[38]

Apparently, Wat and Jay had fallen out "in a private chamber," perhaps in a London ale-house or eating establishment, with Jay receiving a perilous wound. After his recovery "some four or five months" later, Jay challenged Wat, who eagerly accepted.

At the time of these events, Jay seems to have been a rather unsavory character, and he did not improve with age. The oldest son of a propertied Wiltshire clergyman, Thomas Jay (Jeay) was three years younger than Wat, being a nominal Oxford student at the time of their quarrel.[39] Following his return from the Low Countries after the prohibited duel, Jay behaved with "reckless abandon," marrying a widow of means whom he lived off, alienating his father, cultivating a disastrous style of excess, and ultimately being reduced (after much chicanery on his part) to selling two family manors. The author of some commendatory poems, he is dismissed by a modern scholar as "a minor society poet of some pretensions but little ability."[40] An enemy graced his grave with an obscene, doggerel epitaph: "Here lieth Thomas Jay, knight, / Who being dead, I upon his grave did shite." At the risk of reading too much into a single, early acquaintance, we can surmise that Wat's relationship with Jay suggests an unsettled, dark side to his life, and it certainly does not portend a happy future.

In his letter to Secretary Winwood, Wotton does not ask his superior for guidance or propose a plan of action for dealing with Wat and Jay. Since he thought the differences between them to be "irreconcilable," Wotton apparently resolved the problem by separating them, sending Jay back to England and holding Wat at The Hague. That Wat was not returned to England is a plausible inference because he was at The Hague in the middle of July, and the simplest explanation is that he had remained there for the intervening seven weeks. The curious reader may wonder about Wat's doings in the span we have jumped over—between his London wounding of Jay in January or February and his arrest in Leiden before his planned duel with him in May. If the reader surmises that in the interim Wat could not resist involvement in yet another incident involving rapiers, she would be correct. This new episode was a first for Wat—a duel that was actually consummated.

Wat's new opponent was Robert Tyrwhitt (usually pronounced and spelled as Tirrit or Terret), who belonged to an ancient and honorable Lincolnshire house. Tyrwhitt was a second son, and following an old aristocratic custom he was placed in the household of a more powerful family: that of Thomas Howard, the earl of Suffolk, who was also chamberlain and lord treasurer to King James.[41] (Since the death of Robert Cecil in 1612, the Howards had exercised a growing, largely unchecked sway over the king's government.) Suffolk was also one of Ralegh's greatest enemies, since the Howard family had been instrumental in turning James against him and in prosecuting him for treason. In itself, the antagonism between the families would have been enough to account for the fight, since Wat would have been keen to protect his family's threatened honor.

But there is a more immediate, more personal reason why the two young men quarreled. As we have seen, at Ralegh's downfall in 1603 the family's hopes for Wat were dashed when the betrothal that Ralegh had arranged for him with Elizabeth Bassett—the only child of a wealthy and recently deceased father—was forfeited.[42] As master of the king's wards, Robert Cecil made an arrangement whereby a friend of Suffolk's would serve as Elizabeth's guardian until she came of age, when the precious commodity would be transferred to the Howards as a bride. In January of 1614 Elizabeth Bassett was duly married to Henry Howard, the dashing third son of Suffolk. Since Robert Tyrwhitt was the same age as Henry Howard and soon to be a legendary horseman (later he became equerry for Prince Charles), it is likely that the two young men knew and respected each other. Since his own grandmother was a Bassett, Tyrwhitt would have known the details of Wat's confounded hopes, and it seems quite likely that he taunted him about his failure and his lord's great success. One wonders what Sir

Walter, the great historian of divine vengeance, thought two years after the wedding, when "Master Henry Howard died sodainly at the table without speaking one word as most say."[43]

Two brief records of the duel between Wat and Robert Tyrwhitt are extant. One is the letter (mentioned earlier with regard to Thomas Jay) in which Sir Henry Wotton also informs William Trumbull that "Sir Walter Rawleys sonne, whoe had some fewe dayes since fought by London with Mr Robert Terrett, is come hether this weeke to fight with one Jaye."[44] The sequence, then, is that first Wat had wounded Jay in London, which was followed by his duel with Tyrwhitt in the fields beyond London's walls ("*by* London") and then by the proposed duel with Jay in Utrecht that Wotton prevented. Apart from the fact that he fought with both of them, there is no reason to connect Tyrwhitt and Jay as opponents of Wat, and certainly the altercations were very different, one being a fray in a "private chamber" and the other a formal duel. What the fights had in common was Wat's pugnacity.

It is a testimony to Wat's lack of regard for his own safety that, after his arraignment in Star Chamber for attempting to duel with Knollys in the Low Countries, he would—in Britain—fight a duel with Tyrwhitt as well as wound Jay in a scuffle. As his father knew, it was crucially important to get Wat out of England, and we learn how this was done when George Lord Carew is recounting the recent news in a letter to Sir Thomas Roe, the English Ambassador to Mughal India. Carew, a friend of Sir Walter's, says that "Yonge Walter Ralegh in duel hathe wounded Robert Tirwett, my Lord Threasurer's servant. Raleghe fled into the Low Countries, where he is entertayned by the Prince Maurice."[45] For the second time, Wat flees from England into the region he had toured with Ben Jonson several years earlier. This time, however, Wat was apparently "entertayned" by none other than the political and military leader of the United Provinces.

From Carew's letter to Roe, William Stebbing plausibly inferred that "Ralegh sent him [Wat] to the Netherlands, with letters of introduction to Prince Maurice."[46] If so, this would not be the last time that Ralegh was to bail his son out of trouble, and he certainly knew the prince. Shortly before his downfall Ralegh had met with Maurice on what was perhaps a covert diplomatic mission to the Low Countries. Moreover, in his recently published *History of the World* he paid Maurice a very handsome compliment, describing him as "one of the greatest captains and of the worthiest princes that either the present or preceding ages have brought forth."[47] For his part, Prince Maurice must have respected Ralegh as an inveterate opponent of his own mortal enemy, Spain.

It looks as if Wat had taken advantage of his father's solicitude and Maurice's extended hospitality by indulging his passion for dueling. It was during his stay in The Hague that Wat must have made the final arrangements for his duel with the now recovered Jay, who was soon to cross over to the Low Countries to fight him. Needless to say, Wat's planning of the duel would have displeased both of his benefactors. In one very efficient trip to the Low Countries, he had contrived both to flee from the legal consequences of a recent duel (with Tyrwhitt) and also to position himself for a duel (with Jay) that he had been looking forward to fighting. In a tight corner, Wat seems happy enough to receive his father's aid, but this does not mean that he was willing to behave according to paternal behest.

Ralegh's attempt to smooth his son's path may have been more thorough than meets the eye, for he appears to have worked with Sir Henry Wotton and Robert Trumbull to minimize reports of Wat's misdoings. This would explain a curious phrase that Sir Henry Wotton used in his letter to Secretary Winwood when he said that Wat was "so far from avoiding the challenge [of Jay], that (*as it is thought*) he hath only gotten leave to travel for this purpose" (italics added). It seems likely, however, that what Wotton wrote was not really what *he* thought. (Wotton had written to Trumbull two weeks earlier, saying that Wat had "fought by London with Mr Robert Terrett.") In reality, Wat had travelled to the Low Countries in order to flee (with his father's aid) the English law as well as to engage with Jay, and evidently Wotton was attempting to diminish the magnitude of Wat's lawlessness.

It must be said that the attempts by Ralegh and his well-wishers to shield Wat from the consequences of his actions were counterproductive, for his career as a duelist in the Low Countries was still not finished. The evidence for a final duel is provided by another letter from Sir Henry Wotton to William Trumbull—we can imagine Trumbull cursing softly and reaching for a larger tumbler of claret. In the postscript to a letter of 15 July 1615, Wotton writes:

> Yesterday young Mr Rawlegh and a gentleman of the Count Hollocks race (who have contracted heere much familiaritie) fought in thease fieldes with a French Captayne and his Liuetenant. The Captayne and Rawlegh were the principals, but the secondes (to avoyde idlenesse) went likewise together by the eares. Some hurtes theare were on bothe sides, but owre cocke had the better of it.[48]

The gentleman "of the Count Hollocks race" must have been German, and so this formal, bloody duel involved soldiers from three nations, all of them presumably supporters of Prince Maurice and untroubled by major religious differences.[49] Since soldiers in garrison towns were sensitive to insults to their honor and lived in a constricted, boring environment, duels among them were common. The cause of this one could have been anything, and in the wild melée following the engagement of the two seconds it was fortunate there were no injuries more serious than "some hurtes ... on bothe sides," with Wat (as usual) having "the better of it."

As Wotton's detached, mocking diction suggests, he and Trumbull were all too familiar with what they deemed the pointless aggression of young men, and of course with Wat Ralegh's exploits in particular. In his first letter to Trumbull (6 May 1615) Wotton noted that he had prevented the duel with Jay by having Wat—on the authority of His Excellency, Prince Maurice—brought "hither" to The Hague, and now (only two months later) Wat was causing serious disruption among the troops. At this point, it is plausible to assume that Prince Maurice felt that Wat had overstayed his welcome and that he no longer owed Ralegh the courtesy of harboring his dangerously fractious son. It is probably no coincidence that this four-man duel outside The Hague is our last notice of Wat's presence in the Low Countries. When he next surfaces in the historical record, it will be in London in May of 1616, when a young widow accuses him of violent assault.

The obvious question is how Wat returned, or was returned, to England. His potential legal liability was complex, since he had never been punished for the duel outside London that he fought with Robert Tyrwhitt very soon after his frustrated but nevertheless illegal attempt to fight Robert Knollys in the Low Countries. And of course he could have been arraigned for either his actual fight in the private chamber with Jay, or his later planned duel with him in Utrecht. Fortunately for Wat, it may be that the only people who were aware of his full crime sheet were Sir Henry Wotton and William Trumbull, decent men who had no interest in publicizing the whole story. In any event, Wat's return to England seems to have been inconspicuous, since no one commented on it and none of the possible judicial punishments was levied. Fortunately for the Raleghs, a major distraction was happening in England, and—better yet—happening to their most hated enemies, the Howards.

Ralegh must have relied on at least one English official in the Low Countries to facilitate Wat's (probably unofficial) return, and a fascinating piece of evidence points to William Trumbull. This evidence takes the hefty form of a folio volume, an autographed gift copy of Ralegh's *History of the World*, which had appeared in print in November of 1614. This volume is remarkable because, as Trumbull's biographer notes, it appears to be "the only presentation copy of any of Ralegh's works."[50] Revealing nothing of its circumstances, Ralegh's undated inscription reads "*Ex dono Authoris, for Mr. W Trumbull.*" Not being aware of the letters about Wat that Sir John Throckmorton and Sir Henry Wotton had sent to Trumbull, the diplomat's biographer noted no connection between him and Ralegh "other than the routine assistance given by Trumbull to Ralegh's son Walter and his tutor Ben Jonson when they travelled through the Low Countries in 1613." But Ralegh's unprecedented token of appreciation—from a proud man not given to expressions of gratitude—indicates that Trumbull had done father and son a service that was far from routine.

For his part, the admirable Trumbull must have developed a deep respect for Ralegh that he shared with his many confidants, for two of them sent him from England detailed accounts of the great man's speech at his execution.[51] Probably not long afterwards, Trumbull performed an act of memorialization of his own. On the final blank page of his copy of *The History of the World*, Trumbull transcribed the poignant poem of Ralegh's entitled "His Epitaph written by himselfe the night before he suffered":

> Even such is Time which takes in trust
> Our youth, our joys, and all we have,
> And pays us but with age and dust;
> Who in the dark and silent grave
> When we have wandered all our ways
> Shuts up the story of our days.
> And from which earth and grave and dust
> The Lord shall raise me up I trust.[52]

• ELEVEN •

From Thomasine to Guiana

It would be melodramatic to say that on March 19, 1616, Ralegh was reborn, but on that day he did receive a new lease on life. After thirteen years of imprisonment, he was released from the Tower. The letter notifying him of his deliverance was signed by the Privy Council, not King James, and thus could not be mistaken for a royal pardon. His sentence of death remained in place. Moreover, Ralegh's release is hedged about with provisos indicating the king's fear of his old enemy: that he travel always in the company of a keeper and that he "should not presume to resort either to his Majesty's Court, the Queen's or Prince's, nor goe into any publique assemblies wheresoever" without the king's approval.[1] The letter of release allows for only one activity on Ralegh's part: "to followe the businesse which yow are to undertake...." That "businesse" was very substantial—to organize and lead an expedition to Guiana that would return with ballast of gold and silver sufficient to fill the coffers of a cash-strapped monarch. For Ralegh, it was an enormous gamble. Success would likely spell pardon and unconditional freedom; failure might lead to the longstanding sentence of death finally being carried out.

Ralegh's release was made possible by a series of disasters that befell the hated Howard family, which had come to dominate James's court. For Ralegh, the windfall began with the death in 1614 of his more than bitter enemy, Henry Howard, earl of Northampton, who had been instrumental in poisoning the mind of King James against Ralegh and his wife. More decisive was the spectacular downfall of Northampton's nephew, Thomas Howard, the prolific earl of Suffolk, whose many children included the Henry Howard who had married Wat's intended, Elizabeth Bassett. Suffolk's apparently impregnable fortunes quickly collapsed after his daughter Frances married Robert Carr, the former favorite of James and recipient from him of the seized Sherborne. In one of the most lurid crimes of

James's reign, the couple was convicted of having poisoned in the Tower Sir Thomas Overbury, a critic of Frances. Ralegh, the connoisseur of history as irony, must have smiled when he learned that, only a week after his own release from the Tower, Frances Howard was clapped into his former quarters.[2] Perhaps his sour tobacco smoke was still hanging in the air.

The fall of the Howards was a necessary but not sufficient cause for Ralegh's good fortune. Following the death of Prince Henry and printing of the *History of the World*, he began to focus his still impressive energies on convincing the king and his advisors to allow him to undertake a major expedition to Guiana. Of course, the new project entailed Ralegh's winning of his (at least temporary) freedom, since it could be organized and led only by him. But the release that the expedition promised him extended beyond escape from physical incarceration, essential as that was. It was also personal and imaginative, a chance to rediscover the largeness in life and in himself that he had found in Guiana thirty years earlier. A second voyage carried the promise of restoration, a return of Ralegh's forceful middle age as well as a financial return that would purchase his life from the king and establish his good name beyond dispute.

Because Ralegh's hopes were already quite complex without considering Wat, the father's biographers have paid too little attention to the son's place in the expedition. For Ralegh, any dream of restoring the past would seem fatally incomplete if it did not include the recuperation of what Wat had lost. As they always had been, Wat's fortunes were tied to his father's, and a successful voyage might lead to a reversal of the corruption of blood that had robbed Wat of his paternal inheritance. But there was also a dimension to their relationship that, while intimately related to wealth, transcended it. Ralegh must have hoped that what had become a sadly frayed and diminished bond with his son could be restored to the fullness it had enjoyed before his own downfall eclipsed the future he had planned for Wat.

In Ralegh's imagination, Wat had been linked with Guiana long before his release from the Tower. Even on his first voyage, when Wat was only two years old, Ralegh's responsiveness to the relations of indigenous fathers and sons reflected his hopes and fears for his little son, who was left behind in Sherborne but in his father's mind was part of the enterprise.[3] After his return to England, Ralegh regularly dispatched ships to monitor Guiana, and it is suggestive that the pinnace he sent in late 1597 was called the *Watte*.[4] Of course the ship's name bespeaks the father's proud wish to make known his affection for his child, but it also may suggest Ralegh's instinctual connection of the boy to the rich future that Guiana promised, a future that his son could perhaps help to shape.

Ralegh's thoughts of Wat prospering in Guiana did not end with his son's childhood. According to a well-informed Spanish spy in London, apparently still unidentified, when Ralegh was a prisoner in the Tower he considered arranging an expedition to Guiana under the leadership of his long-serving follower, Lawrence Kemys. The spy saw fit to mention that Ralegh intended to send Wat on the voyage.[5] That bit of information sounds plausible because in 1612—the time of the planned expedition—Wat was living at loose ends after Oxford, and Ralegh may well have seen a Guiana expedition as a potentially dangerous but also valuable experience. (At this time he was beginning to hope he could be released from the Tower to lead a Guiana voyage of his own.) In the event, however, the Guiana expedition did not materialize for Wat, being replaced by a considerably less dangerous Continental tour with Ben Jonson.

In the spring of 1616, Ralegh's association of Wat with Guiana took on a new urgency. Having won his own freedom thorough his proposed voyage, Ralegh thought the plan could be leveraged to aid Wat at a most difficult time of transition—at once geographical, legal, and maturational. To understand Wat's situation, we must return to his undisciplined, multinational duel (replete with seconds) outside The Hague in early July 1615. This was the incident that soured Wat's welcome with Prince Maurice, convincing him that all of his obligations to Sir Walter had been more than met. Several weeks later, Ralegh wrote a letter to Secretary Winwood strongly advocating the voyage to Guiana that would take shape in the months to come.[6] Ralegh does not mention Wat in the letter, and the link between his courting of the privy council and Prince Maurice's rolling up of Wat's welcome mat may be entirely coincidental. But Ralegh could be a good strategic thinker, and it seems likely that his sense of the unpromising future facing Wat—a future without prospects—was a spur to make the voyage an immediate reality.

Ralegh's aid to his son has gone largely unremarked upon because it was conducted as a stealth campaign on the fringes of the law and thus is not addressed explicitly in surviving documents. Obliquely, however, we can divine Ralegh at work, Wat's unrecorded return to England from the Low Countries being the first of many instances. The unobtrusiveness, even secrecy, of Wat's repatriation makes eminent sense because his legal status in King James's England was, at best, quite problematic. Even if we assume that—in a no longer extant document—Wat had been formally pardoned for his attempted duel with Robert Knollys, there were more recent infractions for which he could have been prosecuted, beginning with his wounding of Robert Tyrwhitt in a duel outside London and including the fray in which he dangerously wounded Thomas Jay, which led to his and Jay's attempt to arrange a secret duel in Utrecht. The authorities easily could have found reason to bring Wat into custody, had they wished to do so.

In the absence of documentary evidence (including the month in which it occurred), we can only guess that Wat's return involved an intercession with English authorities on his father's part. There would be a pleasing symmetry in Ralegh's intervening to bring Wat home, since his difficult son's presence in the Low Countries was the result of an earlier intervention with Prince Maurice, perhaps with the connivance of Secretary Winwood and others. For Wat's return, Ralegh had a strong bargaining chip, the king's forthcoming approval of the Guiana voyage. It may be, as A.L. Rowse hypothesized, that there was an unrecorded negotiation in which Wat "was pardoned to come back and serve on his father's—and his—last voyage."[7] It is also possible, as Andrew Thrush has suggested, that such a negotiation involved the Crown's silent dropping of the Star Court proceedings against Wat (concerning the earlier duel with Knollys).[8] What seems clear is Ralegh's victorious insistence that Wat be allowed to accompany him to Guiana.

If Ralegh declared to James and Secretary Winwood that Wat's participation in the voyage was a *sine qua non*, he may have been tempted to bite his tongue. No one knew better than he how resistant Wat had been to good advice and how inclined he had been to subvert authority. His attitude to Wat was, at best, mixed: deep love but mounting frustration with the young man's insistence on going his own way. Ralegh would have been rare in the annals of fathers—for the most part a self-justifying lot—if he had never reflected that his care about providing for his son's future had received only disrespect in return. Notwithstanding his misgivings, in an act of love, hope, and folly Ralegh was to make his untested son the captain of the troops on the *Destiny*, the flagship of the expedition—built to his father's design and named by him.

One wonders what Lady Ralegh's attitude was to the arrangement that her husband had made concerning her son. Without supportive evidence, a biographer recently ascribed to the Raleghs neatly differing attitudes: "She had fought to keep Wat at home, but Sir Walter saw the expedition as an ideal opportunity to harness his son's hot blood."[9] But just as Ralegh must have harbored misgivings about Wat's competence to command his fellows, Lady Ralegh is likely to have had complicated feelings of her own about her son's participation. Naturally, she would have resisted the impulse to place her son in harm's way. But she must have known about

Wat's various duels in England and the Low Countries, which had placed him in considerable danger, both physical and legal. She understood enough about the world of men to know that Wat's current course of more or less aimless violence would come to no good end. At least the expedition held the promise of great rewards to offset the legal and physical dangers of Wat's thirst for conflict in the old world.

Another consideration weighs heavily against Lady Ralegh's putative resistance to Wat's participation: that she was a prime financial supporter of the project. As Ralegh acknowledged after his return, his wife had committed most of the £8000 that she and Wat were granted when they surrendered Sherborne to the king in 1610.[10] Moreover, she sold the house at Mitcham that was her own and pestered even distant relatives for cash. If she had opposed Wat's participation strongly, it seems unlikely that she would have invested so much of her own fortune in the undertaking, money that she could have withheld. Even though her eyes were clearer than her husband's, she must have felt that the desperate risk was worth the taking. She scarcely could have been free of private misgivings, but perhaps the venture offered possibilities for her husband and her son to regain their lost standing and even to renew the family relationship they had enjoyed years earlier.

And what did Wat think? His response, like that of his parents, could scarcely have been simple. One reason he spent so much time in the Low Countries, first with Ben Jonson and then with Prince Maurice, must have been a desire to be safely absent from his father's beck and call, to say nothing of his advice. In an expedition to Guiana he would be seen, inevitably, as his father's son, an identity he was not eager to embrace. And on board the *Destiny* he would—despite his formal captaincy—be under the command of his father, the General, whose long experience conferred on him a well-earned authority. Ralegh could not be easily challenged by a son whose seamanship consisted of being a passenger in a handful of Channel crossings and whose military service was negligible, if it existed at all. There could hardly be a more unpromising environment for asserting his rebellious individuality.

To be sure, Wat could not have been unaware of his father's commitment to him, since Ralegh had extricated him from some difficult legal situations. (As we will see, Ralegh would soon do so again.) But the attempts of his father to shield him from the consequences of his actions appear not to have elicited much filial gratitude. Far from it. Given his desire to define himself against his father, Wat must have felt an element of (unintended) humiliation in Ralegh's rescues. As Wat proved repeatedly, in a fight he was very capable of defending himself and punishing his foe in the process. But that violence was outside the law, and it was from the law that Wat had to be rescued.

These tensions between father and son were memorably captured in an anecdote told by John Aubrey in his well-informed "brief life" of Ralegh. Although Aubrey does not provide a date for it, the story must derive from the period between Ralegh's release from the Tower and the sailing of the Guiana fleet. Desperate to gain backers, Ralegh was making the rounds of wealthy Londoners, and on one occasion he took Wat with him to a dinner, but not before lecturing him:

> He sayd to his Son, Thou art such a quarrelsome, affronting creature that I am ashamed to have such a Beare in my Company. Mr Walt humbled himselfe to his Father, and promised he would behave himselfe mightily mannerly. So away they went....

From what we know of Wat, the phrase "quarrelsome, affronting creature" could hardly be improved on, and it has the genuine ring of Ralegh's censure. Given Wat's customary resistance to his father's edicts, there is every reason to suspect irony in his commitment to be "mightily mannerly"—and we are not disappointed.

According to Aubrey, the dinner went well for awhile. Wat "sate next to his Father and was very demure at lease halfe dinner time," but then he casually observed that

> I this morning, not having the feare of God before my eies, but by the instigation of the devill, went to a Whore. I was very eager of her, kissed and embraced her, and went to enjoy her, but she thrust me from her, and vowed I should not, *For your father lay with me but an hower ago.*

Making an excellent story even better, Aubrey adds that,

> Sir Walt, being so strangely supprized and putt out of his countenance at so great a Table, gives his son a damned blow over the face; his son, as rude as he was, would not strike his father, but strikes over the face of the Gentleman that sate next to him, and sayed, *Box about, 'twill come to my Father anon.* 'Tis now a common used Proverb.

Aubrey attributes the story to Benjamin Rudyerd, who plausibly could have attended such an event, and in this period there are records of Ralegh dining with financiers and well-born friends as he searched for funding.[11]

The story is so satisfying that one strives to remember that it is uncorroborated and quite possibly fictitious. But, if it is invented, its inventor—whether Rudyerd or someone else—must have been someone who knew the two Walter Raleghs well and was aware of the tensions between them. Certainly Ralegh's warning to Wat is completely in character, and his son's quick-thinking retaliation accords with other performances in which he reveals the hypocrisy of his elders, most notably his display of his drunken governor through Paris streets. Moreover, the frustrated visit to the prostitute symbolizes the problem from which Wat suffered—as with so much else, his father had preceded him. Finally, at the risk of psychoanalytic over-interpretation, Wat's clever striking of a blow that will find its way to his father is eerily suggestive of the way his acts of violence against his contemporaries may have been displacements of an anger aimed at his progenitor. And, in one way or another, these combats did always come to his father.

Fortunately for the Guiana enterprise, Wat appears to have been a more successful recruiter when he was not accompanied by his father. A jotting in Lady Anne Clifford's diary allows a glimpse of a social gathering in Sussex at which Wat's recruiting may well have mixed with young gentlemen's easy bonhomie. In May 1616—two months after Sir Walter's release—Lady Anne speaks of "a great meeting at Lewes," at which "my Lo. Compton, my Lo. Mordaunt, Tom Nevil, Jo. Herbert & all that crew with Wat. Raleigh, Jack Lewice & a multitude of such company where [were] there. There was bowling, bull baiting, cards & dice with such sports to entertain the time."[12] Anna Beer has pointed out that several gentlemen in "that crew" were to join the Guiana expedition, and it seems likely that Wat was doing some recruiting during the festivities.[13] In hindsight, however, there were shadows over the celebration. Most immediately, Lady Clifford was worried about her ailing mother (who had already died, though the news had not yet reached her daughter), which may help to explain her tacit disapproval of the men's "sports." And of course the expedition itself was to involve privations and mortal sickness that were impossible to imagine on a summer's day in Sussex.

As one would guess, Wat did not spend all of his time advancing (or perhaps hindering) the expedition for Guiana. Shortly before the festivity in Sussex, he was the aggressor in a violent incident that had nothing directly to do with the project but was to trouble himself (and his father) until the fleet sailed from Plymouth a year later (June 1617). Once again, Wat's impulse to violent action came athwart of the law, and once again his father would quietly intervene to minimize the consequences. This episode was different from all the earlier ones, however, because his antagonist was unarmed and a woman.

The person who brought the charge of assault was a forceful adversary who, as Wat was to learn, already possessed hard-won experience in the courtroom. She was a young widow named Thomasine Ostler, and her experience stemmed from a suit she had mounted against her father, John

Heminges. Thomasine is similar to Wat in that she, too, is known primarily for a fractious relationship with a historically significant father. John Heminges' principal claim to fame is his co-editorship (with his theatre colleague Henry Condell) of the First Folio of Shakespeare's plays (1623). Were it not for this invaluable volume, the text of roughly half of Shakespeare's plays would not have survived.[14] Heminges had a solid business background, and after joining the troupe as an actor he became the efficient manager for the King's Men, the company to which Shakespeare belonged and for which he wrote. The principal members of the company relied on each other so devotedly that they functioned as a family, and hence the First Folio was primarily a loving homage to a deceased colleague. As his daughter was to learn, the theatre family took precedence over the claims of flesh and blood.

In 1611, Heminges' daughter Thomasine married William Ostler, a gifted young actor in the King's Men, who was so reliable that he quickly was made a shareholder in the company. Unfortunately, Ostler died only three years later, leaving Thomasine with a baby named Beaumont, after his father's favorite playwright. Ostler's death was apparently sudden, for he did not leave a will. After being named her husband's administrator, a role she probably insisted upon, Thomasine took steps to secure her husband's shares in the King's Men, which would have been easily the most valuable part of his estate.

The lawsuit that followed was long and complex, with a resolution for which evidence is sadly lacking. In brief outline, Heminges refused to release to his daughter the shares in the Blackfriars and Globe theatres belonging to her husband, saying that (unbeknownst to Thomasine) Ostler had granted them to him in trust. After Thomasine had brought a bill of complaint against her father, she alleges that he agreed to pay her six hundred pounds for the shares after she had gone to her parents and "bent the knee, & with tears dropping from her eyes performed & did her duty with all reverence & humility...."[15] But then, according to her second bill of complaint, he reneged on his word, "endeavouring & fraudulently intending subtilely & craftily to deceive & defraud the same Thomasina." Early in 1616, the parties agreed on a trial by jury, and at this point the evidence ends. Whatever the ruling, the relationship between father and daughter was ruptured, and in John Heminges' will (9 October 1630) Thomasine is the only one of his five daughters who is not mentioned.[16] It may be that she predeceased her father, but there is also no mention of her son Beaumont in the will (unlike other grandchildren), so there is a good possibility that mother and son were not forgiven for her rebellion.

Because her suit stipulated the value of the contested shares, Thomasine has a place in the economic history of English popular drama, and especially of the Globe and Blackfriars theatres, which were, respectively, the public and private venues for the King's Men. The documentary evidence of her suit was discovered in the Public Records Office (now the National Archives) in London by a most intrepid and successful team of archival researchers, Charles William Wallace and his long-suffering wife, Hulda.[17] Wallace was an American bardolater who dedicated himself and his wife to the search for traces of Shakespeare in archival legal documents that had never been systematically read through. Their diligence was rewarded by the discovery of a number of important Shakespeare documents (including the Mountjoy-Belott case, which Charles Nicholl explored in his fascinating *The Lodger Shakespeare: His Life on Silver Street*) as well as many relating to other dramatists and actors.[18]

In a piece published in *The Times* of London in 1909, Wallace announced with great fanfare his discovery of the suit about the theatre shares contested by Thomasine and her father.[19] Also, he mentions in passing that, after the action with Heminges, Thomasine had brought a suit against Wat Ralegh. Presumably worried that competitors might poach his discoveries before he made full use of them, he did not give the specific location of the documents for either suit. Wallace soon followed up on the case against Heminges, but he never mentioned Thomasine's suit against Wat again, and so the location of this document concerning Wat never became public knowledge. (Like many Jacobean law cases, it has never been catalogued, and so finding it would have required a dedication equal to that of the Wallaces.) Luckily, the Wallaces' daughter had bequeathed his papers to the Henry E. Huntington Library (San Marino, California), and Gayle M. Richardson, the library's archivist, was able—after a challenging search—to locate the two note cards on which he had jotted down the contents and locations of the two cases concerning Thomasine and Wat: first, her action against him and subsequently her action against the men who had stood surety for him.[20]

The two documents summarized on Wallace's cards, like the one chronicling Thomasine's action against her father, are from Coram Rege Rolls in the Court of King's Bench. Each rotulus is composed of hundreds of long parchment sheets carefully stitched together into a weighty and cumbersome (but surprisingly well-preserved) whole. Like the document concerning Heminges, they are written in a highly abbreviated, legal Latin that is indecipherable to the non-specialist. (I am indebted to Professor Helen Bradley for her invaluable translation of the two documents.) In a sense, Thomasine's action against Wat takes up where she left off with her father, since she is bringing the new case with the same lawyer (William Farrar) in the same court (King's Bench) only four months after the action against her father had gone to jury.

The key document identified by Professor Wallace is a legal memorandum that effectively lays out the history of the case. For our purposes, the crucial section is the all too brief account of the episode leading to the "plea of transgression" that Thomasine had brought against Wat:

> On 10 May in the 14th year of the present King James' reign [1616], he set upon her by force of arms in London, that is in the parish of St Mary-le-Bow in Cheap ward. And at that time in the same place he beat her and ill-treated her, and made so many taunts and other abusive maltreatments that she was unable to go about her business publicly by herself, and inflicted other outrages upon her contrary to the King's peace to her damage, £500.[21]

The rediscovery of this document is very important because in its absence commentators have been forced to repeat Wallace's printed description of Thomasine's suit as being for "insult and slander."[22] However, as the document makes clear—she alleged that Wat "set upon her by force of arms" and "beat her"—Wallace's characterization diminishes the seriousness of Wat's offense, for which he was held until trial "in custody of the Marshal of the King's Marshalsea," the prison in which Ralegh had been held thirty-five years earlier and Thomasine's father only recently. While we are given no details of the alleged assault, Wat's past behavior makes the charge of violence all too likely.

Wallace makes a second, rather Victorian interpretation that may be plausible but is certainly not the fact he presents it to be: that Thomasine ("probably an attractive young woman") was "involved in a romance with young Walter Raleigh."[23] To be sure, Wat may well have found her attractive for various reasons: she was close to him in age (younger by a little more than a year), sexually experienced, and—perhaps best of all—she was at least his match in independence, being spirited enough to defy *her* father in court. It is also plausible that (before May 10th) she had been attracted to Wat. The miniature portrait of Wat that his mother was to wear in a locket in her advanced years depicts a young man with the look of a matinee idol, and if family lore is to be believed, Wat was irresistible to women. According to legend, when the *Destiny* was lying in Cork harbor, waiting for favorable winds on its journey to Guiana, Wat exerted such sway over the women in the Earl of Cork's family that later the Earl would "cuff his younger daughters for swearing to marry no one but young Wat Raleigh."[24] And perhaps a considerable degree of amorous success—as well as misogyny—is evidenced by Ben Jonson's description of Wat parading through the streets of Paris with ladies' favors attached to his cod piece.

The relationship between Thomasine and Wat was personal enough to beget slanderous words, and worse, but their conflict may have arisen from differences about money rather than—or as well as—the travails of "romance." At this time, Thomasine was lodging in the home of her older married sister, Judith Merifield, in Cony Hope Lane, which was in Cheap Ward and not far from the scene of the alleged attack.[25] Perhaps Thomasine and Wat fell out on their way to or from her dwelling. How they met is an open and interesting question. It would add a welcome degree of complexity to Wat's life if we could say he was a haunter of the theatre who sat on the stage, or even shared a tavern with the acting community. But the theatre is not a likely connection, since the chances are that—after her bruising lawsuit with her father—Thomasine was not eager to engage in the world in which he was so prominent. A more pedestrian link is likely. Her sister Judith's husband, Ralph Merifield, was a professional scrivener, and perhaps while seeking his services Wat met Thomasine.[26] One guess is as good as another.

What is certain is the court's final ruling against Wat in Thomasine's suit. At first, in response to Thomasine's charge of violent transgression, he pleaded not guilty and "put himself upon his country," that is, he asked for a trial by jury. Thomasine agreed. It is unfortunate, but not unusual, that an account of the trial does not exist, but the outcome is clear. As the King's Bench document indicates, "a jury was tried and sworn, and they said on oath that Walter Rawleigh was guilty of the transgression exactly as Thomasine had recounted." Thomasine was awarded £250 (only half of what she had asked for), an award that may indicate the jury's sense that her initial claim was excessive. With the addition of her costs, her award came to £260—money that Wat could ill afford and probably did not possess.

This adverse judgment engendered a new legal strategy: that Wat would delay the proceedings (and thus paying the damages) for as long as possible. At the root of this strategy was of course the expectation that Wat would soon be sailing to the Orinoco, well beyond the reach of any English court. In a first step, his counsel asked an appellate court for a writ of error, which was granted. As was customary, this writ moved the case to a higher court (from King's Bench to the Court of Exchequer), and so all the earlier proceedings had to be laboriously copied and passed along. (Lower courts refused to surrender their unique records of litigation.) By this time—the spring of 1617—the days in which Wat was vulnerable to the law could easily be counted. A date for the proceedings was given (May

24), but when it arrived Wat's lawyer asked for a postponement and was granted another week. On the 31st, Wat failed to appear in court, whereupon Thomasine was awarded 50 shillings in addition to the previously awarded damages, and the Court of the Exchequer was adjourned. Two weeks later Wat sailed from Plymouth, without having paid a penny.

Where, one wonders, was Ralegh in all of this? Of course, there is no mention of him in the legal proceedings, but it would scarcely be surprising to learn that—as had long been his practice—he used his good offices to smooth his son's rocky way. At the outset, Wat would not have been proud of having attacked a woman—who proceeded to take him to court—and so he may not have chosen to inform his father of the episode. (This would explain why his lawyer, John Hughes, appears to have had no prior connection with the Raleghs.) But his father's discreet aid is apparent in the strategic end-game that Wat played. For the second time, Ralegh had to pull strings so that his son could participate in the (ill-fated) expedition. After spiriting him back to England from the Low Countries, he now had to get him clear of the law.

Two documents, one known only to the Wallaces and the other printed in Ralegh's letters but previously not understood, illuminate Ralegh's aid to Wat. The little known one is, like the account of Thomasine Ostler's legal proceedings against Wat, a King's Bench manuscript discovered by the intrepid Charles William Wallace.[27] Since the document did not directly involve Elizabethan theatre, Wallace never referred to it in his published work. Fortunately, however, when he found the document he made a note which the Huntington Library archivist found alongside his note on the memorandum chronicling Thomasine's case against Wat. This document concerns a second suit by the persistent Thomasine—a suit to recover the still unpaid portion of the £260 in "damages, expenses, and costs" that earlier she had won. (The document was written on 20 October 1619, almost two years after Wat's death in January 1618 and a full year after Ralegh's in October 1618.) The suit is directed at the two men who, the document says, "came personally to our court to act as pledges for Walter [Wat]." These men who stood surety are identified as "William Stone of the parish of St. Olave Southwark, blacksmith, and Thomas Jennings of the parish of St Olave Old Jewry London, draper." One may well wonder how a blacksmith and a draper (a dealer in cloth) would even know Wat Ralegh, much less risk their well-being by swearing to make good a default on his part. If they knew anything about Wat's history, they would have had ample cause for suspicion. But, as a letter by Ralegh reveals, the financial arrangement was with the father, not the son.

In the hectic days before he left London to join his fleet at Plymouth, Ralegh found time (on 19 March 1617) to write a brief letter to an associate concerning debts for supplies. After reminding him of "the monie dew [due] to Tite, the anker [anchor] smith," he says "ther is fifty pound that this bearer, Wi[llia]m Ston[e], hath given bond for to a linnen draper for shirts for the companie."[28] He goes on to make an arrangement for Stone's bond to be paid, which will "free this poore man [the draper] who hath bine arested for it." The editors of the *Letters* identify "Tite" as the Lewis Tite (or Tayte) who supplied the ironwork and the anchor for the *Destiny*, but in a phase that appears only very rarely in their admirably detailed notes, they note that William Stone (as well as the unnamed draper) is "not identified."

If we bring to bear Thomasine's suit against the two men who stood surety for Wat, we can identify the William Stone who is bearing Ralegh's letter as the "William Stone ... blacksmith" whom she was suing for damages. This identification is supported by the likelihood that the unnamed "linnen draper" with whom Stone was engaged was the "Thomas Jennings ... draper," who shared Wat's surety with Stone. Jennings, it would seem, had a hard time of it, apparently first being arrested for Stone's failure to make the bond good and later being pursued (with Stone) by the sheriff of Middlesex for assets to make good on the remainder of the surety for Wat. To round off Thomasine's story, if Stone and Jennings had assets, the sheriffs of Middlesex were not able to find them within their jurisdiction. Upon the default of Stone and Jennings, "it was decided that Thomasine should have execution £114 14s 6d according to the aforesaid recognisance, by their default." In other words, this was the amount of money she was still owed and could seize in the form of their assets. As with her earlier suit against her father, it is not clear if Thomasine was able to find the satisfaction that was her due.

It would require an economic historian—with more documents than are now at hand—to unpack Ralegh's web of financial arrangements with Stone and Jennings, but some inferences can be drawn. It appears that, following Wat's conviction for assaulting Thomasine, Ralegh arranged with Stone and Jennings to stand surety for his son, which would secure his release from the Marshalsea. In return, Ralegh must have promised some form of quid pro quo, such as preferential treatment for Jennings in his purchase of necessary supplies (such as the durable seaman's shirts that he bought) and for Stone in his blacksmithing work on the *Destiny*.[29] It is typical of Ralegh's concern about debts to relatively unimportant people that he took pains to free Jennings from arrest before the expedition departed. Of course, the deaths of the two Raleghs left Stone and Jennings on the hook for the sizable portion of Wat's surety they had not yet paid. As in the suit against her father, Thomasine must have been disappointed with the outcome, since Stone and Jennings defaulted on a court appearance and since the sheriffs of Middlesex had not been able to find assets in the court's jurisdiction that could be seized in lieu of payment.

We can safely assume that Ralegh's involvement in dealing with Thomasine Ostler's lawsuit exacerbated differences between father and son that were already significant. With considerable justice, Ralegh would have felt that Wat's attack on Thomasine reflected an obvious lack of commitment to the expedition for which he was being groomed—and on which Ralegh's own future depended entirely. Little could be said to mitigate Wat's violence, since the demands of honor, whether personal or familial, could scarcely justify an attack on a woman, and especially a widow supporting a little child. On this score, one wonders how much Lady Ralegh knew of the Thomasine affair and what she thought of her son's behavior. Whether or not his mother noticed it, there is a suggestive resemblance between herself and Thomasine; the widow's plucky confrontation of her father to recover the theatre shares for herself and her small son is very similar to the largely solo campaign Bess mounted against the king to retain Sherborne for herself, Wat, and Carew. One wonders as well if temperamental similarities of the two women played a part in the attraction—whatever its particulars—that Wat had felt for Thomasine.

The best exculpation that either of his parents could have advanced would have been to say that Wat's impulsiveness had gotten the better of him, but Ralegh must have grown tired of making (and hearing) this excuse. And it may be that, despite feeling an affection for Wat less judgmental than her husband's, Lady Ralegh was becoming increasingly worried about his violent behavior. Such a worry need not, of course, have compelled from her the concession that her husband had been right about Wat's dangerous lack of discipline. Moreover, there is—as is usually the case with children—plausible evidence for shared parental culpability. In this regard, Ralegh's repeated rescues of his son from the consequences of his actions were no less deleterious than the ill effects of whatever "cockering," uncritical love Lady Ralegh could be accused of. Nor could she be blamed for giving their impulsive, ill-disciplined son the command of a troop of soldiers on the *Destiny*.

For Wat's part, it seems unlikely that his father's solicitude for him was cause for either gratitude or endearment, since—deliberately or not—it emphasized his own dependency. As the *Destiny* set sail, both father and son must have sensed—beneath the exhilaration of being finally underway—a distance that the close quarters of the ship did little to mitigate. There is no record in Ralegh's daily ship journal or any other surviving document of a personal interaction between father and son on the long journey to the Orinoco. It is scarcely imaginable that they completely avoided each other—if nothing else, Ralegh would have conferred with his son regarding the troop of soldiers on board, who were devastated by a tropical fever. Their silence does appear to have a story behind it.

• TWELVE •

Destiny

As well as opening the gate to the Tower, the second Guiana expedition freed Ralegh's energies and awakened his still considerable powers. Twenty years earlier, Robert Cecil—a decade younger but always much frailer than his colleague—had marveled at how Ralegh "can toil terribly" when he threw himself into a project.[1] By Tudor standards Ralegh was now an old man in his middle sixties, having outlived Cecil and most of the others who had brought him down, but he was still a force to be reckoned with. The challenge of mounting another major expedition would have helped to restore his old combativeness. Certainly the demands of his new project returned him to a familiar state of mind in a London that outwardly had changed so much in the long years of his absence. A week after his release, a letter-writer conveyed Ralegh's wonder and perhaps also his disorientation as he went "up and downe seeing sights and places built or bettered since his imprisonment."[2] It was in dealing with a thousand demands—supplying the master shipbuilder Phineas Pett with specifications for his new flagship, the *Destiny*, securing gentlemen soldiers and ordinary seamen, drawing up surprisingly detailed lists of necessary supplies, and shaking every money tree within his reach—that Ralegh returned to his element.

Unlike more circumspect figures—again, Robert Cecil comes to mind—Ralegh never attempted to winnow his dreams out of his rational calculations, which meant he had great powers of persuasion regarding projects that were not likely to succeed and often did not. He was always loath to acknowledge, or perhaps even to see, failure. Ralegh's *Discoverie of the Large, Rich, and Bewtiful Empyre of Guiana* (1596) was so successful in evoking the wonders of the region that it was easy for him as well as his readers to forget that the first Guiana expedition had returned without the gold that was its prime objective. As a modern commentator drily noted, "The ease with which the gold of Guiana could be mined is a recurrent theme in all of Ralegh's writing about his project, and the further the voyage of 1595 receded into the past the easier seemed the enterprise."[3] Of course, the success of the second Guiana voyage was extremely unlikely, since his earlier expedition was far more auspicious and had financial support from many wealthy backers, even the skeptical Cecil. Since that time, the Spanish authorities had enjoyed plenty of time to look for gold and also to increase their defenses along the Orinoco. Moreover, the conditions imposed by King James—especially that Ralegh was somehow to avoid conflict with hostile Spanish forces—scarcely augured well for discovering and securing deposits of gold. It was only after seizing documents in the Caribbean that Ralegh learned of King James's transmission to Madrid of detailed information about his plans, thus making a perilous reception even more likely.

Ralegh's decision to include Wat in the expedition was shaped by both rational and imaginative impulses, with the latter distinctly predominating. He had practical reasons to include his son on the voyage, including the legal and financial difficulties Wat had created for himself with Thomasine Ostler. As well, he could see that Wat's future in England was not likely to promise advancement of any kind, thanks in part to the dubious status in which his own conviction for treason had left him. These practical concerns helped to stimulate Ralegh's imagination, as the restraints he and his son faced in England encouraged his concentration on the limitless possibilities of Guiana. Though Ralegh never said as much, surely part of the attraction of the second voyage was the opportunity it offered the two of them to restore the relationship that had been so important in earlier years. If the first expedition took him away from his two-year-old son, the second would bring the two of them together on the same ship in pursuit of a shared goal, or so went the father's dream.

For Ralegh, if not for Wat, their voyage to Guiana fulfilled the commitment to adventure that—from the confines of the Tower—he had encouraged in his young son. Soon after his conviction for treason, Ralegh had enjoined the suddenly disinherited Wat to become the father of his own fortunes by actively taking risks in a world full of peril. In the pervasive seafaring imagery of his exhortation, he acknowledges how men "ever and anon are shipwrakt and seasick" as well as "toyled and hazarded with tempests

Opposite: **In the second (1617) and succeeding editions of his *History of the World*, Ralegh appears as commander of the Guiana expedition (courtesy the Thomas Fisher Rare Book Library, University of Toronto).**

The true and lively portraiture of the honourable and learned Knight Sr. Walter Ralegh.

and stormes that arise abroad."[4] He closes by calling upon Wat to "take harte and courage to thee. Strive if thou canst to make good thy station in the upper decke. Those that live under hatches are ordained to be drudges and slaves." He had encouraged Wat to set sail on an adventurous course of life, which his son had not done, and now they would make the great voyage together on the *Destiny*, turning metaphor into vibrant reality.

In addition to the trope of life as a voyage of exploration, there was a second paradigm alive in Ralegh's imagination, a heroic and historical legend of a father and son coming together on a battlefield. It was the legend of a renowned warrior-father and his unproven, same-named son: Sir John Talbot and young John Talbot. We can be sure that the Talbot story was fresh in Ralegh's mind because in the final book of his *History of the World* he had at some length favorably compared Sir John Talbot to a Roman general.[5] Ralegh also had a personal reason to be interested in the legendary John Talbots; the amanuensis to whom he dictated the *History* was almost certainly his devoted servitor and friend John Talbot, descendant and namesake of the hero.[6] This living John Talbot had been Wat's tutor in the Tower, and now he accompanied his master and his old pupil on the *Destiny*. The contemporary John Talbot's presence would have been at least a subliminal reminder of the heroic father and son who bore the name.

Though the two legendary John Talbots were well-known from historical chronicles, the most memorable version of their story was an extremely popular enactment on the Elizabethan stage. This depiction provides the emotional core of one of Shakespeare's earliest plays, Part One of *Henry VI*, which was a resounding success on the London stage shortly before Wat's birth.[7] Shakespeare's depiction of the relationship of the two John Talbots is eerily relevant to the two Walter Raleghs if we substitute Spanish forces in the Caribbean for French armies of the Hundred Years' War. Sir John Talbot is depicted (as Ralegh justifiably saw himself) as a renowned warrior and legendary scourge of his enemies who is growing old and calls to his side his untested son to learn the ways of war. Father and son have not seen each other for some time, and Shakespeare leaves the suggestion that an (unspecified) breach has distanced them. On the battlefield, certain differences between them remain, as young John refuses his father's command to flee and save himself, retorting that—unlike his celebrated father—he has not yet made a name for himself, so flight would be a kind of death.

In a series of battle scenes, Shakespeare's staging and imagery suggest that the two John Talbots have become one in spirit, as they stand alone, surrounded by the French and betrayed by their envious English peers. The battles begin with a scene depicting an experience with which Ralegh was very familiar: the authoritative father rescues his untrained son from great danger. Soon afterward, the young John Talbot reciprocates the favor, as his suddenly aged and helpless father describes his recent rescue from certain death by his now experienced warrior-son. These mutual rescues amount to a symbolic representation of the changing relations of father and son over time, with the son in effect repaying his father for the intervention that had saved his life. It is easy to see how this scenario would appeal to Ralegh as an affirmation of the bond between father and son, even though—or perhaps because—the two John Talbots are soon surrounded by a sea of French soldiers and killed. As Sir John's last words proclaim, they die as one: "Soldiers, adieu! I have what I would have, / Now my old arms are young John Talbot's grave."[8]

Not surprisingly, the reality lived by the two Walter Raleghs failed to re-enact the fabled heroism of the two John Talbots, and from the outset one prosaic (but crucial) difference proved to be decisive. Unlike Sir John Talbot, who brings his inexperienced son to France as an ordinary soldier, Ralegh awarded his equally untried son a position of command, naming him captain of the soldiers on his flagship, the *Destiny*. (On the Guiana expedition, each ship carried a captain who was in charge of its military complement, while the vessel's "master" was in charge of its crew.)

Wat had conspicuously less experience than his fellow captains, including his first cousin George Ralegh. Sir Walter exaggerated only slightly when he characterized George (his brother Carew's son) as having "served longe with singular commendations in the Low Countries" under Prince Maurice.[9] Wat's dubious promotion is probably another instance of the father's renown having an (unintentional) ill-effect on his son; Ralegh presumably felt that his own status as General of the expedition entailed an officer's rank (and share of the spoils) for his son and heir, a feeling that Lady Ralegh would have shared. As well, he must have assumed that his own presence on the *Destiny* afforded protection against Wat's inexperience and impulsiveness, and we can be sure that he spoke sternly to Wat of the duties his position carried. But, as no one knew better than Ralegh himself, Wat was accomplished at resisting paternal direction.

The nature of their on-board relationship is very much open to surmise since no record exists of their face-to-face interactions on the voyage. It is likely that Ralegh maintained an appropriate distance between his son and himself as a means of visibly manifesting his evenhanded authority, but there may well have been a degree of personal coldness between them. In the journal he kept, Ralegh makes only a single, passing reference to "my sonne" (in conjunction with a skirmish in which some resistant islanders were driven off). To be sure, the book that he maintained was considerably less personal than the term "journal" suggests for modern readers; it was a log-book or day-book largely taken up with the recording of facts that could serve as the framework for a polished, triumphant account of the expedition. Nevertheless, Ralegh's silence about Wat suggests an absence of intimacy—not a surprising situation given their recent differences. The closeness that Ralegh had imagined, it would seem, failed to materialize.

Though he was no stranger to suffering at sea, Ralegh could not have imagined the trials that his fleet would face. After weighing anchor at Plymouth, the ships had a hard time of it. The winds were so violently opposed that everyone was angry and on edge. After finally seizing an opportunity to leave Plymouth, the fleet was driven by contrary winds into Falmouth harbor, and tempers were already wearing thin. In a letter sent from Falmouth to London, an adventurer complains that "Heare is no verreitie [variety] of newes but conteneuall quarrles and fighting amongst our owne companye with many dangerous hurttes…."[10] Apparently no one was killed, but not for want of trying. The disciplinary problems were compounded by the motley make-up of the crew, whom Ralegh took to dismissing—especially as conditions worsened—as "scum."[11] When the ships finally set sail from Falmouth, the foul weather persisted, and the fleet was blown into the harbor of Cork, where the winds pinned them in for seven weeks. Fortunately, the men were fed and entertained by the earl of Cork, Richard Boyle, who had bought Ralegh's Irish holdings for a song just before his trial and conviction for treason. It was at this time the earl's daughters developed their crush on the dashing young Captain Ralegh.

But it was also in Cork that Wat enters the historical record in a more serious way—in the service of Mars, not Venus. In an echo of his Low Country combats, Wat was involved in a quarrel with a fellow captain that could easily have resulted in bloodshed. His opponent was the most unreliable figure in the expedition, a privateer and scoundrel named Captain John Bailey, who chafed at the enforced peacefulness of the long, financially unrewarding stay at Cork. Always with an eye to the main chance, Bailey seized any ship that came within his grasp, with no concern for niceties of nationality. Near Cork, as it seems, Bailey "had robbed a Scottish ship and had stolen a shallop."[12] Next, Bailey seized some French ships, which General Ralegh promptly released because they were protected by treaty. Soon Captain Bailey went from bad to worse, deserting the expedition in the Canaries and returning to London, where he was promptly jailed after brazenly proclaiming Ralegh to be a pirate.

Early in the expedition, perhaps when it was still at Cork, Wat confronted Bailey in a fashion that would have both pleased and troubled his father. In a brief statement that leaves everything to the imagination, an observer reported that Bailey had quarreled with Wat and "fled his challenge."[13] In light of Wat's recent history, the "challenge" he gave to Bailey sounds like the prologue to a duel. Given Bailey's rogue conduct, this quarrel may have been unlike Wat's earlier ones, involving not merely his personal honor but also the integrity of his father and of the expedition itself. Nevertheless, Ralegh could not have been happy to see his son impugning the good faith of a fellow captain, even a deplorable one. He had no ships to spare. Whatever the outcome, a duel would have been disastrous, and Ralegh must have worried about a return of Wat's old disruptive ways.

Even before fever broke out and decimated the crew, the voyage was challenging for everyone. Although they enjoyed advantages as officers, the two Walter Raleghs faced difficulties of their own. Despite his experience of long voyages, Sir Walter had always been vulnerable to seasickness and had particular difficulty sleeping at sea. We are reminded of his advanced years when we hear that, later in the voyage, he fell and badly injured his head. But at least he had relatively comfortable quarters and the trunk of books that he always took with him on voyages. For Wat, however, there was no engaging diversion from the endless roll of the sea and the repetitive military drills. Worst of all for this physically ebullient young man, there was no opportunity for the action he craved, no form of freedom in which he could expend his abundant energies. If he had access to them, his father's books would have left him supremely bored.

When the Canary Islands were finally sighted, the fleet was in desperate need of water and supplies. Unfortunately, Barbary pirates had recently attacked several settlements, and Ralegh had to cajole and threaten the authorities for provisions. On the island of Lancerota, a party from the *Destiny* was ambushed while taking on fresh water, and a handful of English soldiers—"seconded by Sir Warham St. Leeger and my sonne" (Ralegh's reference to Wat noted earlier)—"made fortie of them runne away."[14] For his part, Wat must have appreciated the chance to throw himself into combat, especially since his small group put a much larger force to headlong flight. This enthusiasm would prove to be dangerous, however, when the opposition included Spanish troops equipped with muskets.

After the fleet left the Canaries and crossed the equator, the lethal enemy that attacked the becalmed vessels was not Spanish warships but a tropical fever that swept through the ships, hitting the *Destiny* especially hard. Ralegh himself barely survived. Upon reaching land in Guiana, he sent a letter to his wife, his first extant message to her since the voyage had begun. It begins by stressing his own weak condition, since "I have suffered the moste violent calenture for fifteene dayes that ever man did and lived."[15] (A calenture was a burning fever accompanied by delirium—the afflicted sometimes attempted to throw themselves into the sea.) After an overview of the casualties among the crew and soldiers (forty-two dead, with many more sick and uncertain of recovery), finally he writes the words she was hoping to see: "Your sonne had never soe good helth, havinge no distemper in all the heate under the line [south of the equator]." Their son's vigorous constitution, which had protected him in the Tower when the plague took a child in the room next to his, fended off the tropical diseases that had devastated so many men of authority, including his father. Doubtless, Lady Ralegh desired to hear more about her son, but nothing was forthcoming. Beyond its address to her ("Deare heart" or in most copies "Sweet heart"), the letter is primarily public in nature, expressing little personal affection and ending briskly with "Commend me to poore Carew, my sonne. Soe God blesse yow."[16]

The bulk of the letter is taken up with Ralegh's matter-of-fact listing by name and rank of the "menn of the better sort" from the *Destiny* who have died. At the end of the catalogue, however, a rare note of personal feeling obtrudes when he comes to the final two names: "but to mine inestymable greife Hamond and Talbot." The word "but" indicates the depth of Ralegh's loss; his immeasurable ("inestymable") grief comes from losing not officers but ordinary men who are friends. Ralegh does not need to specify who Hammond and especially Talbot are because Lady Ralegh knew them well. Like his brother Robert, who was Wat's lieutenant, Christopher Hammond served on the *Destiny*, and John Talbot was of course Wat's old tutor and Ralegh's devoted companion throughout the Tower years and on the voyage. When Talbot died of the fever that was ravaging the ship, Ralegh praised him in one of the Journal's most poignant passages as "my honest friend Mr. John Talbot, one that had lived with me eleven years in the Tower, an excellent general scholar and as faithful true man as lived."[17]

After he had returned to England and to the Tower, Ralegh wrote a note recommending actions to be taken on behalf of various people to whom he felt beholden. (When his keeper copied it for the eyes of his superiors he described it as written "for discharge of his [Ralegh's] conscience.")[18] In that message, Ralegh remembered the families of Hammond and Talbot, specifying "I desire that my wife if she enjoy her goods may have consideration of Christopher Hamons wyfe" and that "my wyfe do in any case according to her ability relieve Mr Jo. Talbots mother, who I feare me (her sonn being deade) will otherwise perish." For years Lady Ralegh lived in close proximity to members of the Talbot family on Tower Hill and would have known the mother of John well. In this revealing passage, Ralegh's loyalty to the men who died in service to him takes the form of solicitude for the women they have left vulnerable and in need. Unlike the contemporary Talbots (and Raleghs), there were no wives or mothers in the accounts of the legendary Sir John Talbot and his son John.

After the fleet's arrival at the coast of Guiana (7 November), Ralegh's surviving men began to heal, and a mission to find and defend the desired gold mine could be set in motion. The obstacles to success were many, beginning with a fundamental problem: no one was sure of the location of the supposedly easily available source of gold. (That the voyagers seem not to have decided whether it was a mine or a surface seam did not bode well for their venture.) This uncertainty was greatly compounded by the nearly impossible political constraints dictated by King James, who made it clear that this very well-armed fleet was not to engage in hostilities with the presumably inhospitable Spanish who controlled the region in which the gold was thought to exist.

Ralegh decided to send a force of five small ships capable of negotiating the shallows of the Orinoco's delta, each carrying a company of fifty soldiers. Since no one knew what lay ahead with regard to Spanish fortifications, effective leadership was essential. It was also problematic. Ralegh himself would have been the obvious person to lead the small fleet, but he had not fully recovered his strength and was never to do so. The command went to Lawrence Kemys, a loyal follower who had served Ralegh in many capacities over three decades, including a major role in his financial transactions after his imprisonment. Originally a scholar and a chemist, Kemys had accompanied Ralegh on the first Guiana voyage, and he led a small expedition to reconnoiter the area more fully soon after Ralegh's initial "discovery" in 1595.[19] Kemys knew the terrain better than anyone else—but not nearly well enough. Unbeknownst to the English, Spain had fortified the little town of San Thomé and perhaps moved its location as well, thus necessitating quick decision-making. Kemys lacked the force of character to impose military discipline on his men and demonstrated a fatal indecisiveness when his original assumptions proved to be incorrect.

Down the chain of command, the quality of leadership remained questionable. Ralegh's original Sergeant Major (a kind of field commander superior to the various captains) had been the utterly reliable John Pigott, an officer who had distinguished himself in the Low Countries. But Pigott had recently died of the fever. Since the next in command (Warham St. Leger) lay grievously ill, Ralegh conferred the post on his nephew, George Ralegh. While no one doubted George's courage, he was viewed by veterans as a hothead. The unproven reliability of George as the leader of a substantial force meant that Captain Wat Ralegh was not subjected to the authoritative control of an experienced leader. In his very brief account of the military conduct of the expedition, Sir Walter was to praise George, but with the tactful qualification that he "was not so well obeyed as the enterprize required."[20]

After he dispatched this force up the Orinoco, Ralegh and his remaining ships—dangerously undermanned—patrolled the sea, watching for the Spanish fleet rumored to be on its way. Since the soldiers' destination of San Thomé was 150 miles up the river, any news of Wat and the others would have to come from Spanish-speaking natives, and soon Ralegh was sending out skiffs in search of tribesmen who may have heard something. With every passing day, his uncertainty grew. Finally some information came from a native in touch with a tribe living close to San Thomé— Ralegh had seized him and threatened him with torture.

The tale Ralegh heard was very disturbing, and it proved to be true. He carefully recorded the details in his journal: that "the English in the Orinoco had taken St. Thome, slain Diego de Palmita, the governor, slain Captain Erenetta and Captain John Rues, and that the rest of the Spaniards, their captains slain, fled into the mountains, and that two English captains were also slain."[21] Following the specificity with regard to Spanish casualties, the uncertain reference of the final words must have been excruciating. Ralegh was a gambling man, and he would have known that the mathematical odds that Wat was one of the deceased captains—six had journeyed up the Orinoco—were increased by his son's boldness and lack of experience.[22] But keeping to the objective nature of his journal, Ralegh makes no mention of Wat, nor of his concern.

From the same settlement, Ralegh's men soon brought him another captive, who confirmed the previous report and added (Ralegh writes) "divers other particulars, which I forbear to set down till I know the truth...." There is no way to know if this additional information included the identity of the slain English captains, but one suspects it did. Ralegh's silence is ominous. Evidently he had heard something so disturbing that— even in the relative privacy of his journal—he had to "forbear" committing it to paper. That Wat might no longer be breathing would have been unthinkable, certainly too painful to be mentioned as a possibility.

After the original report about two English captains being killed,

Twelve • Destiny

Ralegh desperately sought more information. Two weeks later, on February 13, he writes that he had sent a large force to the "Indian town" to capture some escaped prisoners who may have been in San Thomé when the battle took place. After this entry, the journal suddenly breaks off. There is no entry for February 14th, nor any day after it. Ralegh must have learned the terrible truth, and the act of objective recording that had come so easily to him (and may have been a source of satisfaction) was now irrelevant and impossible.

In a Spanish legal deposition concerning the fall of San Thomé, we catch a glimpse of Ralegh at the moment he received the crushing news. In his testimony, a government witness recalls a tribesman telling him that "while he was held prisoner on board the ship of the general, whose name was Walter Ralegh (Guaterral), he had seen a launch arrive with news of what had happened, and that the General, on hearing it, began to weep for the death of his son."[23] The supreme self-possession that had always been Ralegh's strength and shield was, with the loss of Wat, gone.

After he had first learned of the battle at San Thomé—which violated the explicit conditions under which he had sailed—Ralegh knew he was likely to be tried and put to death upon his return to England. But still he continued to act decisively and to record events that he hoped might ultimately turn out well. After the confirmation of Wat's death, however, none of that mattered, and the journal stopped. Instead of making his son's fortunes, the father's expedition had killed him.

For Lawrence Keymis, who had served Ralegh since well before his son's birth and worked closely with him when he was in the Tower, Wat's death must have been deeply disturbing. As well as anyone, he knew what the young man meant to his father, and as Wat's commander he must have felt responsible for his death. After the fatal battle Keymis seems to have lost his moorings, becoming withdrawn and ineffectual, not knowing where or how to look for the mine. Having avoided doing so for a week, Keymis sent the letter to Ralegh that may have confirmed—when it arrived a month later—the terrible truth.

Keymis's narrative bears witness to the disturbing nature of Wat's death in its strategic silences, a recurring feature in many accounts. After opening with a long, opaque disquisition about the nature of the "humane condition" and "fatal necessity," Keymis gives a brief account of the episode that is completely free of specifics.[24] In a tortuous sentence, he writes of Wat that

> had not his extraordinarie vallor and forwardnes which with constant vigour of mynde, being in the hands of death, his last breath exprest in these words, Lord have mercy on

> me and prosper your enterprise ledd them all on, when some beganne to pause and recoyle shamefully, this action had neither bene attempted as it was, nor performed as it is, with his surviveing honor.

As Ralegh would have noticed, Keymis's strained emphasis on Wat's exemplary heroism seems to be shadowing a negative critique of his behavior. There is no context for the situation in which the suddenly dying Wat's "last breath" inspires his comrades, and there is no sense of the battle's result, apart from the "surviveing honor" that Wat achieved. As well, Keymis's coupling of "extraordinarie vallor" and "forwardnes" creates an ambiguity, since the latter term often carries negative connotations not present in the totally laudatory phrase preceding it.[25] Moreover, the odd, anxious phrasing—"this action had neither bene attempted as it was, nor performed as it is"—indicates Keymis's unwillingness to describe the "action" that Wat seems to have precipitated, much less praise it. Although he was fearful of Ralegh's response, the too gentle Keymis could not have imagined the fury that awaited him.

There is another eyewitness account of Wat's death, and in its disrespectful frankness it is as different from Keymis's as it could be. It was written by Captain Charles Parker, one of the leaders of the assault and a professional soldier whom Ralegh respected. Parker's account was not written for his General's eyes, and he does not worry about offending a father's love. (He is writing to a fellow captain on the expedition who had been sent back to England for treatment of a wound.) According to Parker, in the middle of the night

> we made an assaulte, wher we loste Captaine Ralegh and Captain Cosmor, but Captaine Raleghe lost him selfe with his unadvised daringnes as you shall heare for I will acquinte you, how we were ordered. Captain Cosmor led the forlorne hope with some 50 men, after him I brought upe the first devission of shotte, next brought up Captaine Raleigh a devission of Pikes who no sooner hearde us charged but indiscreetely came from his commaunde to us, where he was unfortunately welcomed with a bullet, which gave him no tyme to call for mercye to our hevenly father for his sinfull lyfe he had ledde....[26]

We should be wary of lucid accounts of battles fought at night, but Parker's account has the virtue of specifying the circumstances behind the "forwardnes" that Keymis had vaguely acknowledged. There can be no doubt that, notwithstanding his father's cautions, Wat had been spoiling for a fight. In his deposition before the Privy Council in London, Captain Roger North later declared that the English forces landed only five miles away from the town "by commandment of the Sergeant Major [George Ralegh] and the forwardness of young Walter Ralegh."[27] In this context, the word definitely tilts into the pejorative.

Evidently Wat's company had been placed as the third company in the battle formation (perhaps to protect him and to minimize his inexperience), but he instinctually responded to the Spanish charge with one of his own, alone. For a military man like Parker (whose place in the battle plan was usurped by Wat), this was not bravery but "unadvised daringnes" and a desertion of command. After reading Parker's scornful description, we can better understand why Keymis's account to Ralegh was so studiously vague.

There is, however, one phrase in Parker's account that raises troubling questions: his closing characterization of Wat as a person who had need to pray for mercy because of the "sinfull lyfe he had ledde." Most Elizabethans believed that all people are sinful and require mercy to be saved, but the harshness of Parker's words is unsettling. Nothing we know of Wat supports the charge that his life was uncommonly sinful. He never killed or, as far as we know, maimed an opponent in a duel, and it seems unlikely that (had he known of it) Captain Parker would have considered the assault on Thomasine a damnable sin.

The remainder of Parker's letter illuminates his charge. He immediately launches into a scorching vituperation against Lawrence Keymis, who fumblingly had committed suicide after Ralegh later blamed him for Wat's death and failure to find the mine. Given everything we know of Keymis's life, Parker's description of him as a "mear machevill [a totally evil machiavellian]" sounds crazed, and his explanation adds little: Keymis "was false to all men and moste odious to him selfe, for moste ungodly he butchered himselfe lothinge to live since he could doe no mor villany; I wil speake no more of this hatefull fellow to God and man...." Parker's excoriation of the pathetic Keymis is so furiously uncharitable—he condemns him, as he had blamed Wat, for destroying himself—that his vindictive religiosity is repellant.

Surely this man's assessment of Wat's military conduct is more trustworthy than his judgment of the young man's soul. It is impossible to know what Ralegh understood to have been the circumstances of Wat's death. He would not have seen Parker's letter, but he could have discussed the episode with Parker and the other surviving captains. Certainly he would have discussed it with his nephew George Ralegh, his brother Carew's son, who apparently failed to exercise a discipline commensurate with his command; Ralegh noted that "by my absence and Sir Warhams" George was "not so well obayed as the enterprize required."[28] Of course, Ralegh would have had ample opportunity to discuss the fatal battle with Keymis, but perhaps he was not inclined to listen to his faithful lieutenant's account, being determined (as we will see) to blame him for causing the battle and bringing about Wat's death.

Two months passed before Ralegh was able to write a letter informing Secretary Winwood of Wat's death and the aborted mission. (His words fell on deaf ears since Winwood himself had died, thus depriving Ralegh of his strongest supporter on the privy council.) Ralegh's account of the battle is considered and circumspect, exculpating the actions of both his son and the English forces. He says the Spaniards

> begann the warr and shott at us, both with their ordnance and muskets, whereupon the companies were forced to charge them and soone after beate them out of theire towne, in the assalt whereof my sonne, haveinge more desyre of honour then of saftie, was slayne, and with whom (to saie the truth) all respect of the world hath taken end in me."[29]

To describe Wat as "haveinge more desyre of honour then of saftie" is not untrue, but of course the formulation masks his son's fatal indiscipline.

The truest part of Ralegh's account is his sense of numbed personal loss. In the aftermath of his attainder for treason, we recall, Ralegh had often spoken of himself as a nonentity, but he did so with a certain melodramatic self-display. Here, however, he observes simply that the world has ceased to engage him. His comment that "all respect of the world hath taken end in me" is more stunned and devastated than "I have lost all interest in the world" would have been. The words he had written to Lady Ralegh fifteen years earlier—"He is parte of me and I live in him"—have altered unthinkably. The son in himself has died, and the father will have no continuance.[30]

On the day after his letter to Secretary Winwood, Ralegh wrote the letter to Wat's mother that he had been postponing. Perhaps he thought (correctly) that she already may have learned of her son's death, since he had asked Winwood to "take some pittie on my poore wife, to whom I dare not write for renewinge of her sorrow for her sonne...." Without salutation or preparation, he begins abruptly: "I was loath to write because I know not how to comfort you." In its contrast to the many occasions over the years in which Ralegh had insisted (not always convincingly) on the magnitude of his suffering, the simple statement of his grief for Wat is stunning: "And God knows I never knew what sorrow meant till now."[31]

After reminding her of the duty to obey God's will, as Queen Anne had borne the loss of Prince Henry "with a magnanimous heart," he returns to a more personal vein: "Comfort your hart (deare Bess): I shall sorrow for us both and I shall sorrowe the lesse because I have not long to sorrowe, because not long to live." If she desires to know what has happened, he asks her to obtain a copy of the letter he had sent to Winwood, since "my braines are broken and tis a torment to mee to write, espetially of miserie." Movingly, Ralegh closes his brief letter to Bess by addressing solely her grief: "The Lord blesse you and comfort you, that you may beare patientlie the death of your most valient sonne." He signs it "Your W Ralegh." Nothing more need be, or can be, said.

Ralegh sealed the letter, but before he could pass it on he had second thoughts which led him to break the seal and—despite having said "tis a torment to mee to write"—he adds a postscript much longer than the original message. This addition reveals another, less attractive side of Ralegh— the Ralegh who knew he must defend himself. The transition from a private to a public mode is apparent in the postscript's opening words: "I protest before the Majestie of God...." He is now addressing his wife but really speaking to an imaginary jury. Ralegh observes that great heroes like Sir John Hawkins and Sir Francis Drake died heartbroken after they were defeated, and he says he would have died as well, "did I not contend ag[ains]t sorrow to comfort and releive you. If I live to return, resolve yourself that it is the care for you that hath strengthened my heart." In these lines, Ralegh seems to be detaching himself from the loving sorrow he had just expressed, and indeed he says he will "contend" against it for his wife's sake. But the rest of the postscript is really a rebuttal of the charges that he expects to be brought against him. This long justification in no way annuls the tender sensitivity of his words to Bess, but it does reveal another side of Ralegh—his impulse to protect himself by disclaiming responsibility for his actions.

In this long postscript, Ralegh parenthetically adds a new (uncorroborated) detail about their son—he says that "my sonne Watt" killed one of the Spanish captains who were slain in the engagement, a declaration that Lady Ralegh may have found to be consoling proof of Wat's bravery and prowess. It is notable that nowhere in the letter does Ralegh mention the twelve-year-old Carew, whom he easily (and justly, as it happens) could have cited as a hope for the future and a compelling reason for his wife and himself to remain strong. It is probable that, never having lived with Carew, Ralegh had not come to know his younger son well. But the truth is that for his father it was Wat alone who had always represented the future.

Conclusion:
Last Words and Silences

The mortal remains of young Captain Wat Ralegh, along with those of his slain colleague, Captain Cosmor, were buried with appropriate military solemnity—"muffled drums beating, pikes trailing, and banners borne before them, to signify they were captains."[1] But this young mocker of ceremonies would have appreciated a silent note of discord: he was buried in front of the high altar in the church in San Thomé, the most hallowed Catholic ground in the village. Presumably the distraught Lawrence Keymis, fearing Ralegh's wrath, sought the greatest honors for Wat that the village afforded, and perhaps he thought this sanctified earth might protect the grave from future desecration. (It would be interesting to know if, several weeks later, the church was spared when the English forces torched the village.) In any event, the church has disappeared, as have most traces of the son Ralegh had hoped would extend his own name and the family name to future generations.

Ironically, when Wat Ralegh's life is remembered, it is in conjunction with his father—the man against whom he had struggled to individuate himself. A crowning example of this phenomenon is a stamp issued by British Guiana in 1934. It reproduces in a purplish-brown monotone the double portrait of the two Walter Raleghs from 1602, with Wat's dark-eyed face strikingly lacking in fidelity to the bright-faced lad of the painting. A box under the picture contains the description: "Sir Walter Raleigh and his Son." This hedge against risking an identification of the son is prudent, and greatly preferable to the common mistake of identifying Wat as his brother Carew. But still his name is absent.

The stamp is especially interesting because it appears to be associating the portrait of 1602 with the father and son who attempted to claim Guiana for England in 1617. Of course the subjects of the early painting and the adventurers of 1617 are in legal terms the same persons. But the intervening years had brought great changes to both father and son, and their relationship in Guiana was much more complex than it had been in Sherborne. Although one senses in the young Wat of the double portrait an inchoate resistance to his father, in Guiana the lie is clearly given to the paternal vision—we see a rebellion against Ralegh by his son. This rebellion led, directly or indirectly, to the deaths of both of them; the stamp is a poignant reminder of the relationship that had been lost.

It appears that Wat's sudden death at San Thomé was above all an act of defiance—defiance of the Spanish defenders, of military discipline, and of his father's will. All of the English accounts agree that when Wat led his charge, which was perhaps a charge of one, he was acting of his own volition. His death was his own. He fearlessly exposed himself to great danger and perished. The act was perhaps foolish, and certainly it was ill-considered, but for Wat it must not have been pointless. By helping to precipitate a battle for the town, Wat had contravened his father's (and his king's) express command. But his willful engagement was an act of filial disobedience with unintended consequences. He could not have guessed that (in a modern biographer's words) he "more than anyone, had been responsible for the attack that was his father's death warrant."[2]

When Ralegh returned to England, King James and his ministers showed a strong interest in Wat's dying words, but the point of this apparent interest in the son was really a concern about his father. In their search for evidence that would justify putting Ralegh to death, the king's clear intention, James's lawyers and privy counsellors deposed a number of the voyage's commanders. Apparently an officer (not identified in the documents) reported overhearing Wat's final words as he threw himself into combat, and the lords deemed these words to be highly incriminating. After Ralegh's execution, James and his counsellors wrote a *Declaration* in which they attempted to defend their lethal justice. (The fact that they wrote such a document—despite their opening axiom that "kings be not bound to give account of their actions to any but God alone"—indicates a good deal of popular opposition to their condemnation of Ralegh.)[3] Intriguingly, one of their charges against Ralegh referenced Wat, not with regard to anything he had done but to something he had said—a battle-cry before he rushed into combat and was slain.

We have already encountered a version of Wat's dying words that was anodyne and incriminated no one. In the careful, perhaps sanitized, account sent by Lawrence Keymis in the Orinoco to Ralegh on the *Destiny*, the mortally wounded Wat's "last breath [was] exprest in these words, *Lord have mercy upon me, and prosper your enterprise.*"[4] This sounds like a generic speech-of-a-dying-hero, and unless Wat took on a different nature as he lay dying, one has to be suspicious of such entirely appropriate, well-mannered words. Indeed, one should be skeptical of any dying words at all, since Wat was apparently felled by a musket ball in the neck, which in Captain Parker's smug phrase "gave him no tyme to call for mercye to our hevenly father."[5] But Keymis's version of the final words did not interest James's lawyers because it supplied no grounds for condemning Ralegh.

The earliest surviving evidence of this new, alternate version of Wat's final words appears to be a note written by the king, which he added to his instructions urging the Privy Council to produce a plausible case for Ralegh's execution. In a slightly cryptic suggestion, the king recommends that the lords refer to "his [Ralegh's] son's oration when they [English troops] came to the town."[6] When the Council arraigned Ralegh a few days later (22 October 1618), James's suggestion had been accepted (and clarified) by his learned henchmen. In the outline of charges to be brought against Ralegh, one general heading is "His impostures," and under it the first subheading is "Hee never intended a mine." James's central allegation was that Ralegh gained his freedom through deception, since his intent was never to discover a mine but rather to engage in piracy and raids against Spanish settlements. The importance of Wat's words is made clear in a following subsection of the document: "His sonnes speeches to the soldiers to attend the spoile of St. Thomas, for that was the mine they sought after."[7] The charge is that Ralegh's son knew there was no mine, so he declared that the only mine (source of riches) to be had was the wealth to be taken from sacking the town.

In a later tract by the king and lords—the *Declaration* of Ralegh's crimes that was drawn up after his execution—Wat's words undergo a new and improved iteration. We learn that "young Mr Ralegh ... when he led his soldiers upon the town, used these or the like words: "*Come on, my hearts, here is the mine that you must expect; they that look for any other mine are fools.*"[8] Of course, there is no compelling reason to accept this supposed speech by Wat as genuine; in any of its forms, it was never attributed to a specific listener, and the phrase "these or the like words" suggests editorial activity. But, if these words were *not* spoken by Wat, they are very convincingly ventriloquized, especially the explosive dismissal of gullible believers in the mine as "fools." Like much else in his life, these words would have set Wat apart from his fellows, and they certainly sound more authentic than the conventional final words that Keymis attributed to him. And if the words were the invention of the lords, who among them would have known Wat well enough to mimic him so convincingly?

This *Declaration* finally makes explicit the reasoning behind the crown's emphasis on the damning nature of these words when it asserts that Wat "was likest to know his father's secret." The lords are assuming that the son is speaking as an extension of his father, a patrilineal idea that had been attractive to Ralegh but was much less so to Wat. Over the years, Wat had resisted the acceptance of this shared identity, and it is plausible that his reputed words—if actually spoken by him—do not betray his access to his father's secret but rather express his mockery of what he felt was his father's self-deluding ambition. It may be that, from this limited but cogent perspective, Wat looked upon the Guiana voyage as his father's ego-trip. But there is no more evidence to bring to bear—the rest is silence.

As we have seen, Ralegh's first response to Wat's death was a devastated silence of his own. To a remarkable degree, he maintained this reticence throughout the final year of his life, saying no more than he was required to say. In his announcement of Wat's death to Secretary Winwood (quoted in the previous chapter), Ralegh's comment on Wat is simply that in the assault on San Thomé "my sonne ... was slayne, and with whome (to saie the truth) all respect of the world hath taken end in me."[9] This account is less forthcoming than Keymis's in that it gives us less detail about Wat and makes no reference to a dying speech. His single description of Wat—"haveinge more desyre of honour then of saftie"—is followed immediately by his poignant remark that "all respect of the world hath taken end in me." The world has died to Ralegh, and with it his desire to speak of his son.

For both personal and political reasons—his loss was raw and Wat was being used by his enemies to undo him—Ralegh sought to avoid public discussion of his son's death in Guiana. It is interesting that, when he appeared before the Privy Council in Westminster to respond to its questions, he rebutted many of their charges but apparently said nothing about Wat, nor about the incriminating speech to the soldiers he had supposedly made.[10] Moreover, Ralegh did not contest the issue in the speech he made at his execution, though he combatted other charges made by the lords. In his address to Council, Ralegh's only reference to Wat was in a charge aimed at Keymis: that he knew the location of the mine but "would not discover [disclose] it, when he saw that my Son was slain."[11] A cynic might argue that, at the end, Wat mattered to his father only as an arguing point—which is how he mattered to James and his lords—but this view ignores the depths of Ralegh's silence.

In formal and public circumstances, Ralegh avoided expressing his emotional response to Wat's death, emphasizing merely the fact of the loss. After his return to England, Ralegh published his *Apologie* in defense of his intentions and conduct, which contained his most widely circulated account of Wat's death. According to Ralegh's brisk narrative, the encamped English force was attacked by a Spanish troop, and in pursuit it found itself at the gates of the town, counter-attacked by the governor and his captains:

> my sonne not tarrying for his Musketeers, came upp in the head of a Company of pykes, where he was first shott, and pressing upon a Spanish Captaine with his sword, called Errinetta, who taking the small end of his musket in his hand, struck him on the head, and with the stroake felled him; whome againe John Plessington my sonnes serjeant thrust through with his halbert....[12]

In this brutal, matter-of-fact reportage (which does not contradict the essentials of Captain Parker's negative account), Ralegh does not attempt to praise Wat. In language stripped of adjectives and adverbs, Wat was "not tarrying" and "came upp in the head of a Company," with no mention of either his valor or forwardness.[13] Instead Ralegh's eye goes to small details, such as that of Errinetta (the name of the Spanish captain, not of Wat's sword) swinging his musket from its barrel. In this passage Ralegh is writing with an historian's cold eye, perhaps to prevent his own emotional engagement. It is significant that Wat is "first shott" and then "felled" in the middle of a long sentence, with no reference to his death. Even here, a silence is present.

In other public letters and speeches, Ralegh is careful to maintain an avoidance of expressive emotion when he counts Wat among his "losses." In a letter to King James, he mentions having "spent my poore estate, lost my sonne, suffered by sicknesse and otherwise a world of miseries" in a long list of privations he suffered in commanding the expedition for the king's benefit.[14] He uses a similar phrase when he addresses the judiciary on the day before his execution, declaring that he had undertaken the voyage for the king, though it "had no other success [outcome] but what was fatal to me, the loss of my son and the wasting of my whole estate."[15] In both formulations, we glimpse the patrilineal Ralegh in the coupling of lost son and failed estate, especially since his estate essentially had been spent decades earlier. Perhaps he is expressing the least he must say in order to insist on his sincere intention to have found the goldmine.

Since Ralegh said so little of it himself, one has to infer by indirect means the depth of his mourning. One such oblique manifestation occurs in a book he appears to have read on the long, grief-filled voyage back to

England.[16] The volume was a recently published folio of the collected works of Ralegh's old friend and fellow poet from his Irish days, Edmund Spenser. (It is touching that, later, Lady Ralegh proudly annotated the text to identify for young Carew the poet's allusions to his father.) Ralegh appears to have lost himself in Spenser's *Faerie Queene*, a long, leisurely allegory of Elizabeth's England, but late in the poem he came upon a passage that mirrored his own response to the loss of Wat. Spenser describes the response of an old knight when his wounded, apparently deceased son is brought before him. Ralegh would have seen himself in the aged warrior, who had "borne great sway in armes amongst his peares [peers]: / But now weake age had dimd his candle light."

But it is the description of the knight's lament for his son that would have held Ralegh's attention. In a stanza that he marked by a line in the margin and also a pointing hand, Ralegh read that the knight

> Was inly touched with compassion deare,
> And deare affection of so doolefull dreare
> That he these words burst forth: Ah sory boy,
> Is this the hope that to my hoary heare [hair]
> Thou brings? aie me, is this the timely joy
> Which I expected long, now turnd to sad annoy [grief]?[17]

Spenser's passage, written two decades earlier, bears an uncanny resemblance to Ralegh's circumstances: a white-haired knight who was once a great warrior mourns the son who had always represented his hope for the future. The words of his long-deceased friend articulate the lament that Ralegh cannot express in his own words. But there is a poignant difference between life and art, for in Spenser's poem the son regains consciousness and returns to life.

A second, much more troubling index to the force of Ralegh's bereavement took the form of a devastating guilt and rage. After Wat's death, Ralegh turned with unrelenting fierceness against Lawrence Keymis, whom he had named to lead the expedition to find, occupy, and defend the mine. To that point, Ralegh had trusted Keymis entirely, and for good reason since his lieutenant loyally had served him in many offices for thirty years. But Ralegh insisted on blaming Wat's death and the failure to find the mine on Keymis. In the *Apologie* (meaning apologia rather than the modern "apology") that Ralegh later wrote in his defense, he recounts how a distressed Keymis came to his cabin after he had been severely reprimanded by Ralegh.[18] When the distraught Keymis, Ralegh writes, "prayed me for to allowe of his Appollogie… I told him that he had undone me by his obstincie and that I would not favour or colour in any sort his former follie." After Ralegh confirmed that this was his resolution, Kemys "replied in these words, 'I knowe then, Sir, what course to take.'" Whereupon he retired to his cabin, first shooting himself with his pistol and then killing himself with a stab of his long knife. Ralegh expresses no remorse, and indeed charges that Keymis was a man "farr from careing to please or satsfie any man but himselfe," a charge that over the years Ralegh's own enemies had levelled against him.

Ralegh had many grounds for mordant self-accusation with regard to Wat's death, and he could not have escaped feeling some degree of responsibility for it. His guilt is most apparent in the cold rage with which he attacked Keymis for botching the entire enterprise at San Thomé. This rage is probably a displacement of his own (unacknowledged) guilt, in which self-reproach is directed outward at a figure very like himself. This interpretation helps to explain several strange passages in which Ralegh ascribes to Keymis the devastation he himself felt at Wat's death. Thus he says of Keymis that "the death of my sonne ... made him resolve not to open the myne" and that "after my sonne was slaine I knewe that he had noe care att all of any man surviveing."[19]

Since Ralegh had always valued Kemys highly, this transference of anger must have been powerfully motivated by his loss. In the letter he had written bidding farewell to Lady Ralegh before his expected execution fifteen years earlier, there is painfully ironic evidence of his deep regard for the man whom he was later to undo; in his final paragraph, he asks his wife to "be good to Kemis for he is a perfecte honest man and hath [suffered] much wronge for my sake."[20] While it in no way excuses Ralegh's appalling reversal, the death of Wat must have been instrumental in his denial of his old friend.

In the Ralegh family there was fortunately a third voice, silent in most biographies but heard clearly within her family—that of Lady Ralegh. She left behind her very little written evidence to illuminate her feelings for her husband and her elder son—no correspondence with Wat survives, and only a business-like note or two to Ralegh, which she knew would be read and transcribed for prosecutors' eyes by prison officials. In the years in which Sherborne was being disposed of, or tussled over, she was of course careful to voice her claims and indictments in the loudest register she could muster. After the family finally surrendered Sherborne, there was little she could do for Wat, beyond (one would guess) making over to him the better part of the £400 grant they received each year. For her husband, who was buried in his *History of the World* when he was not actively courting Prince Henry with tracts on warfare and politics, there was even less call for her engagement.

As Wat grew older and more independent, it would have become difficult for Lady Ralegh to navigate the increasingly conflictual relationship between him and her husband. Her prime motive must have been to reconcile their differences as best she could. The Guiana expedition that Ralegh organized was a golden opportunity for bringing them together, although its dangers posed a test to her good wishes. We can well imagine that Lady Ralegh had misgivings about the expedition—as she had expressed concerning the first Guiana expedition twenty years earlier—but the evidence does not support the assertion that "She had fought to keep Wat at home."[21] Her financial support, after all, was crucial for the expedition; without her initial commitment of much of the £8,000 settlement for Sherborne, it is unlikely that adequate funding could have been raised, and she supplemented it by selling a property in Mitcham (Surrey) that had come to her through her Throckmorton relations. One can feel Ralegh's shame when, as evidence of the seriousness of his endeavor, he cites the death of his son and the expenditure of his wife's resources.

In addition to emotional reasons for supporting Wat's participation, Lady Ralegh was shrewd enough to perceive that his future looked increasingly unpromising. His recent conviction for assaulting Thomasine Ostler, when added to his rash of duels at home and abroad, indicated her son's pressing need to find a new direction—or a new opponent—for his combative energies. As well, she must have hoped, a goldmine would go a long way to alleviating Wat's financial problems and opening a future for him.

Of Sir Walter Ralegh's short, eventful journey from departure at Plymouth to the scaffold at Westminster, many fascinating pages have been written, and this is not the place for more.[22] In lieu of a narrative, let one poignant detail stand for the whole. The road from Plymouth to London brought Ralegh and his travelling party—which included his wife and son Carew—within sight of Sherborne, as if it were retracing the stages of his career. Upon seeing his treasured home and grounds, Ralegh turned to a companion and exclaimed "that all that was his, and that the king had unjustly taken it from him."[23] If rash, this sounds a natural enough comment, and it was nothing that the king had not heard before, often enough from Lady Ralegh. But now, under close guard, everything that Ralegh said or did had consequences. In the list of charges against Ralegh that included Wat's supposed final words, we have his companion's recollection of his fatal remark and the lords' conclusion that "Sir Walter Raleigh was nowe unworthie of any further continuance of his Majesty's favour towards him." If this dubious withdrawal of the king's favor helped to bring Ralegh to the executioner's block, it was an unintended favor from his old enemy.

Conclusion

After Ralegh's return, the family was immediately confronted by two difficult, shared experiences: the loss of Wat and the noxious exposure to interrogation by the crown. Of course, Ralegh had the lion's share of judicial attention, but his wife and son were not overlooked. At the end of August 1618, an associate wrote to William Trumbull in Brussels that, in addition to Ralegh, "Sir Walters sonne [Carew], and his sons [Wat's] man that attended him when he was slayne" were questioned.[24] It is not clear what crown's men expected (or hoped) to learn from little Carew, who was hardly an expert on his brother, but the interrogation of Wat's servant on the *Destiny* suggests that the crown was pursuing evidence to support the view that Ralegh's son (and hence Ralegh himself) believed there was no mine in Guiana. Nothing appears to have come of this questioning.

It goes without saying that the crown would attempt to squeeze as much information from Lady Ralegh as it could. To that end she was held under house arrest, as William Trumbull learned when a friend informed him (18 September 1618) that Ralegh's "poore Lady and sunne are still close prisoners," and they remained confined for another month.[25] Being no stranger to imprisonment and interrogation, she gave her enemies nothing they could use against her husband, but she must have chafed against the confinement since there was so much for her to do. Once again, the responsibility to protect her family fell on her, and she responded with the same energy she had shown when Ralegh was first convicted. Possessions (including Ralegh's valuable books) had to be protected from the circling vultures, and she resisted the fatalism that had overtaken her husband.

On the eve of her husband's execution, Lady Ralegh was allowed access to him, the last visit to the Tower in a series stretching over a decade and a half. Lady Ralegh left no record of their conversation—she was always careful not to write or speak publicly about her husband's inner life. Inevitably, Ralegh would have had a list of tasks for her to take care of, and according to a contemporary letter she reassured him that "The Lords have granted me the disposing of your body." To which he responded, "It is well, Bess, that thou mayst dispose of it dead, that hadst not always the disposing of it when it was alive."[26] Behind Ralegh's little jest is his acknowledgment of how much time he had spent away from her, how often he had pursued grand designs that did not include her. She left his cell after midnight.

One of the most telling characterizations of Ralegh's life came—obliquely—from his own pen. While describing Rome's escalation of the war against Carthage, Ralegh paused to generalize (and to comment on himself):

It is the disease of Kings, of States, and of private men, to covet the greatest things, but not to enjoy the lest; the desire of that which we neither have nor neede, taking from us the true use and fruition of what we have already.[27]

The truth of Ralegh's observation in the *History of the World* was soon confirmed by his own actions. The second voyage to Guiana, the expedition that destroyed so much of what he had lived for, was already beginning to take shape in his mind. When he mounted the scaffold at Westminster, he moved toward release. To use another phrase of his own, finally he laid down "the burden of ambition."

For Lady Ralegh, a final office for Wat remained to be performed, a duty that recalls (and silently comments on) the family's early days. In his will of 1597, Ralegh had named designates to act as executors if he should die before Wat came of age; it seems likely that he did not trust Lady Ralegh (perhaps in tandem with a new husband) to administer the will with sufficient regard for Wat's future. It is poignant, then, that after Wat's death (without a will) she was appointed to be administrator of his effects. Presumably Lady Ralegh would have submitted an inventory to the Prerogative Court of Canterbury listing Wat's belongings, but "relatively few inventories survive for the period before 1661," and Lady Ralegh's inventory for her son has not been found.[28] It is unlikely that Wat left much, but one can hope that his mother was able to retain some of his valued possessions, perhaps his sword and shield.

After the business of organizing their estates was finished, Lady Ralegh felt a need to express her devotion to her husband and son in lasting terms, and she commissioned two works of visual art to memorialize them. One is a very large, anonymous painting that is known only through a single, fifty-year-old photograph.[29] This intriguing painting is quite dominated by the seated figure of Lady Ralegh, who wears black mourning garments, including what appears to be a widow's cap and a very fine, long mantilla. In a lovely, pensive gesture, the outstretched fingers of her right hand almost touch her inclined face, which is distinguished by intelligent, inquisitive eyes that engage the viewer's gaze. Her right elbow rests on the lid of a tomb that bears on its front the Ralegh arms and on its lid a rather formal remembrance (in rhyme) of her husband. Rather surprisingly, Lady Ralegh stresses how Ralegh's "wisdome, valour, Faith and high desert / Did place thee neare in thy Queens woorthy harte." No friend of Elizabeth herself, Lady Ralegh generously memorializes the relationship that meant so much to her husband in his happy days at court (before their marriage). The short poem ends with praise for Ralegh's "worth that did excell."

Perhaps the painting alludes to the early double portrait of father and

Remembrances of her deceased husband and son encompass the figure of Lady Ralegh in mourning with her young son Carew (unknown collection, courtesy National Portrait Gallery, London).

son, for under her elbow—as Wat stood under his father's—stands a small Carew, who is remarkably fresh-faced in this dark canvas and looks younger than his thirteen or fourteen years. In an action that contrasts him with his older brother, he intently reads a book. Since Wat's weapons are also depicted—on the other side of Lady Ralegh—the suggestion is that the

Ralegh line encompasses both aspects of the common Renaissance formula for masculine accomplishment: arms and arts.

The white hand of Lady Ralegh's extended left arm draws attention to artifacts associated with her elder son: Wat's sword, shield, and a few clods of earth underneath. Balancing the untitled lines for her husband, Lady Ralegh claims Wat as "my eldest Sonne" in a concise sepulchral epigram:

> To my eldest Sonne Walter Ralegh
> Guianas mould interred thy valours story
> Where thou exchangdst life for martiall glory.

The brevity of the couplet allows Lady Ralegh to forgo any detail about the circumstances of Wat's death. In its place is an afterlife, beginning in "Guianas mould" and ending with Wat's elevation into "martiall glory." As Anna Beer aptly remarked, "When it is remembered that, for different reasons, neither Ralegh nor Wat had received conventional burials and that neither had been commemorated in any material way, then this portrait becomes their monument."[30]

In addition to this large painting, Lady Ralegh commissioned a less weighty, more personal remembrance of her husband and her eldest son: a locket in which a beautiful cloisonné case held a portrait in miniature of each. The early provenance of the locket is not known, but it was apparently acquired by one of the eighteenth-century Dukes of Rutland, and it has remained in the Manners collection at Belvoir Castle. In lieu of an illustration of the case, Victoria Manners's description of its lid (quoted from the catalogue of an 1897 exhibition) must suffice: "Oval miniature case of gold, about 2¼ inches × nearly 4 in. English Cloisonné…. The pattern is a floral arabesque, worked in gold cloisons, on a black background, with flowers in translucent green. In the centre is a heart-shaped lozenge, under a W., while beneath is the monogram E.R., all in green translucent enamel."[31] If, as a recent biographer has surmised, this beautiful case in which the initials W and ER are entwined, was "a gift from Ralegh to his wife in happier times," there is great poignancy in her repurposing it into a memorial to him and to their union's first child who lived beyond infancy.[32]

Beautiful and suggestive as this cover is, the treasure is within: the portraits of Lady Ralegh's husband and son. The portraits are anonymous, painted by one of the many gifted miniaturists working in London. They are carefully matched, a sign not of the artist's limited ability but rather of Lady Ralegh's evident desire to convey the similarity of the two men being memorialized. (One could think of these paired miniatures as being Lady

These portrait miniatures of the two Walter Raleghs (c. 1619) were commissioned by Lady Ralegh and worn by her in a locket (courtesy His Grace, the Duke of Rutland [Belvoir Castle, Grantham, Leicestershire]).

Ralegh's version of the double portrait in which Wat imitates his father—but here their independence is paramount.) Both figures are represented chest-high against an identical cerulean blue backdrop. Both are bareheaded, facing to the left and wearing armor enhanced with gold (the father's more ornate than the son's), each with a sash of command over the right shoulder. In both portraits, an inscription in gold lettering runs inside the edge of the oval, giving the subjects' common date of death (1618) and their ages, 24 for Wat and 68 for Ralegh (several years older than most biographers believe).

These commonalities in presentation invite careful attention to the similarities and differences of their faces, each turning slightly to his left. One can detect shared features such as their light-grey eyes and curly hair, but the vicissitudes of age make it difficult to see each face in the other. Moreover, the "like father, like son" formula is undercut by character as well as years. In Wat we see a young man whose striking handsomeness is inseparable from the robust insouciance of his manner. His prominent nose and jaw suggest a habit of superiority, and his steady stare at (or through) the viewer refuses engagement. This is portrait as icon. By contrast, the face in Ralegh's portrait invites a sympathetic response. Though he wears armor inlaid with gold, his authority of command is not dominant; unlike the engraving of him leading the Guiana expedition, this aged man with thinning white hair does not hold a baton of command. Nor does he impose himself on his viewer. The length and narrowness of his face, emphasized by the shadowed left cheek, suggest a vulnerability not denied by the subject. Unlike his son, he looks to the side, declining direct eye contact and suggesting a bemused sadness. It is easy to see why Lady Ralegh loved both of them.

Beneath each oval portrait is a small compartment containing a battle scene in which each subject led British troops to victory over Spanish forces. (A French engraving of Ralegh, with a cartouche underneath depicting his victory at Cadiz, may have provided the seed for the idea.[33]) For Wat, the scene depicts, perhaps inevitably, the fatal attack on San Thomé. In the foreground we see the English forces rushing forward, while the center of the background is dominated by a lone figure who lies on the ground—arms flung out—in the empty space between the fleeing Spaniards and the attacking English. Sword in hand, Wat has fallen while rallying his men, as accounts of the battle sympathetic to the Raleghs depict him.

For Ralegh, the options for a combat scene are numerous, and Lady Ralegh's choice of a battle which the miniature identifies as "Fial" (Fayal) is very significant. An island in the Azores, Fayal was the location of the battle in which Ralegh's behavior was most like his son's in Guiana. Acting without the permission of his absent Admiral, the earl of Essex, Ralegh led a perilous (and victorious) attack on foot against the fort, his clothes apparently being perforated by Spanish shot. (It was before this voyage that he had drawn up his will, an act very nearly prescient.) As the remark she made to Ben Jonson about her son in Paris indicates, Lady Ralegh was aware of Wat's similarity to Ralegh in his boisterous youth. From her perspective, the parallel of Ralegh's charge with Wat's more recent one would have been striking—in both cases, a successful attack is led by a valiant Walter Ralegh who disregards the chain of command and the danger of Spanish muskets. Every aspect of the locket suggests the equivalency of her husband and her child in her love.

For more than a century Lady Ralegh's locket has been disassembled, perhaps first taken apart so that both portraits could be seen when the miniature collection of Belvoir Castle was displayed in panels in its Elizabeth Saloon.[34] In her careful commentary (1903) on the collection, Victoria Manners added a useful detail: that the portrait of Wat "originally fitted into the back of the case, its present frame being a more modern one."[35]

We can imagine, then, a beautifully crafted locket in which Sir Walter's image was attached to the inside of the cover, while the miniature of Wat—similar in so many ways—faced it from the back of the case. After the entwined deaths of her husband and eldest son, Lady Ralegh's devotion realized in art what could not be accomplished in life: the union of this father and son who were so like each other, and so unlike.

Chapter Notes

Introduction

1. *The Letters of John Chamberlain.* Edited by N.E. McClure. 2 vols. (Philadelphia: American Philosophical Society, 1939), ii: 185.
2. Anna Beer, *My Just Desire: The Life of Bess Ralegh, Wife to Sir Walter* (New York: Ballantine Books, 2003). Also notable is the important, literature-focused essay by Judith Owens, "Patrilineal Ralegh," in *Literary and Visual Ralegh,* ed. Christopher M. Armitage (Manchester: Manchester University Press, 2013), 302–26.
3. For the painting (at Knole House, Kent), see Roy Strong, *Tudor & Jacobean Portraits.* 2 vols. (Her Majesty's Stationery Office, 1969), i: 258.
4. *The Letters of Sir Walter Ralegh,* ed. Agnes Latham and Joyce Youings (Exeter: University of Exeter Press, 1999), 249.
5. Friedrich Nietzsche, *The Portable Nietzsche,* trans. Walter Kaufmann (New York: Viking, 1968), 212.

Chapter One

1. The date of Wat Ralegh's birth has not been established. The Elizabethan prayer book admonished parents to baptize infants no later than the first Sunday or holy day after the birth, but often a second week was required. David Cressy, *Birth, Marriage, and Death: Ritual, Religion, and the Life-Cycle in Tudor and Stuart England* (Oxford: Oxford University Press, 1997), 101. Damerei, the Raleghs' short-lived first child, was born on 29 March and baptized on 10 April, 1592.

A.L. Rowse, *Ralegh and the Throckmortons* (London: Macmillan, 1962), 160–61.
2. My thanks to Mark Ashley-Miller, the churchwarden of St. Martin of Tours in Lillington, for photographs of this entry and the church.
3. "Wat" was a common Elizabethan nickname for "Walter." In a poem, Queen Elizabeth addresses Sir Walter as "my Wat." *Queen Elizabeth I, Selected Works,* ed. Steven W. May (New York: Washington Square Press, 2004), 16.
4. Sir Robert Naunton, *Fragmenta Regalia, or Observations on Queen Elizabeth: Her Times and Favorites,* ed. John S. Cerovski (London: Associated University Presses, 1985), 72.
5. *Elizabeth: The Golden Age.* Directed by Shekhar Kapur (Universal Studios 2007).
6. *The Letters of Sir Walter Ralegh,* ed. Agnes Latham and Joyce Youings (Exeter: University of Exeter Press, 1999), 70.
7. P.E.J. Hammer, "Sex and the Virgin Queen: Aristocratic Concupiscence and the Court of Elizabeth I," *Sixteenth Century Journal* 31 (2000), 77–97.
8. Alison Weir, *The Life of Elizabeth I* (New York: Ballantine Books, 1998), 408.
9. Anna Whitelock, *Elizabeth's Bedfellows: An Intimate History of the Queen's Court* (London: Bloomsbury, 2013), 269–70.
10. Ralegh, *The History of the World* (London: Walter Burre, 1614), II. iv. 6. Thomas Fisher Rare Book Library at the University of Toronto.
11. *Sir Walter Raleighs Instructions to his Sonne and to Posteritie.* The Second Edition (London: Benjamin Fisher, 1632), 27.

12. *The Complete Essays of Montaigne,* trans. Donald M. Frame (Stanford: Stanford University Press, 1965), 289.
13. Ralegh, *Instructions to his Sonne,* 86.
14. Ralegh, *History of the World,* "Preface."
15. Gervase Holles, *Memorials of the Holles Family, 1493–1656,* Camden 3rd Series, vol. 55 (1937), 2.
16. *Letters of Ralegh,* 265.
17. Joyce Youings, "Ralegh's Devon," in *Ralegh and Quinn: The Explorer and his Boswell,* ed. H.G. Jones (Chapel Hill: University of North Carolina Press, 1987), 75.
18. Helen Miller, "Ralegh, Walter (1504/5–81)," *History of Parliament Online,* Members, 1509–1558.
19. The document is quoted at some length in T.N. Brushfield, "Notes on the Ralegh Family," *Notes and Transactions of the Devonshire Association,* xv (1883), 173–74. The lease stipulates a yearly rent of £5.
20. Naunton, *Fragmenta Regalia,* 72.
21. *Holinshed's Chronicles,* 1808, vol. 6, 105.
22. Michael J.G. Stanford, "The Raleghs: Father and Son," in *Raleigh in Exeter,* ed. Joyce Youings (Exeter: University of Exeter Press, 1985), 93.
23. Stanford, "The Raleghs: Father and Son," 93.
24. *Holinshed's Chronicles,* 1808, vol. 3, 942.
25. For differing accounts, see Eamon Duffy, *The Stripping of the Altars,* 2nd ed. (New Haven: Yale University Press, 2005), 488–89 and Nicholls and Williams, *Sir Walter Raleigh: In Life and Legend* (London: Continuum, 2011), 5.
26. Michael J.G. Stanford, "The Raleghs Take to the Sea," *Mariner's Mirror* 48 (1962).
27. Raleigh Trevelyan, *Sir Walter Raleigh* (London: Allen Lane, 2002), 5–6.
28. Scott Smith-Bannister, *Names and Naming Patterns in England, 1538–1700* (Oxford: Clarendon, 1997), 58–59, 65.
29. *Letters of Ralegh,* 249.
30. Desiderius Erasmus, *Adages IV iii 1 to V ii 51.* Ed. John N. Grant. *Collected Works of Erasmus,* vol. 36 (Toronto: University of Toronto Press, 2006), 25 and 185. For the pressure on Elizabethan sons to imitate their fathers, see Fred B. Tromly, *Fathers and Sons in Shakespeare: The Debt Never Promised* (Toronto: University of Toronto Press, 2010), 25–33.
31. Robert Walker, *The Namesake: A Biography of Theodore Roosevelt, Jr.* (New York: Brick Tower, 2008), 19, 41.
32. *Discoveries,* ed. Lorna Hudson, in *The Collected Works of Ben Jonson,* vol. 7 (Cambridge: Cambridge University Press, 2012), 514. Apparently, the relevance of Wat Ralegh to Jonson's remark has never been noted.
33. Franz Kafka, *Letter to his Father,* trans. Ernst Kaiser and Eithne Wilkins (New York: Schocken, 1963), 115.

Chapter Two

1. William Oldys, *Life of Sir Walter Raleigh,* in *The Works of Sir Walter Raleigh,* 8 vols. (Oxford: Oxford University Press, 1829), i: 180.
2. Sir Robert Cecil to Sir Thomas Heneage, 2 September 1592, quoted in Edward Edwards, *The Life of Sir Walter Ralegh ... together with his Letters,* 2 vols. (London: Macmillan, 1868), i: 154.
3. A.L. Rowse, *Ralegh and the Throckmortons* (London: Macmillan, 1962), 161.
4. Mark Nicholls and Penry Williams, *Sir Walter Raleigh: In Life and Legend* (London: Continuum, 2011), 77.
5. *Letters of Ralegh,* 63.
6. Sir Walter Ralegh, *Instructions to his Sonne.* Second Edition. (London: Benjamin Fisher, 1632), II, 15.
7. Anna Beer, *My Just Desire: The Life of Bess Ralegh, Wife to Sir Walter* (New York: Ballantine, 2003), 69.
8. HMC 71, *Report on the Manuscripts of Allen George Finch,* ed. S.C. Lomas (London: HMSO, 1913), 1: 34.
9. Edwards, *Life of Sir Walter Ralegh,* ii: 397.
10. *Letters of Ralegh,* 119.
11. *Letters of Ralegh,* 24–25.
12. The most comprehensive account of the Raleghs and Sherborne is W.B. Wildman, *A Short History of Sherborne from 705 A.D.,* 2nd ed. (Sherborne: Bennett, 1902), 159–67. Concerning many legal maneuvers, fuller information is to be found in the notes of Agnes Latham and Joyce Youings for the *Letters of Ralegh.*
13. Ben Jonson, "To Penshurst," in *The Complete Poems,* ed. George Parfitt (Harmondsworth: Penguin, 1975), 101.

14. Ralegh's will is usefully included as an Appendix in *Letters of Ralegh*, 381–86.
15. *Letters of Ralegh*, 120.
16. Aubrey, *Brief Lives*, 420.
17. Rowse, *Ralegh and the Throckmortons*, 183.
18. Raleigh Trevelyan, *Sir Walter Raleigh* (New York: H. Holt, 2004), 294.
19. Ralegh, *Instructions to his Sonne*, II, 24–25.
20. *The Wizard Earl's Advices to his Son: A Facsimile and Transcript from the Manuscripts of Henry Percy, Ninth Earl of Northumberland*, ed. Gordon R. Batho and Stephen Clucas (Roxburghe Club, 2002), 48.
21. Ralegh, *Instructions to his Sonne*, II, 25.
22. Lady Ralegh to Robert Cecil (20 March 1595), printed in Edwards, ii: 398–99.
23. See Alice T. Friedman, *House and Household in Elizabethan England: Woolaton Hall and the Willoughby Family* (Chicago: University of Chicago Press, 1989), 46–48.
24. Ralph Houlebrooke, ed. *English Family Life 1576–1716: An Anthology from Diaries* (Oxford: Blackwell, 1988), 111.
25. *The Complete Essays of Montaigne*, trans. Donald M. Frame (Stanford: Stanford University Press, 1965), 280.
26. Anne Buck, *Clothes and the Child: A Handbook of Children's Dress in England 1500–1900* (Carlton, Bedford: Ruth Bean, 1996), 150.
27. Sir Thomas Elyot, *The Book Named the Governor*, ed. S.E. Lehmberg (London: Dent, 1962), 19.
28. Margaret P. Hannay, "'High Housewifery': The Duties and Letters of Barbara Gamage Sidney, Countess of Leicester," *Early Modern Women: An Interdisciplinary Journal*, 1 (2006). Online.
29. *The Wizard Earl's Advices*, xix.
30. Rachel Hassall, archivist at the Sherborne School, noted in a helpful correspondence that, while the early records are incomplete, any indication of the Ralegh and Cecil scions' attendance would have been seized on and claimed long ago.
31. *Letters of Ralegh*, 188.
32. Fred B. Tromly, "Lord Burghley's 'Ten Precepts' for his Son, Robert Cecil: a New Date and Interpretation," *Historical Research*, 88 (2015), 185–91.
33. For Daniel Featley's comments on Wat, see Chapter Eight.
34. Ursula Potter, "Cockering Mothers and Humanist Pedagogy in Two Tudor School Plays," in *Domestic Arrangements in Early Modern England*, ed. Kari Boyd McBride (Pittsburgh: Duquesne University Press, 2002), 244–45.
35. Edward Thompson, *Sir Walter Ralegh: The Last of the Elizabethans* (London: Macmillan, 1935), 274.
36. *The Correspondence of Sir Philip Sidney*, ed. Roger Kuin, 2 vols. (Oxford: Oxford University Press, 2012), 1: 3. In another version of the commonplace, Christopher Wandesford urges his son George to "Learn to obey when you are young, so that you may be fit to govern when you are old." Quoted in Felicity Heal and Clive Holmes, *The Gentry in England and Wales, 1500–1700* (London: Macmillan, 1994), 243.
37. Ben Jonson, *Complete Poems*, 424.
38. Richard Mulcaster, *Positions Concerning the Training Up of Children*, ed. William Barker (Toronto: University of Toronto Press, 1994), 186. I am indebted to Judith Owens for this reference.
39. Richard Carew, *The Survey of Cornwall* (1602), ed. John Chynoweth, Nicholas Orme, and Alexandra Walsham (Exeter: Devon and Cornwall Record Society, 2004), 64. Ralegh, to whom the book was dedicated, was a cousin of Carew.

Chapter Three

1. Natalie Mears, "*Regnum Cecilianum*? A Cecilian Perspective of the Court," in *The Reign of Elizabeth I: Court and Culture in the Last Decade*, edited by John Guy (Cambridge: Cambridge University Press, 1995), 48.
2. Sir Thomas Wilson, *The State of England anno. Dom. 1600*, ed. F.J. Fisher, *Camden Miscellany*. 3rd Series (London, 1936), vol. xvi, 52.
3. *Sir Walter Raleighs Instructions to his Sonne: and to Posteritie*. The Second Edition (London: Benjamin Fisher: 1632), II, 16–17.
4. Ralegh, *History of the World*, I, iv, 5.

5. Ralegh, *Instructions to his Sonne. The Second Edition* (London: Benjamin Fisher, 1632), II, 16.
6. Ralegh, *History of the World*, V, iii, 17.
7. *The Letters of Ralegh*, 247.
8. Margaret P. Hannay, "'High Housewifery': The Duties and Letters of Barbara Gamage Sidney, Countess of Leicester," *Early Modern Women: An Interdisciplinary Journal*, 1 (2006). Online.
9. *OED*, s.v. "kind, n.," I. i. a.
10. *Aubrey's Brief Lives*, ed. Oliver Lawson Dick (Harmondsworth: Penguin, 1972), 422.
11. Anne Buck, *Clothes and the Child: A Handbook of Children's Dress in England 1500–1900* (Carlton, Bedford: Ruth Bean, 1996), 150.
12. *HMC, Sixth Report. Part I: Report and Appendix* (London, 1877), 228.
13. *Letters of Ralegh*, 156.
14. *Letters of Ralegh*, 188.
15. Edward Edwards, *The Life of Sir Walter Ralegh*. 2 vols. (London: Macmillan, 1868), ii: 405.
16. HMC Salisbury MSS, 10: 459. Since Will's charming note ended up in the Cecil archives at Hatfield House, an amused and flattered Ralegh must have forwarded it to the boy's distant father.
17. HMC Salisbury MSS, 10: 459.
18. *History of the World* (Oldys, 8: 57) quoted in Rowse, 261.
19. For an illustration, see Jane Ashelforde, *A Visual History of Costume* (London: Batsford, 1983), i: 84.
20. Buck, *Clothes and the Child*, 159–61.
21. In the National Portrait Gallery, there is a painting of Prince Henry who stands in Ralegh's pose, but with the dark curtain behind him pulled aside to reveal a window looking onto a garden. It is reproduced in Robert Lacey, *Sir Walter Ralegh* (London: Weidenfeld & Nicolson, 1973).
22. Joaneath Spicer, "The Renaissance Elbow," in *A Cultural History of Gesture: From Antiquity to the Present Day*. Edited by Jan Bremmer and Herman Roodenburg (Cambridge: Polity, 1991), 84–128.
23. Spicer, 115, 118.
24. For illustrations of standing portraits in which armor appears under the subject's crooked elbow, see Roy Strong, *Tudor & Jacobean Portraits*. 2 vols. (London: Her Majesty's Stationery Office, 1969), 2: plates 382–83 (the Earl of Leicester by Federico Zuccaro) and plate 589 (the earl of Southampton).
25. Strong, *Tudor & Jacobean Portraits*, 1: 257–58.
26. See, for instance, Jean Wilson, "The Noble Imp: The Upper-Class Child in English Renaissance Art and Literature," *Antiquaries Journal* 70 (1990), 367.
27. The Conveyance of Freehold is to be found in the archives at Sherborne Castle. For detailed commentary on the document, see Mark Nicholls and Penry Williams, *Sir Walter Raleigh: In Life and Legend* (London: Continuum, 2011), 173–74.
28. Raleigh Trevelyan, *Sir Walter Raleigh* (London: Allen Lane, 2002), 170.
29. Timothy Mowl, *Elizabethan and Jacobean Style* (London: Phaidon, 1993), 188.
30. The rather sordid story is told in Joel Hurstfield, *The Queen's Wards: Wardship and Marriage under Elizabeth I* (London: Longmans, Green, 1958), 301–04. Also I am indebted to communications from David Swinscoe, who has written widely on the history of Blore and Staffordshire.
31. Lucy Worsley, *Cavalier: a Tale of Chivalry, Passion and Great Houses* (London: Faber & Faber, 2007), 67. David Swinscoe notes that "With the apparent consent of Cecil and Cobham, the four year old Elizabeth was betrothed" to Wat.
32. Henry Lancaster and Ben Coates, "Dallison, Sir Roger (c.1562–1620)," *History of Parliament Online*, Member, 1604–1629.
33. HMC, Salisbury, 17: 573.
34. *Observations upon Some Particular Persons and Passages in a Book lately made publick written by a Lover of the Truth* (London, 1656), 12.
35. *Montaigne's Essays*, trans. John Florio, 3 vols. (London: J.M. Dent, 1965), ii: 496. A *New Yorker* cartoon turns Montaigne's suggestion into broad comedy. It shows two men whose many similarities include large, malformed posteriors; the younger says to the older, "Thanks, dad, for almost everything."
36. Bodleian Library, Rawlinson MS 47, 54b.

Chapter Four

1. Ralegh's exhortation to Wat is discussed in Chapter Five and his treatise of advice in Chapter Seven.
2. For descriptions of these manuscripts, see Peter Beal's online *Catalogue of English Literary Manuscripts 1450–1700* (www.celm-ms-org.uk), which is also available in printed volumes. Under "Sir Walter Ralegh" the relevant entries are numbered RaW 316–319.
3. Willard M. Wallace, *Sir Walter Raleigh* (Princeton: Princeton University Press, 1959), 267.
4. Respectively, Stephen Coote, *A Play of Passion: The Life of Sir Walter Ralegh* (London: Macmillan, 1993), 329 and Steven May, *Sir Walter Ralegh* (Boston: Twayne, 1989), 70.
5. The excellent biographies by Robert Lacey and by Mark Nicholls and Penry Williams do not mention the poem. Raleigh Trevelyan prints the entire poem but ventures no comment except to observe that Ralegh was "obviously a little alarmed about Wat's behaviour." *Sir Walter Raleigh* (London: Allen Lane, 2002), 422–23.
6. Frost calls the poem "the Wood, the Weed, the Wag." *The Notebooks of Robert Frost*, ed. Robert Faggen (Cambridge, MA: Harvard University Press, 2006), 254.
7. *The Poems of Sir Walter Ralegh*, ed. Agnes Latham (London: Routledge & Kegan Paul, 1951), 49.
8. Linda Gregerson, "Sir Walter Ralegh to His Son," *The Atlantic Online*, http://www.theatlantic.com/unbound/poetry/soundings/ralegh.htm. Accessed 3/3/2009.
9. Judith Owens, "Patrilineal Ralegh," in *Literary and Visual Ralegh*, ed. Christopher M. Armitage (Manchester: Manchester University Press, 2013), 326.
10. "Affectionate teasing" is from May, *Sir Walter Ralegh*, 70.
11. OED, s.v. *part*, I.1.b.
12. Gregerson, "Sir Walter Ralegh to his Son."
13. *The Poems of Sir Walter Ralegh: An Historical Edition*, ed. Michael Rudick (Tempe, AZ: Center for Medieval and Renaissance Studies, 1999), 125.
14. Rudick, 176.
15. On the night before his execution, Ralegh is said to have added two lines to the end of an earlier poem. See *Poems of Walter Ralegh*, ed. Latham, 72, 152–56. This poem is printed at the end of Chapter Ten.
16. This text is RaW 319 (CELM) from Folger MS V.a.162.
17. These texts are RaW 316 and RaW 318 (CELM), the latter of which is printed in Rudick, 125.
18. Text from Rudick, ed., *Poems of Sir Walter Ralegh*, 125.
19. For a subtle reading of this version that emphasizes the speaker's loss of authority, see Owens, "Patrilineal Ralegh," 322–26.
20. Stephen Greenblatt, *Sir Walter Ralegh: The Renaissance Man and his Roles* (New Haven: Yale University Press, 1973).
21. Margaret Irwin, *That Great Lucifer: A Portrait of Sir Walter Ralegh* (London: Chatto & Windus, 1960), 203.
22. R.H. Bowers, "Ralegh's Last Speech: The 'Elms' Document," *Review of English Studies*, n.s., 21 (1951), 215.

Chapter Five

1. The enemy is Anthony Bagot, a supporter of Essex. H.M.C. *Fourth Report*, Appendix (London: 1874), 338.
2. John Aubrey, *Aubrey's Brief Lives*, ed. Oliver Lawson Dick (Harmondsworth: Penguin, 1972), 420.
3. In this and the following two paragraphs, I am indebted to Andrew Thrush for making available his unpublished entry on Lord Cobham for the *History of Parliament*, Members, 1603–1628.
4. Mark Nicholls and Penry Williams, *Sir Walter Raleigh: In Life and Legend* (London: Continuum, 2011), 206. The account of the trial in this volume is notably well-balanced (189–222).
5. *The Letters of Sir Walter Ralegh*, ed. Agnes M.C. Latham and Joyce Youings (Exeter: University of Exeter Press, 1999), 291.
6. *Letters of Ralegh*, 259.
7. For the psychological effects of attainder on Ralegh, see Brady J. Spangenberg, "Civil Death in Early Modern Europe, from Jack Cade to Luther, Hamlet, and Raleigh." PhD diss., Purdue University, 2011.
8. Quoted in Robert Lacey, *Sir Walter*

Ralegh (London: Weidenfeld & Nicolson, 1973), 304.

9. In early modern English, "posterity" in the plural usually refers to multiple future generations (*OED*, 2.b.).

10. *Letters of Ralegh*, 308.

11. William Blackstone, *Commentary on the Laws of England*, 4 vols. (1768), ii: 251.

12. *House of Commons Journal* for 25 March 1651 (London, 1808), vol. 6: 552–53.

13. *Letters of Ralegh*, 249.

14. *Letters of Ralegh*, 287. This claim may have been Ralegh's attempt to avoid recent legislation that declared conveyances null and void if they were devised to circumvent legal penalties.

15. In their introduction to the *Letters*, Latham and Youings plausibly suggest that Ralegh's concern was to avoid guardianship (xlvii).

16. In the Sherborne archives, the document is referred to as the "Deed of Trust 1603" and catalogued as SHR//ML8. My thanks to Mr. K.E. Wingfield Digby for permission to quote from the document.

17. Shakespeare, *Macbeth*, Act Four, Scene One.

18. *Letters of Ralegh*, 308.

19. Ralegh, *Instructions to his Sonne* (London: Benjamin Fisher, 1632), V, 65. For Carew, *House of Commons Journal*, vol. 6: 552–53.

20. *Letters of Ralegh*, 286.

21. John Aubrey, *Aubrey's Brief Lives*, ed. Oliver Lawson Dick (Harmondsworth: Penguin, 1972), 416.

22. *Letters of Ralegh*, 317. Though the exhortation was probably not intended to be a letter, the editors usefully include it in their volume (317–18).

23. For the early date, see Fred B. Tromly, "Sir Walter Ralegh Instructs his Son, Twice," *Notes and Queries*, n.s. 56 (2009), 616–19.

24. See Quentin Skinner, "Political Philosophy" in *The Cambridge History of Renaissance Philosophy*, ed. Charles B. Schmitt and Quentin Skinner (Cambridge: Cambridge University Press, 1988), 421–23.

25. Thomas Nashe, *Works*, edited by Ronald B. McKerrow and F.P. Wilson, 5 vols. (Oxford: Blackwell, 1966), i: 319.

26. Gervase Holles, *Memorials of the Holles Family*, edited by A.C. Wood. (London: 1937), Camden Society, 3rd ser., vol. 55, 4. Holles cites the chapter "On Nobility" in Pierre Charron's *On Wisdome*, a book Ralegh knew.

27. For this meaning of "troublesome," see *OED* 2.a.

28. *History of the World*, "Preface," C4v.

Chapter Six

1. *The Letters of Sir Walter Ralegh*, ed. Agnes Latham and Joyce Youings (Exeter: Exeter University Press, 1999), 263.

2. Ralegh's earlier farewell letter to Bess is discussed in Chapter Three.

3. For family blessings, see Bruce Young, "Parental Blessings in Shakespeare's Plays," *Studies in Philology*, 89 (1992), 179–209.

4. *Letters of Ralegh*, 265.

5. *Letters of Ralegh*, 287.

6. *History of the World*, V. ii: 2.

7. Edmund Tilney, quoted in Sid Ray, "'Those Whom God Hath Joined Together': Bondage Metaphors and Marital Advice in Early Modern England," in Kari Boyd McBride, ed., *Domestic Arrangements in Early Modern England* (Pittsburgh: Duquesne University Press, 2002), 287n and 38–39.

8. A.L. Rowse, *Ralegh and the Throckmortons* (London: Macmillan, 1962), 276.

9. Edward Edwards, *The Life of Sir Walter Ralegh*, 2 vols. (London: Macmillan, 1868), ii: 439.

10. *Works* (1829), viii: 573.

11. *Letters of Ralegh*, 253.

12. Robert Lacey, *Sir Walter Ralegh* (London: Weidenfeld & Nicolson, 1973), 317.

13. Henry Percy, Ninth Earl of Northumberland, *The Wizard Earl's Advices to his Son*, ed. Gordon R. Batho and Stephen Clucas (Roxburghe Club, 2002), xix.

14. *HMC Salisbury MSS* 17, 376 and 379.

15. William Hepworth Dixon, *Her Majesty's Tower*. Sixth Edition (London: Hurst and Blackett, 1870), i: 345.

16. *Letters of Ralegh*, 285.

17. *Letters of Ralegh*, 286. In 1623 she was residing in the neighborhood when fire from the Broad Street storehouse of the monopolist Alderman Cockayne spread to her dwelling, which had to be pulled down. *The*

Letters of John Chamberlain, ed. N.E. Mc-Clure (Philadelphia: American Philosophical Society, 1939), ii: 253–54.

18. Nicholls and Williams, 229.

19. *HMC Salisbury MSS* 17, 548.

20. Respectively, Nicholls and Williams, 235 and Anna Beer, *My Just Desire: The Life of Bess Ralegh, Wife to Sir Walter* (New York: Ballantine, 2003), 84.

21. *HMC Salisbury MSS* 17, 444.

22. For Waad and his patron Cecil, see Fiona Bengtsen, *Sir William Waad: Lieutenant of the Tower & the Gunpowder Plot* (Victoria, B.C.: Trafford, 2005), 24–31.

23. *HMC Salisbury MSS* 16, 193. The note is from the Lieutenant of the Tower to Robert Cecil (30 July 1604).

24. Joseph Foster, *Alumni Oxonienses 1500–1714*, 4 vols. (Oxford: Parker, 1891–92), 4: 454. Also George C. Brodrick, *Memorials of Merton College with Biographical Notices of the Wardens and Fellows*. Oxford Historical Society, vol. 4 (Oxford: Clarendon, 1885), 276.

25. Lady Ralegh was a friend of Mary Talbot, widow of the earl of Shrewsbury and a politically sympathetic neighbor on Tower Hill. After John Talbot's death Ralegh asked Lady Ralegh to aid Talbot's mother, whose relationship to Mary Talbot is not known.

26. *HMC Salisbury MSS* 17, 444.

27. Ralegh, *The Discovery of Guiana and the Journal of the Second Voyage Thereto*, ed. Sir Robert A. Schomburgk (London: Cassell, 1887), 172.

28. The documents are noted in *HMC Salisbury MSS* 18, 459; their significance was pointed out by Pierre Lefranc, *Sir Walter Ralegh, Écrivain: L'oeuvre et les Idées* (Paris: A. Colin, 1968), 269.

29. Henry Percy, *Wizard Earl's Advices*, ed. Gordon R. Batho and Stephen Clucas (Roxburghe Club, 2002), xxxvii.

30. Edward Thompson, *Sir Walter Ralegh: The Last of the Elizabethans* (London: Macmillan, 1935), 213.

31. *Letters of Ralegh*, 286, fn. 2.

32. John Bellamy, *The Tudor Law of Treason* (Toronto: University of Toronto Press, 1979), 216.

33. *Letters of Ralegh*, 285.

34. Edwards, ii: 407.

35. W.B. Wildman, *A Short History of Sherborne*, 2nd. ed. (Sherborne: Bennet, 1902), 162.

36. *Letters of Ralegh*, 272.

37. A.R. Mimardière, "Wingfield, Edward (c. 1562–1603) of Kimbolton, Hunts.," *History of Parliament Online*, Members, 1558–1603.

38. Edwards, ii: 409–11.

39. Wildman, 163. See *Calendar of State Papers Domestic*, 1603–10, vol. 8, p. 138.

40. *The Letters of Philip Gawdy*, ed. Isaac Herbert Jeayes (London: J.B. Nichols, 1906), 152–53. The letter is dated 15 November 1604.

41. For Gawdy's rejected proposal to Elizabeth Throckmorton, see Beer, 32–33.

42. Nicholls and Williams, 230.

43. Brady J. Spangenberg, *Civil Death in Early Modern Europe, from Jack Cade to Luther, Hamlet, and Ralegh* (Unpublished dissertation, Purdue University, 2011), 176. The easiest way to track the narrative of change is in Wildman, 159–67.

44. *Letters of John Chamberlain*, i: 280.

45. "A brief Relation of Sir Walter Ralegh's Troubles: with the taking away of the Lands and Castles of Sherburn," in *The Works of Sir Walter Ralegh, kt.*, 8 vols. (Oxford: Oxford University Press, 1829), viii: 788. The author is Carew Ralegh or an associate of his.

46. *Letters of Ralegh*, 292.

47. Quoted in Nicholls and Williams, 230.

48. *Letters of Ralegh*, 332.

49. *Letters of Ralegh*, 305.

Chapter Seven

1. Ralegh's poem is discussed in Chapter Four and his exhortation in Chapter Five.

2. Edward Thompson, *Sir Walter Ralegh: The Last of the Elizabethans* (London: Macmillan, 1935), 232.

3. Some points in this paragraph (and following ones) are more fully discussed in Fred B. Tromly, "Masks of Impersonality in Burghley's 'Ten Precepts' and Ralegh's *Instructions to his Son*," *Review of English Studies* n.s. 66 (2015), 480–500.

4. The most notable exception is the 'Ten Precepts' that William Lord Burghley

wrote for Robert Cecil, who was his second son (born to a second wife and much preferred to his elder brother).

5. For many examples of paternal instruction in families of the gentry, see Felicity Heal and Clive Holmes, *The Gentry in England and Wales, 1500–1700* (London: Macmillan, 1994), Index, s.v. "advice literature."

6. Sir Walter Raleigh's *Instructions to his Sonne: and to Posteritie*. Second Edition (London: Benjamin Fisher, 1632), V, 61. This remains the best text of the *Instructions*, as there is no reliable modern edition. Since this text is not easily available, I have tried to make my quotations from it more easily locatable in modern texts (such as that in *Advice to a Son*, ed. Louis B. Wright, 1962) by citing chapter numbers (in Roman numerals) as well as page numbers. These references will be cited parenthetically in the text.

7. The passage is discussed in Chapter Three.

8. For examples, see A.L. Rowse, *Ralegh and the Throckmortons* (London: Macmillan, 1962), 326 and Paul Hyland, *Ralegh's Last Journey* (London: Harper Collins, 2004), 218.

9. Agnes Latham, "Sir Walter Ralegh's Instructions to his Son," in *Elizabethan and Jacobean Studies Presented to Frank Percy Wilson* (Oxford: Clarendon, 1959), 210.

10. Latham, "Sir Walter Ralegh's *Instructions*," 210 and Thompson, *Sir Walter Ralegh*, 232.

11. William Cecil, Lord Burghley, "Certain Precepts for the Well Ordering of a Man's Life," in *Advice to a Son*, ed. Louis B. Wright (Ithaca, NY: Folger Library, 1962), 9.

12. For the relevance of Burghley's advice to Robert Cecil, see Fred B. Tromly, "Lord Burghley's 'Ten Precepts' for his Son, Robert Cecil: A New Date and Interpretation," *Historical Research* 88 (2015), 185–91.

13. Fred B. Tromly, "Sir Walter Ralegh Instructs his Son, Twice," *Notes and Queries* ns 56 (2009), 616–19.

14. Burghley, in Wright, 9.

15. Steven W. May, *Sir Walter Ralegh* (Boston: Twayne, 1989), 69.

16. For examples of Ralegh's advice reflecting his own, often unacknowledged, experience, see Tromly, "Masks of Impersonality," 492–93.

17. Philip Edwards, *Sir Walter Ralegh* (London: Longmans, Green, 1953), 143.

18. Latham, "Ralegh's Instructions to his Son," 206–07.

19. Judith Owens, "Patrilineal Ralegh," in *Literary and Visual Ralegh*, ed. Christopher M. Armitage (Manchester: Manchester University Press, 2013), 318.

20. Sir Walter Ralegh, *The Letters of Sir Walter Ralegh*, ed. Agnes Latham and Joyce Youings (Exeter: Exeter University Press, 1999), 249. See the discussion in Chapter Three.

21. Robert Lacey is certain of 1607, assuming it was written "for young Wat's benefit before the boy went off to Oxford." *Sir Walter Ralegh* (London: Weidenfeld & Nicolson, 1973), 343. Cautiously, Mark Nicholls and Penry Williams suggest it was written "in about 1609." *Sir Walter Raleigh: In Life and Legend* (London: Continuum, 2011), 252.

22. Thomas Howard's letter to his children is printed in Neville Williams, *Thomas Howard, Fourth Duke of Norfolk* (London: Barrie and Rockliff, 1964), 239–46.

23. For commentary on this point, see Owens, "Patrilineal Ralegh," 320–21 and the final pages of Tromly, "Masks of Impersonality."

24. *History of the World* (1614), Bk I, Chap. ix, Subsection 1.

25. *The Complete Essays of Montaigne*, trans. Donald M. Frame (Stanford: Stanford University Press, 1965), 291.

26. For Ralegh's tracts for Prince Henry, see Steven W. May, *Sir Walter Ralegh* (Boston: Twayne, 1989), 71–78.

27. Roy Strong, *Henry, Prince of Wales and England's Lost Renaissance* (London: Thames & Hudson, 1986), 51.

28. *History of the World*, V, vi, 12.

Chapter Eight

1. Lawrence Stone, "The Size and Composition of the Oxford Student Body 1580–1910," in Lawrence Stone, ed., *The University in Society*, vol. 1: *Oxford and Cambridge from the 14th to the Early 19th Century* (Princeton: Princeton University Press, 1974), 25.

2. For the changing social function of the universities, see Hugh Kearney, *Scholars and Gentlemen: Universities and Society in Pre-Industrial Britain 1500–1700* (London: Faber and Faber, 1970), esp. 27–28.

3. Ralegh, *Instructions to his Sonne: and to Posteritie*. Second Edition (London: Benjamin Fisher, 1632), 29.

4. John Aubrey, *Brief Lives*, ed. Andrew Clark. 2 vols. (Oxford: Clarendon, 1898), ii: 179.

5. Joseph Foster, *Alumni Oxonienses: The Members of the University of Oxford*, 4 vols. (Oxford: Parker, 1891–1892), iii: 1230.

6. For the age distribution of matriculants at Oxford in 1605–07, see Stephen Porter, "University and Society," in *The University of Oxford in the Seventeenth Century*, ed. Nicholas Tyacke, vol. 4 of *The History of the University of Oxford* (Oxford: Clarendon, 1997), 57.

7. "Sir William Wentworth's Advice to His Son," in *Wentworth Papers 1597–1628*, ed. J.P. Cooper, *Camden Fourth Series*, vol. 12 (London: Royal Historical Society, 1973), 21.

8. For Corpus and the West, see Porter, "University and Society," 195.

9. HMC, Salisbury MSS, 17: 444.

10. Joseph Foster, *Alumni Oxonienses*, ii: 679.

11. For Hawthorne's church career, see *CCEd* (Clergy of the Church of England Database), where he is listed as Person ID: 13076.

12. Joseph Foster, *Alumni Oxonienses*, ii: 741.

13. Thomas Fowler, *The History of Corpus Christi College* (Oxford: Clarendon, 1893), 178.

14. Fowler, *History of Corpus Christi*, 393.

15. Edward Edwards' account of the relationships among Ralegh, Lady Ralegh, and the two Oxford tutors is extremely misleading. *The Life of Sir Walter Ralegh*, 2 vols. (London: Macmillan, 1868), i: 623–24.

16. For Featley's drafts of letters to Ralegh, see n. 18 below.

17. Anna V. Danushevskaya, "The Formation of a Renaissance Nobleman: William Cecil, 2nd Earl of Salisbury 1591–1668," *History of Education* 31 (2002), 509.

18. The Featley manuscript is Bodleian MS Rawlinson 47; the three drafts to Ralegh appear on ff. 54b, 56b, and 57–57b. Quotations from the manuscript are cited parenthetically in the text. The first draft was printed (with a number of errors) in Anthony Wood, *Athenae Oxonienses*, edited by P. Bliss. 4 vols. (London: Rivington, 1813–20), 3: 170.

19. In what is probably his last letter to Ralegh, Featley refers to a "Mr. Dr. Allen," who is the Richard Allen named Doctor of Divinity on 30 June 1608 (Foster, *Alumni Oxonienses*, i: 17). In the same letter, Featley refers to the plague, which a modern historian notes "threatened Oxford and Cambridge in the autumn of 1608, breaking up the term at Cambridge." Victor Morgan, *A History of the University of Cambridge*, vol. 2, *1546–1750* (Cambridge: Cambridge University Press, 2004), 317.

20. *OED*, "carriage," I. 14. 15.

21. Galen, *Hygiene*, trans. Robert M. Green (Toronto: Ryerson, 1951), 82, 86.

22. "Sir William Wentworth's Advice to His Son," *Wentworth Papers*, 21. Ralegh's friend Henry Percy, Earl of Northumberland, also cautioned his son to avoid harmful forms of exercise. Henry Percy, *The Wizard Earl's Advices to his Son*, ed. Gordon R. Batho and Stephen Clucas (London: Roxburghe Club, 2002), 26.

23. For hunting hare on foot, see James McConica, "The Collegiate Society" in *The Collegiate University*, ed. James McConica, vol. 3 of *The History of the University of Oxford* (Oxford: Clarendon, 1986), 651. For tennis, see Robert Dallington, *A Method of Travel* (London: Thomas Creede, 1605), sig. B4v.

24. Stephen Porter, "University and Society," 71–72.

25. HMC, *MSS of the Duke of Rutland* (London, 1888), 1: 195.

26. *OED*, "strange," I. 1, 2, 5.

27. McConica, "The Collegiate Society," 651–52.

28. For the "great horse," see Percy Manning, "Sport and Pastime in Stuart Oxford," in *Surveys and Tokens*, ed. H.E. Salter, Oxford Historical Society, 75 (Oxford: Clarendon, 1923), 116–17.

29. Rosemary O'Day, *Education and Society 1500–1800* (New York: Longman, 1982), 115–16.

30. Aubrey, *Brief Lives*, ed. Clark, ii: 194.
31. Anthony Wood, *Athenae Oxonienses*. Edited by P. Bliss. 4 vols. (London: Rivington, 1813–20), ii: 603.
32. Aubrey, *Brief Lives*, 418, 184. For Chester and Aubrey's anecdote, see Mathew Steggle, "Charles Chester and Ben Jonson," *Studies in English Literature* 39 (1999), 313–26.
33. For the statutory curriculum, see J.M. Fletcher, "The Faculty of Arts," in *The Collegiate University*, vol. 3 of *The History of the University of Oxford*, 165–81.
34. Fletcher, "The Faculty of Arts," 165–66.
35. The document is printed in *Letters of Ralegh*, 314–15.

Chapter Nine

1. A.L. Rowse, *Ralegh and the Throckmortons* (London: Macmillan, 1962), 285.
2. Rowse, *Ralegh*, 285.
3. Anna Beer, *My Just Desire: The Life of Bess Ralegh, Wife to Sir Walter* (New York: Ballantine, 2003), 192–93.
4. See the extensive summary of Throckmorton's travel diary in Rowse, 80–94.
5. Felicity Heal and Clive Barnes estimate the average cost for a student from the gentry at between £30 and £50 a year, but Wat's clothing, social activities, and multiple tutors would surely have amounted to considerably more. *The Gentry in England and Wales, 1500–1700* (Basingstoke: Macmillan, 1994), 262.
6. In his guide to travel in France, Robert Dallington estimated a minimal yearly expense of £80 for a gentleman traveller but cautioned that fashionable activities (fencing, dancing, and especially riding) easily could raise the cost to £150. *A Method of Travell* (London: Thomas Creede, 1605), sig. C.
7. John Stoye identifies Will Cecil, Henry Lord Clifford and William Lord Roos as scions who spent on tour more than £1,000 per annum. *English Travellers Abroad 1604–1667*, rev. ed. (New Haven, CT: Yale University Press, 1989), 34.
8. Anna V. Danushevskaya, "The Formation of a Renaissance Nobleman: William Cecil, 2nd Earl of Salisbury 1591–1668," *History of Education* 31 (2010), 514.

9. In a note to John Aubrey, which is in places confused, the aged Izaak Walton said that Camden had secured Jonson's employment with Ralegh. See *Ben Jonson*, ed. C.H. Herford and Percy Simpson, ten vols. (Oxford: Clarendon, 1925), 1: 181.
10. For Jonson's contribution to Ralegh's *History*, see Brandon S. Centerwall, "A Reconsideration of Ben Jonson's Contribution to Sir Walter Ralegh's *The History of the World* (1614)," *Ben Jonson Journal* 7 (2000), 539–54.
11. Ben Jonson, *The Complete Poems*, edited by George Parfitt (Harmondsworth, Middlesex: Penguin, 1975), from "Epigram 132," 86.
12. "Informations to William Drummond of Hawthornden," ed. Ian Donaldson, in *The Cambridge Edition of the Works of Ben Jonson*, ed. David Bevington et al., 7 vols. (Cambridge: Cambridge University Press, 2008), 5: 372. In ancient Rome *opima spolia* were the arms taken by a general from his defeated counterpart; Jonson's account inflates his heroic stature but is not necessarily untrue.
13. Ian Donaldson, *Ben Jonson: A Life* (Oxford: Oxford University Press, 2011), 285, 287.
14. Clare Howard, *English Travellers of the Renaissance* (London: John Lane, 1914), 152.
15. Jonson, *Complete Poems*, from "A Celebration of Charis in Ten Lyric Pieces," 140.
16. David Riggs, *Ben Jonson: A Life* (Cambridge, MA: Harvard University Press, 1989), 187.
17. *The Cambridge Edition of the Works of Ben Jonson Online, Life Records*, ed. Eugene Giddens and Hester Lees-Jeffries, LR44.
18. Dallington, *A Method of Travell*, sig. C. For the attraction of fencing and dueling for young Englishmen in Paris, see Stoye, 38–40.
19. *Hamlet*, act IV, scene vii, ll. 69–91, in *Hamlet*, ed. G.R. Hibbard (Oxford: Oxford University Press, 1987), 315–16.
20. Andrew Thrush, "Puckering, Sir Thomas, 1st Bt. (1591–1637), of the Priory, Warwick," *History of Parliament Online*, Members, 1604–29.
21. Edward Herbert, *The Life of Edward, First Lord Herbert of Cherbury*, edited by

J.M. Shuttleworth (London: Oxford University Press, 1976), 45.
22. "Informations to William Drummond," *Works of Ben Jonson*, 374–75.
23. *The Poems of Sir Walter Ralegh*, ed. Agnes Latham (London: Routledge & Kegan Paul, 1951), 49.
24. *Ben Jonson*, ed. C.H. Herford and P. Simpson, 1: 165. The story was recounted by William Oldys, Ralegh's first editor, who found it (he says) in a manuscript written by a secretary to Philip Earl of Pembroke, Jonson's patron.
25. *Works of Ben Jonson Online, Life Records*, LR95a. The clergyman was Archdeacon Thomas Plume, who probably set down his little anecdote in the 1650s. He did not have access to Drummond's version.
26. *Ben Jonson*, eds. C.H. Herford and E. Simpson, 10: 141–42.
27. Ben Jonson, *Bartholomew Fair*, edited by Edward B. Partridge (Lincoln: University of Nebraska Press, 1964), 156 (5.4.94–97).
28. Thomas Coryate, quoted in Donaldson, *Ben Jonson*, 298.
29. Riggs, *Ben Jonson*, 190.
30. *Works of Ben Jonson Online, Life Records*, LR45.
31. *Works of Ben Jonson Online, Life Records*, LR46.
32. Upon leaving Oxford, Featley became chaplain for Sir Thomas Edmondes, the English ambassador in Paris. See Hugh Adlington, "Chaplains to Embassies: Daniel Featley, Anti-Catholic Controversialist Abroad," in Hugh Adlington, ed., *Chaplains in Early Modern England: Patronage, Literature and Religion* (Manchester: Manchester University Press, 2013), 83–102.
33. Pierre Lefranc, *Sir Walter Ralegh Écrivain* (Paris: A. Colin, 1968), 339.
34. *Works of Ben Jonson Online, Life Records*, LR47.
35. Daniela Prögler, *English Students at Leiden University, 1575–1650* (Burlington, VT: Ashgate, 1962).
36. Jonson's visit to Leiden was first postulated by David McPherson, "Ben Jonson Meets Daniel Heinsius, 1613," *English Language Notes* 44 (1976), 105–09.
37. Jonson, *Complete Poems*, from line 135 of "An Expostulation upon Vulcan," 185.

38. I am indebted to Dr. Daniela Prögler for confirming that Wat was indeed a student at Leiden and for providing me with the matriculation entry, which appears in MS ASF 7 (Archief van Senaat en Faculteiten, Volumina inscriptionum, 1575–1618) in Universiteitsbibliotheek, Leiden.
39. Wat Ralegh's attendance at the university came to my attention through a passing remark in Benjamin B. Roberts, *Sex and Drugs before Rock 'n' Roll: Youth Culture and Masculinity during Holland's Golden Age* (Amsterdam: Amsterdam University Press, 2012), 132.
40. For the reference to the university court, I am indebted to a communication from Dr. Martine Zoeteman. John Stoye notes that in 1641 John Evelyn matriculated by paying a dollar, which also allowed him freedom from excise duties (*English Travellers Abroad*, 178).
41. Prögler, *English Students at Leiden University*, 234–38.
42. Roberts, *Sex and Drugs*, 119.
43. Dr. Martine Zoeteman kindly ascertained that there are no extant records of students who studied fencing at the university.
44. Herford and Simpson, *Complete Works of Ben Jonson*, 1: 181.
45. Jonson, "Informations to William Drummond," 375.
46. Jonson, "Informations to William Drummond," 370.
47. Jonson, *Complete Poems*, 161.

Chapter Ten

1. For English travelers and the war in the Low Countries, see John Stoye, *English Travellers Abroad 1604–1667*, rev. ed. (New Haven, CT: Yale University Press, 1989), 187–92.
2. John Aubrey, *Brief Lives*, ed. Andrew Clark, 2 vols. (Oxford: Clarendon, 1898), 2: 179.
3. *Acts of the Privy Council of England*, vol. 11: 1578–1580, ed. John Roche Dasent (London: HMSO, 1895), 445, 121, 129.
4. *Acts of the Privy Council*, vol. 11: 384, 121, 129.
5. For the naval expedition and Thomas's subsequent knighthood, see A. H. D.,

"Perrot, Sir John (1528–92)" in *History of Parliament Online*, Members, 1558–1603.

6. *APC*, vol 11, 388–89.

7. *APC*, vol. 11, 421.

8. Ralegh may have had a minor role in the drama, for as a follower of Oxford he was said to have been dispatched to present Sidney with terms for the duel. See D.C. Peck, "Raleigh, Sidney, Oxford, and the Catholics, 1579," *Notes and Queries* 223 (1978), 428.

9. Of several contemporaries of the name, Ralegh's opponent was more likely Edward Wingfield (c.1562–1603) than his cousin (another eldest son) Edward Maria Wingfield (c.1550–c.1614). See their biographies in *History of Parliament Online*, Members, 1558–1603.

10. For the charges made against the Earl of Oxford by Charles Arundell and Henry Howard, see Mathew Lyons, *The Favourite* (London: Constable, 2011), 147 and 161–63.

11. Wingfield was remanded to the charge of the sheriffs of London, pending the Lordships' further pleasure (*APC* 11, 429), and on 25 July he was before the council on another matter.

12. For rapier and broadsword, see Sydney Anglo, *The Martial Arts of Renaissance Europe* (New Haven, CT: Yale University Press, 2000), 91–118.

13. George Silver, *Paradoxes of Defence* (London, 1599) rptd. (Amsterdam: Da Capo, 1968), 64–72. Since Silver was an advocate of the English broadsword, his accounts of these victories over Italian fencing-masters should be taken with a grain of salt.

14. Silver, 64.

15. Ralegh, *Letters*, 34–35 (tentatively dated by the editors as early 1586).

16. Sydney Anglo, "How to Kill a Man at your Ease: Fencing Books and the Duelling Ethic," in *Chivalry in the Renaissance*, ed. Sydney Anglo (Woodbridge: Boydell, 1990), 11.

17. *The Chamberlain Letters*, ed. Elizabeth McClure Thomson (London: John Murray, 1965), 281.

18. M.A. Stevens, "Sir John Burgh (1561/2–1594)" in the *Oxford Dictionary of National Biography Online*.

19. Ralegh, *Letters*, 235.

20. Victor Kiernan, *The Duel in European History* (London: Zed, 2016), 49.

21. Roger B. Manning, *Swordsmen: The Martial Ethos in the Three Kingdoms* (Oxford: Oxford University Press, 2003), 196, 213.

22. For a vivid survey of "Duels and Affrays" in Wat's time, see G.P.V. Akrigg, *Jacobean Pageant* (Cambridge, MA: Harvard University Press, 1962), 249–58.

23. The fullest account of this antiduelling campaign is Markku Peltonen, *The Duel in Early Modern England* (Cambridge: Cambridge University Press, 2003), 80–145.

24. *The History of the World*, 1829, VI, iii, section 17, subsection 2, 454–68.

25. The publication date of 29 March 1614 for Ralegh's "universal history" is recorded in William Camden's *Diary*. See the online text edited by Dana F. Sutton in *The Philological Museum*.

26. For the "Proclamation against Private Challenges and Combats," see *Stuart Royal Proclamations*, ed. James F. Larkin and Paul L. Hughes, 2 vols. (Oxford: Clarendon, 1973), 1: 302–08.

27. For a vivid account of the bad blood between Knollys and Gilbert (as well as his step-brothers), see Lyons, *The Favourite*, 122–35.

28. The details in this paragraph derive from Andrew Thrush, "Knollys, Robert (c.1590–1626), of Abbey House, Reading, Berks." *History of Parliament Online*. Members, 1604–1629. This Robert Knollys is not to be confused with his same-named contemporary, whom Thrush identifies in the same volume as "Knollys, Sir Robert II (1589–1659), of Stanford-in-the-Vale, Berks." In correspondence, Dr. Thrush drew my attention to these accounts and thereby prevented a good deal of confusion.

29. The letter that Throckmorton received from Winwood is evidently not extant. The letter that Throckmorton sent to Sir Robert Sidney (13 May 1614) is printed in HMC 77, *Report on MSS of Lord L'Isle*, vol. 5 (Sidney Papers), ed. William A. Shaw and G. Dyfnallt Owen (1962), 209.

30. HMC 75, Downshire MSS, vol. 4, *Papers of William Trumbull the Elder, Jan. 1613-Aug. 1614*, ed. A.B. Hinds, 408.

31. *APC*, vol. 33 (1613–14), 455–56.

32. *Stuart Royal Proclamations*, i: 304.
33. *Letters of John Chamberlain*, ed. Norman Egbert McClure, 2 vols. (Philadelphia: American Philosophical Society, 1939), ii: 54–55. For the eloquence of the speech, see William Camden's *Diary*, online edition by Dana F. Sutton in *The Philological Museum*.
34. *The Charge of Sir Francis Bacon Knight ... Touching Duells* (London, 1614), 39.
35. PRO 30/53/7, f. 14. The letter is very usefully cited in Andrew Thrush, "Knollys, Robert (c.1590–1626), of Abbey House, Reading, Berks," *History of Parliament Online*, Members, 1604–29. The book referred to is clearly Bacon's recently printed *Charge*, since Danvers's reference to the "Boucher and Baker" alludes to Sir Francis's hope that gentlemen may forego duelling now that it has "come so low as to Barbers-surgeons and Butchers, and such base mechanical persons" (*Charge of Francis Bacon*, 6).
36. Thrush, "Knollys, Robert (c.1590–1626)," *History of Parliament Online*.
37. HMC 75, Downshire MSS. vol. 5, *Papers of William Trumbull the Elder, Sept. 1614–August 1626*, ed. G. Dyfnallt Owen, 1988, 209.
38. Logan Pearsall Smith, *Life and Letters of Sir Henry Wotton*, 2 vols. (Oxford: Clarendon, 1907), 2: 79.
39. With the exception of the comment on his poetry, the information in this paragraph is from Henry Lancaster, "Sir Thomas Jay (1597/8–1639)," *History of Parliament Online*, Members, 1604–1629.
40. Thomas Alexander Dunn, *Philip Massinger* (London: Nelson, 1957), 39.
41. Robert Philip Tyrwhitt, *Notices and Remains of the Family of Tyrwhitt*, corrected ed. (London: Harrison & Sons, 1862), 55.
42. See the discussion in Chapter Three.
43. *The Letters of John Chamberlain*, ii: 24.
44. HMC 75, Downshire MSS, 5: 209.
45. The faulty transcription of "Tirwett" as "Finet" in the *Calendar of State Papers Domestic, 1611–18* (9: 344) has misled many biographers of Ralegh. The transcription of "Tirwett" is accurate in *Letters from George Lord Carew to Sir Thomas Roe 1615–1617*, ed. John Maclean. Camden Society, series 1, no. 76, p. 10.
46. William Stebbing, *Sir Walter Ralegh: A Biography*, rev. ed. (Oxford: Clarendon, 1899), 300.

47. Ralegh, *History of the World*, in *Works*, ed. William Oldys (Oxford: Oxford University Press, 1829), v: 98.
48. HMC 75, Downshire MSS, 5: 277.
49. "Count Hollock" was Philip of Hohenlohe Langenburg (1550–1606), a hated figure among the English for his violent antipathy to the earl of Leicester.
50. Sonia P. Anderson, "The Elder William Trumbull: A Biographical Sketch," *British Library Journal* 19 (1993), 121.
51. John Wolley's and Jean Beaulieu's moving accounts of Ralegh's death are printed in HMC 75, Downshire MSS, 6: 566–69.
52. Trumbull's transcription appears in Peter Beal's listing of manuscript copies of Ralegh's works as RaW 104.

Chapter Eleven

1. *Acts of the Privy Council*, vol. 34, 1615–16, p. 456.
2. Paul Hyland, *Ralegh's Last Journey* (London: Harper Collins, 2004), 8. In another retributive irony, it was Carr who had convinced the king to wrest Sherborne from the Raleghs as a suitable gift for himself.
3. For patrilineal resonances in Ralegh's account of natives with whom he interacted on his voyage, see Judith Owens, "Patrilineal Ralegh," in *Literary and Visual Ralegh*, ed. Christopher M. Armitage (Manchester: Manchester University Press, 2013), 304–15.
4. Nicholl and Williams, 117.
5. See Joyce Lorimer, ed. *Sir Walter Ralegh's "Discoverie of Guiana,"* The Hakluyt Society (London: Ashgate, 2006), 302.
6. *Letters of Ralegh*, 322–24.
7. A.L. Rowse, *Ralegh and the Throckmortons* (London: Macmillan, 1962), 326.
8. Andrew Thrush, in correspondence with the author.
9. Hyland, *Ralegh's Last Journey*, 23.
10. W.B. Wildman, *A Short History of Sherborne* (Sherborne: Bennet, 1902), 166, and Anna Beer, *My Just Desire: The Life of Bess Ralegh, Wife to Sir Walter* (New York: Ballantine, 2003), 202–03.
11. Aubrey says that Rudyerd ("an acquaintance of Sir Walter Raleigh's") was present at the dinner and told the story to James Harrington, who passed it on to him

(418). Aubrey does not identify the "great person" with whom the Raleghs dined, but Secretary Winwood is a likely possibility. For a notice of Ralegh dining at Winwood's (but with no mention of Wat), see *Letters of John Chamberlain*, ed. N.E. McClure (Philadelphia: American Philosophical Society, 1939), ii: 34.

12. *The Diary of Anne Clifford 1616–1619*, ed. Katherine O. Acheson (New York: Garland, 1995), 51.

13. Beer, *My Just Desire*, 202.

14. More specifically, "Of the 39 plays now accepted as either wholly or partly by Shakespeare, 18 have survived only because the First Folio was published." Peter W.M. Blayney, *The First Folio of Shakespeare* (Washington, D.C.: Folger Library, 1991), 1.

15. National Archives KB 27/1454/1, rot. 692, translated by Nina Green (2011), at http//wwwoxford-shakespearecom/ (p. 10). The brief description and summary of the case by Alan H. Nelson is useful. See http://www.shakespearedocumented.org/exhibition/document/ostler-v-heminges (accessed 2017-07-17).

16. Heminges's will is printed in E.A.J. Honigmann and Susan Brock, eds., *Playhouse Wills, 1558–1642: An Edition of Wills by Shakespeare and his Contemporaries in the London Theatre* (Manchester: Manchester University Press, 1993), 164–68.

17. For a lively account of the Wallaces, see S. Schoenbaum, *Shakespeare's Lives* (Oxford: Clarendon, 1970), 645–57.

18. Charles Nicholl, *The Lodger Shakespeare: His Life on Silver Street* (London: Penguin, 2007). Nicholl's brief pages on Wallace are vivid (6–8).

19. Charles William Wallace, "Shakespeare in London," *The Times* (October 2, 1909), 9.

20. For perseverance in locating the material and sending me photocopies, I am indebted to Gayle M. Richardson, Catalog Librarian/Archivist at the Huntington Library (San Marino, California). The location of the cards is in the Huntington's collection of Charles W. Wallace Papers, Box 16 (Black metal File box). For Thomasine's suit against Wat Ralegh, Wallace's card is headed "Thomasina Ostler—Walter Rawleigh, Jun." For her suit against the men standing surety for Wat, the card is headed "Ostler—Raleigh—K.B."

21. For the document, see (National Archives) KB27-1459-1.

22. For an important example, see E.K. Chambers, *The Elizabethan Stage*, 4 vols. (Oxford: Clarendon, 1923), 2: 322–23. Had Chambers not noted Wallace's reference to Thomasine's lawsuit against Wat in his magisterial history, it might have remained buried in the original newspaper article.

23. Wallace, "Shakespeare in London," 9.

24. Margaret Irwin, *That Great Lucifer: A Portrait of Sir Walter Ralegh* (Toronto: Clarke, Irwin: 1960), 271.

25. Yet another document discovered by the Wallaces establishes Thomasine's residence with her sister. The record is in a Requests and Affidavits Book, which Wallace records as "15–18 Jas. I, Misc. Books, 130." Thomasine is one of four people being warned to appear in court to answer to a bill of complaint at the suit of Ralph Treswell (the Younger). According to Gayle Richardson, the references in the Charles William Wallace Papers at the Huntington Library appear in in Box 4 (17) concerning "Osteler-Treswell."

26. J.C. Whitebrook, "Some Fresh Shakespearean Facts," *Notes & Queries* 162 (1932), 94.

27. For the document, see (National Archives) KB 27-1487-1. Wallace's file card is headed "Ostler-Rawleigh-KB."

28. *Letters of Ralegh*, 339

29. In an early itemization of estimated expenses for the voyage, Ralegh lists (for a company considerably smaller than the one he actually mounted), "For 800 spare shirts for the company at ijs vjd the shirt." See Ernest A. Strathmann, "Ralegh Plans His Last Voyage," *Mariner's Mirror* 50 (1964), 265.

Chapter Twelve

1. Cecil to Sir Thomas Heneage, 21 September 1592, in Edward Edwards, *The Life of Sir Walter Ralegh ... Together with his Letters*, 2 vols. (1868), i: 154. Cecil is commenting on Ralegh's tireless direction of the processing of the plunder from the Spanish Great Carrack, which the queen had freed him from the Tower to oversee.

2. *The Letters of John Chamberlain*, ed. N.E. McClure, 2 vols. (Philadelphia: American Philosophical Society, 1939), i: 617.

3. Ernest A. Strathmann, "Ralegh Plans His Last Voyage," *Mariner's Mirror* 50 (1964), 267. Some of the "surprisingly detailed lists" of necessary supplies mentioned in the previous paragraph are printed in this article.

4. *Letters of Ralegh*, 317–18. This exhortation to Wat is discussed more fully in Chapter Five.

5. For Ralegh's comparison of Talbot with Aemilius Paulus (in their responses to defeat) see the *History of the World*, Book V.

6. For Talbot as Ralegh's amanuensis see Pierre Lefranc, *Walter Ralegh, Écrivain* (Paris: A. Colin, 1968), 269–70.

7. For a fuller discussion of the two John Talbots in *1 Henry VI*, see my *Fathers and Sons in Shakespeare: The Debt Never Promised* (Toronto: University of Toronto Press, 2010), 41–67.

8. *1 Henry VI*, IV, vii, 31–32 from *The Riverside Shakespeare*, ed. G. Blakemore Evans, 2nd ed. (Boston: Houghton Mifflin, 1997).

9. *Letters of Ralegh*, 348.

10. Vincent T. Harlow, *Ralegh's Last Voyage ... and the Fatal Consequences of the Same* (London: Argonaut Press, 1932), 143.

11. For instance, Ralegh characterizes the men whom he sent back to England before his own return as "these scumme of men" (*Letters of Ralegh*, 352).

12. Raleigh Trevelyan, *Sir Walter Raleigh* (New York: H. Holt, 2004), 486. Trevelyan does not cite his source, which I have not been able to identify. A shallop was a slooplike boat.

13. Trevelyan, 486.

14. Harlow, 320–21 (from Ralegh's *Apologie*).

15. *Letters of Ralegh*, 345.

16. For differences among the salutations and closings of copies, see *Letters of Ralegh*, 346–47.

17. Sir Walter Ralegh, *The Discovery of Guiana and the Journal of the Second Voyage Thereto*, ed. Sir Robert Schomburgk (London: Cassell, 1887), 172.

18. Harlow, 284.

19. For an excellent thumbnail account of Keymis, see Charles Nicholl, *The Creature in the Map: Sir Walter Ralegh's Quest for El Dorado* (London: Vintage, 1996), 74–76.

20. *Letters of Ralegh*, 348.

21. *Journal*, 189.

22. *Journal*, 185. In addition to these six, Ralegh mentions Keymis as a captain, but says his chief charge is on the river.

23. Harlow, 198.

24. Harlow, 343–44, printing the text of Keymis' letter that Ralegh included in his own *Apologie* (written after his return to England).

25. In Ralegh's time, forwardness could mean simply "readiness, promptness, eagerness" (*OED* 3), but it was increasingly taking on negative meanings, such as "over-readiness, presumptuous self-confidence; hence lack of becoming modesty" (*OED* 4).

26. Harlow, 231.

27. Harlow, 258.

28. *Letters of Ralegh*, 349. "Sir Warham" was Sir Warham St. Leger, who "lay sicke without hope of life" (*Letters*, 348).

29. *Letters of Ralegh*, 349.

30. Mark Nicholls' beautifully written account of the journal begins with the memorable observation that "The boy in Sir Walter Ralegh dies with his son." "Last Act? 1618 and the Shaping of Sir Walter Ralegh's Reputation," in *Thomas Harriot and his World*, ed. Robert Fox (Burlington, VT: Ashgate, 2012), 165.

31. *Letters of Ralegh*, 353.

Conclusion

1. Edward Thompson, *Sir Walter Ralegh: The Last of the Elizabethans* (London: Macmillan, 1935), 299.

2. Robert Lacey, *Sir Walter Ralegh* (London: Weidenfeld & Nicolson, 1973), 357.

3. Vincent T. Harlow, *Ralegh's Last Voyage* (London: Argonaut Press, 1932), 335

4. Harlow, *Ralegh's Last Voyage*, 343–44.

5. Harlow, *Ralegh's Last Voyage*, 231.

6. Harlow, *Ralegh's Last Voyage*, 297 fn.

7. Harlow, *Ralegh's Last Voyage*, 298.

8. Harlow, *Ralegh's Last Voyage*, 344.

9. *The Letters of Sir Walter Ralegh*, ed. Agnes Latham and Joyce Youings (Exeter: University of Exeter Press, 1999), 349.

10. The lords' list of charges contains a summary of "Sir Walter's answere" to them. While Ralegh challenges their claim that he never intended a mine, his brief rebuttal does not mention the words ascribed to Wat (Harlow, *Ralegh's Last Voyage*, 300).

11. Harlow, *Ralegh's Last Voyage*, 309.

12. Harlow, *Ralegh's Last Voyage*, 326.

13. It should be noted that, on the same page of the *Apologie*, Ralegh printed without comment the letter in which Keymis described Wat's death.

14. *Letters of Ralegh*, 363.

15. Peter Hyland, *Ralegh's Last Journey* (London: HarperCollins, 2004), 200.

16. Walter Oakeshott, "Carew Ralegh's Copy of Spenser," *The Library*, 5th series, 26 (1971), 1–21. Oakeshott shows that the freshly printed volume appeared early enough for Ralegh to have taken it with him for the long, sleepless voyage to Guiana.

17. *Faerie Queene* VI.vi.3–4 in *The Poetical Works of Edmund Spenser*, ed. J.C. Smith and E. de Selincourt (London: Oxford University Press, 1926).

18. Harlow, *Ralegh's Last Voyage*, 328.

19. Ralegh's *Apologie*, in Harlow, 327–28. In his speech before his execution, again Ralegh ascribes a devastating power to the effect of Wat's death on Keymis, saying that he "knew the Head of the Myne [but] would not discover it, when he saw that my Son was slain, but made himself away" (Harlow, 309).

20. *Letters of Ralegh*, 249. Aptly, the editors note that Keymis had been interrogated lengthily (and unsuccessfully) after Ralegh's arrest for treason.

21. Hyland, *Ralegh's Last Journey*, 23.

22. In *Ralegh's Last Journey* Peter Hyland tells the story with flair and much documentary evidence.

23. King James, *A Declaration of the Demeanour and Carriage of Sir Walter Ralegh, Knight*, in Harlow, *Ralegh's Last Voyage*, 348.

24. HMC, Downshire MSS, *Papers of Sir William Trumbull the Elder, Sept. 1616–December 1618*, ed. G. Dyfnallt Owen and Sonia P. Anderson (London: HMSO, 1995), 6: 487.

25. Downshire MSS, 6: 515; Hyland, 189.

26. *The Letters of John Chamberlain*, ed. N.E. McClure, 2 vols. (Philadelphia: American Philosophical Society, 1939), ii: 180.

27. *History of the World*, V. i. 6.

28. Personal correspondence from Nigel Taylor of the National Archives, for whose help I am grateful.

29. The photograph is in the files of the Heinz Archive of the National Portrait Gallery in London. I wish to thank Catharine MacCleod for aid in my (long and unsuccessful) attempt to locate the painting and Paul Cox for arranging the scanning of the photograph.

30. Anna Beer, *My Just Desire: The Life of Bess Ralegh, Wife to Sir Walter* (New York: Ballantine, 2003), 228.

31. This description—from "the Catalogue of the Exhibition of European Enamels held by the Burlington Fine Arts Club in 1897"—is quoted in Victoria Manners, *Collection of Miniatures at Belvoir Castle* (Grantham: Clarke and Marshall, 1903), under "Panel 1."

32. Beer, *My Just Desire*, 227.

33. The print of Ralegh is by Thomas de Leu. British Museum (P, 1. 106).

34. In 1896, J.J. Foster noted that the miniatures of the Raleghs "were found by the writer detached from their enamelled case..." "Miniature Painting in England," *The Art Journal* (April 1896), 103. The miniatures remain detached from the locket.

35. Manners, *Collection of Miniatures*, Panel I.

Bibliography

Manuscripts

Bodleian Library: MS Rawlinson 47
British Library: MS Additional 23229; 22587
Huntington Library: Charles W. Wallace Papers, Box 16 (black metal file box); Box 4 (17)
National Archives (London): KB 27–1459–1; KB 27–1487–1; SP 30/53/7
Sherborne Castle Archives: SHR/ML8; SHR/ML11—Courtesy of E.K. Wingfield Digby, Sherborne Castle
Universiteitsbibliotheek, Leiden, Archief van Senaat en Faculteiten, Volumina inscriptionum, 1575–1618, MS ASF 7
Woburn Abbey Collection: ALN 30/11/5—Courtesy of His Grace, the Duke of Bedford

Historical Manuscripts Commission (HMC)

De L'Isle, HMC 77: *Report on the MSS of Lord De L'Isle and Dudley*
Downshire, HMC 75: *Report on MSS of the Marquess of Downshire*, vols. 4, 5, 6 (Papers of William Trumbull the Elder)
Finch, HMC 71: *Report on the MSS of Allen George Finch*, vol. 1
Fourth Report of the Royal Commission on Historical MSS, Appendix
Rutland: *MSS of His Grace the Duke of Rutland*, vol. 1
Salisbury: *Calendar of MSS of ... Marquess of Salisbury*, vols. 10, 16. 17, 18
Sixth Report of the Royal Commission on Historical MSS, Appendix

Books and Periodicals

Adlington, Hugh. "Chaplains to Embassies: Daniel Featley, Anti-Catholic Controversialist Abroad." In *Chaplains in Early Modern England: Patronage, Literature and Religion*. Edited by Hugh Adlington. Manchester: Manchester University Press, 2013. 83–102.
A.H.D. "Perrot, Sir John (1528–92)." *History of Parliament Online*. Members, 1558–1603.
Akrigg, G.P.V. *Jacobean Pageant: Or, The Court of King James I*. Cambridge: Harvard University Press, 1962.
Anderson, Sonia P. "The Elder William Trumbull: A Biographical Sketch." *The British Library Journal* 19 (1993). 115–32.
Anglo, Sydney. *Chivalry in the Renaissance*. Woodbridge, England: Boydell Press, 1990.
_____. *The Martial Arts of Renaissance Europe*. New Haven, CT: Yale University Press, 2000.

Anon. *Observations upon Some Particular Persons and Passages in a Book lately made publick written by a Lover of the Truth.* London, 1656.
Aubrey, John. *Aubrey's Brief Lives.* Edited by Oliver Lawson Dick. Harmondsworth: Penguin, 1972.
_____. *Brief Lives: Chiefly of Contemporaries, Set Down by John Aubrey, between the Years 1669 & 1696.* Edited by Andrew Clark. 2 vols. Oxford: Clarendon Press, 1898.
Bacon, Sir Francis. *The Charge of Sir Francis Bacon Touching Duells.* Rptd. London: Theatrum Orbis Terrarum, 1968.
Beal, Peter. *CELM (Catalogue of English Literary Manuscripts 1450–1700).* http://www.celm-ms.org.uk.
Beer, Anna. *My Just Desire: The Life of Bess Ralegh, Wife to Sir Walter.* New York: Ballantine Books, 2003.
Bellamy, John. *The Tudor Law of Treason.* Toronto: Toronto University Press, 1979.
Bengtsen, Fiona. *Sir William Waad: Lieutenant of the Tower & the Gunpowder Plot.* Victoria, B.C.: Trafford, 2005.
Blayney, Peter W.M. *The First Folio of Shakespeare.* Washington, D.C: Folger Library, 1991.
Bowers, R.H. "Ralegh's Last Speech: The 'Elms' Document." *Review of English Studies* n.s. 21 (1951): 209–16.
Brodrick, George C. *Memorials of Merton College with Biographical Notices of the Wardens and Fellows.* Oxford Historical Society, vol. 4. Oxford: Clarendon, 1885.
Brushfield, T.N. "Notes on the Ralegh Family." *Notes & Transactions of the Devonshire Association for the Advancement of Science, Literature and Art,* vol. 15 (1883):163–79.
Buck, Anne. *Clothes and the Child: A Handbook of Children's Dress in England 1500–1900.* Carlton, Bedford: Ruth Bean, 1996.
Camden, William. *Journal.* In Dana Sutton, ed. *The Philological Museum.* Birmingham: University of Birmingham, Shakespeare Institute, 1999. http://www.philological.bham.ac.uk/
Carew, George. *Letters from George Lord Carew to Sir Thomas Roe 1615–1617.* Edited by John MacLean. London, 1860. Camden Society, Series I, vol. 76.
Carew, Richard. *The Survey of Cornwall (1602).* Edited by John Chynoweth, Nicholas Orme, & Alexandra Walsham. Exeter: Devon and Cornwall Record Society, 2004.
Cecil, William, Lord Burghley. "Certain Precepts for the Well Ordering of a Man's Life." In *Advice to a Son: Precepts of Lord Burghley, Sir Walter Ralegh, and Francis Osborne.* Edited by Louis B. Wright. Ithaca: Folger Library, 1962. 9–13.
Centerwall, Brandon S. "A Reconsideration of Ben Jonson's Contribution to Sir Walter Ralegh's *History of the World.*" *Ben Jonson Journal* 7 (2000): 539–54.
Chamberlain, John. *The Chamberlain Letters: A Selection of the Letters of John Chamberlain Concerning Life in England from 1597 to 1626.* Edited by Elizabeth McClure Thomson. London: Murray, 1966.
_____. *The Letters of John Chamberlain.* Edited by N.E. McClure. 2 vols. Philadelphia: American Philosophical Society, 1939.
Chambers, E.K. *The Elizabethan Stage.* Reprinted with corrections. 4 vols. Oxford: Clarendon, 1951.
Clifford, Anne. *The Diary of Anne Clifford, 1616–1619.* Edited by Katherine O. Acheson. New York: Garland, 1995.
Coote, Stephen. *A Play of Passion: The Life of Sir Walter Ralegh.* London: Macmillan, 1993.
Cressy, David. *Birth, Marriage, and Death: Ritual, Religion, and the Life-Cycle in Tudor and Stuart England.* Oxford: Oxford University Press, 1997.
Croft, Pauline. "Cecil, Robert, First Earl of Salisbury (1563–1612), Politician and Courtier." *Oxford Dictionary of National Biography Online.*
Dallington, Robert. *A Method of Travell.* London: Printed by Thomas Creede, 1605.

Danushevskaya, A.V. "The Formation of a Renaissance Nobleman: William Cecil, 2nd Earl of Salisbury 1591–1668," *History of Education* 31 (2002): 505–20.
Dixon, William Hepworth. *Her Majesty's Tower*. 6th ed. London: Hurst and Blackett, 1870. vol. 1.
Donaldson, Ian. *Ben Jonson: A Life*. Oxford: Oxford University Press, 2011.
Duffy, Eamon. *The Stripping of the Altars: Traditional Religion in England, 1400–1580*. 2nd ed. New Haven, CT: Yale University Press, 2005.
Dunn, Thomas Alexander. *Philip Massinger: The Man and the Playwright*. London: Nelson, 1957.
Edwards, Edward. *The Life of Sir Walter Ralegh, Based on Contemporary Documents ... Together with His Letters*. 2 vols. London: Macmillan, 1868.
Edwards, Philip. *Sir Walter Ralegh*. London: Longmans, Green, 1953.
Elizabeth I. *Queen Elizabeth I: Selected Works*. Edited by Steven W. May. New York: Washington Square Press, 2004.
Elyot, Sir Thomas. *The Book Named the Governor*. Edited by S.E. Lehmberg. London: Dent, 1962.
Erasmus, Desiderius. *Adages IV iii 1 to V ii 51*. Edited by John N. Grant. In *Collected Works of Erasmus*. Edited by J.K. McConica and R.M. Schoeffel. vol. 36. Toronto: University of Toronto Press, 2006.
Fletcher, J.M. "The Faculty of Arts." In *The Collegiate University*. Edited by James McConica. Vol. 3 of *The History of the University of Oxford*. Oxford: Clarendon, 1986. 157–99.
Foster, J.J. "Miniature Painting in England." *Art Journal* (April 1896): 101–04.
Foster, Joseph. *Alumni Oxonienses: The Members of the University of Oxford, 1500–1714*. 4 vols. Oxford: Parker, 1891–92.
Fowler, Thomas. *The History of Corpus Christi College: with Lists of Its Members*. Oxford: Clarendon, 1893.
Friedman, Alice T. *House and Household in Elizabethan England: Woolaton Hall and the Willoughby Family*. Chicago: University of Chicago Press, 1989.
Frost, Robert. *The Notebooks of Robert Frost*. Edited by Robert Faggen. Cambridge, MA: Harvard University Press, 2007.
Galen, Claudius. *Hygiene*. Translated by Robert M. Green. Toronto: Ryerson, 1951.
Gawdy, Philip. *The Letters of Philip Gawdy*. Edited by Isaac Herbert Jeayes. London: J.B. Nichols, 1906.
Greenblatt, Stephen. *Sir Walter Ralegh: The Renaissance Man and his Roles*. New Haven, CT: Yale University Press, 1973.
Gregerson, Linda. "Sir Walter Ralegh to His Son." *The Atlantic Online*. http://www.theatlantic.com//unbound/poetry/soundings/ralegh.htm Accessed March 3, 2009.
Hammer, P.E.J. "Sex and the Virgin Queen: Aristocratic Concupiscence and the Court of Elizabeth I." *Sixteenth Century Journal* 31 (2000): 77–97.
Hannay, Margaret P. "'High Housewifery': The Duties and Letters of Barbara Gamage Sidney, Countess of Leicester." *Early Modern Women: An Interdisciplinary Journal Online*. 1 (2006).
Harlow, Vincent T. *Ralegh's Last Voyage ... and the Fatal Consequences of the Same*. London: Argonaut Press, 1932.
Heal, Felicity, and Clive Holmes. *The Gentry in England and Wales, 1500–1700*. London: Macmillan, 1994.
Herbert, Edward. *The Life of Edward, First Lord Herbert of Cherbury*. Edited by J.M. Shuttleworth. London: Oxford University Press, 1976.
Holinshed, Raphael. *Holinshed's Chronicles of England, Scotland, and Ireland*. 1807. 6 vols., rpt. New York: AMS Press, 1965.

Holles, Gervase. *Memorials of the Holles Family, 1493–1656*. Edited by A.C. Wood. Camden Society, 3rd ser. vol. 55. London: 1937.
Houlebrooke, Ralph, ed. *English Family Life 1576–1716: An Anthology from Diaries*. Oxford: Blackwell, 1988.
Howard, Clare. *English Travellers of the Renaissance*. London: J. Lane, 1914.
Hurstfield, Joel. *The Queen's Wards: Wardship and Marriage under Elizabeth I*. London: Longmans, Green, 1958.
Hyland, Paul. *Ralegh's Last Journey: A Tale of Madness, Vanity and Treachery*. London: HarperCollins, 2004.
Irwin, Margaret. *That Great Lucifer: A Portrait of Sir Walter Ralegh*. Toronto: Clarke, Irwin, 1960.
James I. "Proclamation against Private Challenges and Combats." In *Stuart Royal Proclamations*. Edited by James F. Larkin and Paul L. Hughes. 2 vols. Oxford: Clarendon, 1973. 1: 302–08.
Jonson, Ben. *Bartholomew Fair*. Edited by Edward B. Partridge. Lincoln: University of Nebraska Press, 1964.
_____. *The Cambridge Edition of the Works of Ben Jonson*. Edited by David M. Bevington, et al. 7 vols. Cambridge: Cambridge University Press, 2014.
_____. *The Cambridge Edition of the Works of Ben Jonson Online*. Life Records. Edited by Eugene Giddens and Hester Lees-Jeffries.
_____. *The Complete Poems*. Edited by George Parfitt. Harmondsworth: Penguin, 1975.
Kafka, Franz. *Letter to his Father*. Translated by Ernst Kaiser and Eithne Wilkins. New York: Schocken, 1963.
Kapur, Shekhar, Director. *Elizabeth: The Golden Age*. Universal Studios, 2007. Motion picture.
Kearney Hugh. *Scholars and Gentlemen: Universities and Society in Pre-Industrial Britain, 1500–1700*. London: Faber & Faber, 1970.
Kiernan, Victor. *The Duel in European History: Honour and the Reign of Aristocracy*. Reprint. London: Zed, 2016.
Lacey, Robert. *Sir Walter Ralegh*. London: Weidenfeld & Nicolson, 1973.
Lancaster, Henry. "Sir Thomas Jay (1597/8–1639)." *History of Parliament Online*. Members, 1604–29.
Lancaster, Henry, and Ben Coates. "Dallison, Sir Roger (c. 1562–1620)." *History of Parliament Online*. Members, 1604–29.
Latham, Agnes M.C. "Sir Walter Ralegh's *Instructions to his Son*." In *Elizabethan and Jacobean Studies Presented to Frank Percy Wilson*. Oxford: Clarendon, 1959. 198–218.
Lefranc, Pierre. *Sir Walter Ralegh, Écrivain: L'oeuvre et les Idées*. Paris: A. Colin, 1968.
Low, Jennifer A. *Manhood and the Duel: Masculinity in Early Modern Drama and Culture*. New York: Palgrave Macmillan, 2003.
Lyons, Mathew. *The Favourite*. London: Constable, 2011.
Manners, Victoria. *The Collection of Miniatures at Belvoir Castle*. Grantham: Clarke and Marshall, 1903.
Manning, Percy. "Sport and Pastime in Stuart Oxford." In *Surveys and Tokens*. Edited by H.E. Salter. Oxford Historical Society, 75. Oxford: Clarendon, 1923. 85–135.
Manning, Roger B. *Swordsmen: The Martial Ethos in the Three Kingdoms*. Oxford: Oxford University Press, 2003.
May, Steven W. *Sir Walter Ralegh*. Boston: Twayne, 1989.
McConica, James. "Elizabethan Oxford: The Collegiate Society." In *The Collegiate University*. Edited by James McConica. Vol. 3 of *The History of the University of Oxford*. Edited by T.H. Aston. Oxford: Clarendon, 1986. 645–732.
McPherson, David. "Ben Jonson Meets Daniel Heinsius, 1613." *English Language Notes* 44 (1976): 105–09.

Mears, Natalie. "Regnum Cecilianum? A Cecilian Perspective of the Court." In *The Reign of Elizabeth I: Court and Culture in the Last Decade.* Edited by John Guy. Cambridge: Cambridge University Press, 1995. 46–64.
Miller, Helen. "Ralegh, Walter (1504–81)." *History of Parliament Online.* Members, 1509–1558.
Mimardière, A.R. "Wingfield, Edward (c.1562–1603) of Kimbolton, Hunts." *History of Parliament Online.* Members, 1558–1603.
de Montaigne, Michel. *The Complete Essays of Montaigne.* Translated by Donald M. Frame. Stanford: Stanford University Press, 1965.
———. *Montaigne's Essays.* Translated by John Florio. 3 vols. London: J.M. Dent, 1965.
Morgan, Victor. *A History of the University of Cambridge. Vol. 2. 1546–1750.* Cambridge: Cambridge University Press, 2004.
Mowl, Timothy. *Elizabethan and Jacobean Style.* London: Phaidon, 1993.
Mulcaster, Richard. *Positions Concerning the Training Up of Children.* Edited by William Barker. Toronto: University of Toronto Press, 1994.
Nashe, Thomas. *Works.* Edited by Ronald B. McKerrow and F.P. Wilson. 5 vols. Oxford: Blackwell, 1966.
Naunton, Sir Robert. *Fragmenta Regalia, or Observations on Queen Elizabeth: Her Times and Favorites.* Edited by John S. Cerovski. London: Associated University Presses, 1985.
Nicholl, Charles. *The Creature in the Map: Sir Walter Ralegh's Quest for El Dorado.* London: Vintage, 1996.
———. *The Lodger Shakespeare: His Life on Silver Street.* London: Penguin, 2007.
Nicholls, Mark. "Last Act? 1618 and the Shaping of Sir Walter Ralegh's Reputation." In *Thomas Harriot and His World.* Edited by Robert Fox. Burlington, VT: Ashgate, 2012. 165–82.
———, and Penry Williams. "Ralegh, Sir Walter (1554–1618), Courtier, Explorer, and Author." *Oxford Dictionary of National Biography Online.*
———, and ———. *Sir Walter Raleigh: In Life and Legend.* London: Continuum, 2011.
Nietzsche, Friedrich. *The Portable Nietzsche.* Translated by Walter Kaufmann. New York: Viking, 1968.
Nye, Robert. *The Voyage of the Destiny.* London: H. Hamilton, 1982.
Oakeshott, Walter. "Carew Ralegh's Copy of Spenser." *The Library.* 5th series 26 (1971): 1–21.
O'Day, Rosemary. *Education and Society, 1500–1800: The Social Foundations of Education in Early Modern Britain.* London: Longman, 1982.
Owens, Judith. "Patrilineal Ralegh." In *Literary and Visual Ralegh.* Edited by Christopher M. Armitage. Manchester: Manchester University Press, 2013. 302–26.
Peck, D.C. "Raleigh, Sidney, Oxford, and the Catholics, 1579." *Notes and Queries* 223 (1978): 427–31.
Peltonen, Markku. *The Duel in Early Modern England: Civility, Politeness and Honour.* Cambridge: Cambridge University Press, 2003.
Percy, Henry, Earl of Northumberland. *The Wizard Earl's Advices to his Son: A Facsimile and Transcript from the Manuscripts of Henry Percy, Ninth Earl of Northumberland.* Edited by Gordon R. Batho and Stephen Clucas. London: Roxburghe Club, 2002.
Porter, Stephen. "University and Society." In *The University of Oxford in the Seventeenth Century.* Vol. 4 of *The History of the University of Oxford.* Edited by Nicholas Tyacke. Oxford: Clarendon, 1997.
Potter, Ursula. "Cockering Mothers and Humanist Pedagogy in Two Tudor School Plays." In *Domestic Arrangements in Early Modern England.* Edited by Kari Boyd McBride. Pittsburgh: Duquesne University Press, 2002. 244–78.

Prögler, Daniela. *English Students at Leiden University, 1575–1650.* Burlington, VT: Ashgate, 2013.
Ralegh, Carew. "A brief Relation of Sir Walter Ralegh's Troubles: with the taking away of the Lands and Castles of Sherburn." In *The Works of Sir Walter Ralegh.* 8 vols. Oxford: Oxford University Press, 1829. Vol. 8.
Ralegh, Sir Walter. *The Discovery of Guiana and the Journal of the Second Voyage Thereto.* Edited by Sir Robert Schomburgk. London: Cassell, 1887.
———. *The History of the World.* London: Walter Burre, 1614.
———. *The Letters of Sir Walter Ralegh.* Edited by Agnes Latham and Joyce Youings. Exeter: University of Exeter Press, 1999.
———. *The Poems of Sir Walter Ralegh: A Historical Edition.* Edited by Michael Rudick. Tempe, AZ: Center for Medieval and Renaissance Studies, 1999.
———. *Poems.* Edited by Agnes Latham. London: Routledge and Kegan Paul, 1962.
———. *Sir Walter Ralegh's Discoverie of Guiana.* Edited by Joyce Lorimer. Burlington, VT: Ashgate for the Hakluyt Society, 2006.
———. *Sir Walter Raleigh's Instructions to his Sonne: and to Posteritie. The Second Edition.* London: Benjamin Fisher, 1632.
———. *Works, Now First Collected: To Which Are Prefixed The Lives of the Author.* Edited by William Oldys and Thomas Birch. 8 vols. Oxford: Oxford University Press, 1829.
Ray, Sid. "'Those Whom God Hath Joined Together': Bondage Metaphors and Marital Advice in Early Modern England." In *Domestic Arrangements in Early Modern England.* Edited by Kari Boyd McBride. Pittsburgh: Duquesne University Press, 2002. 15–47.
Riggs, David. *Ben Jonson: A Life.* Cambridge, MA: Harvard University Press, 1989.
Roberts, Benjamin B. *Sex and Drugs Before Rock 'n' Roll: Youth Culture and Masculinity During Holland's Golden Age.* Amsterdam: Amsterdam University Press, 2012.
Rowse, A.L. *Ralegh and the Throckmortons.* London: Macmillan, 1962.
Schoenbaum, Samuel. *Shakespeare's Lives.* Oxford: Clarendon, 1970.
Shakespeare, William. *Hamlet.* Edited by G.R. Hibbard. Oxford: Oxford University Press, 1987.
Sidney, Sir Philip. *The Correspondence of Sir Philip Sidney.* Edited by Roger Kuin. 2 vols. Oxford: Oxford University Press, 2012.
Silver, George. *Paradoxes of Defense.* (1599). New York: Da Capo, 1968.
Skinner, Quentin. "Political Philosophy." In *The Cambridge History of Renaissance Philosophy.* Edited by Charles B. Schmitt and Quentin Skinner. Cambridge: Cambridge University Press, 1988. 390–452.
Smith, Logan Pearsall. *Life and Letters of Sir Henry Wotton.* 2 vols. Oxford: Clarendon, 1907.
Smith-Bannister, Scott. *Names and Naming Patterns in England, 1538–1700.* Oxford: Clarendon, 1997.
Spangenberg, Brady J. "Civil Death in Early Modern Europe, from Jack Cade to Luther, Hamlet, and Raleigh." PhD diss., Purdue University, 2011.
Spenser, Edmund. *The Poetical Works.* Edited by J.C. Smith and E. de Selincourt. London: Oxford University Press, 1926.
Spicer, Joaneath. "The Renaissance Elbow." In *A Cultural History of Gesture: From Antiquity to the Present Day.* Edited by Jan Bremmer and Herman Roodenburg. Cambridge: Polity, 1991. 84–128.
Stanford, Michael J.G. "The Raleghs Take to the Sea." *The Mariner's Mirror* 48 (1962): 18–35.
———. "The Raleghs: Father and Son." In *Raleigh in Exeter: Privateering and Colonisation in the Reign of Elizabeth I.* Edited by Joyce Youings. Exeter: University of Exeter Press, 1985. 91–97.

Stebbing, William. *Sir Walter Ralegh: A Biography*. Reissue with a Frontispiece and a List of Authorities. Oxford: Clarendon, 1899.
Steggle, Mathew. "Charles Chester and Ben Jonson." *Studies in English Literature* 39 (1999): 313–26.
Stevens, M.A. "Sir John Burgh (1561/2–1594)." *Oxford Dictionary of National Biography Online*. Members, 1558–1603.
Stone, Lawrence. "The Size and Composition of the Oxford Student Body 1580–1910." In *Oxford and Cambridge from the 14th to the Early 19th Century*. Vol. 1 of *The University in Society*. Edited by Lawrence Stone. 2 vols. Princeton: Princeton University Press, 1974. 3–110.
Stoye, John. *English Travellers Abroad, 1604–1667: Their Influence in English Society and Politics*, rev. ed. New Haven, CT: Yale University Press, 1989.
Strathmann, Ernest A. "Ralegh Plans His Last Voyage." *The Mariner's Mirror* 50 (1964): 261–70.
Strong, Roy. *Henry, Prince of Wales and England's Lost Renaissance*. London: Thames and Hudson, 1986.
———. *Tudor & Jacobean Portraits*. 2 vols. London: Her Majesty's Stationery Office, 1969.
Thompson, Edward. *Sir Walter Ralegh: The Last of the Elizabethans*. London: Macmillan, 1935.
Thrush, Andrew. "Knollys, Robert (c.1590–1621) of Abbey House, Reading, Berks." *History of Parliament Online*. Members, 1604–29.
———. "Knollys, Sir Robert II (1589–1659), of Stanford-in-the-Vole, Berks." *History of Parliament Online*. Members, 1604–29.
———. "Puckering, Sir Thomas, 1st Bt. (1589–1637) of the Priory, Warwick." *History of Parliament Online*. Members, 1604–29.
Trevelyan, Raleigh. *Sir Walter Raleigh*. London: Allen Lane, 2002.
Tromly, Fred B. *Fathers and Sons in Shakespeare: The Debt Never Promised*. Toronto: University of Toronto Press, 2010.
———. "Lord Burghley's 'Ten Precepts' for his Son, Robert Cecil: A New Date and Interpretation." *Historical Research* 88 (2015). 185–91.
———. "Masks of Impersonality in Burghley's 'Ten Precepts' and Ralegh's *Instructions to His Son*." *Review of English Studies* n.s. 66 (2015): 480–500.
———. "Sir Walter Ralegh Instructs his Son, Twice." *Notes and Queries* n.s. 56 (2009): 616–19.
Tyrwhitt, Robert Philip. *Notices and Remains of the Family of Tyrwhitt*. London: Harrison and Sons, 1862.
Walker, Robert. *The Namesake: A Biography of Theodore Roosevelt, Jr*. New York: Brick Tower, 2008.
Wallace, Charles William. "Shakespeare in London: Fresh Documents on the Poet and His Theatres." *The Times* (October 2, 1909): 9.
Wallace, Willard M. *Sir Walter Raleigh*. Princeton: Princeton University Press, 1959.
Weir, Alison. *The Life of Elizabeth I*. New York: Ballantine Books, 1998.
Wentworth, William. "Sir William Wentworth's Advice to his Son." In *Wentworth Papers 1597–1628*. Edited by J.P. Cooper. Camden Fourth Series, vol. 12. London: Royal Historical Society, 1973. 9–35.
Whitebrook, J.C. "Some Fresh Shakespearean Facts." *Notes and Queries* 162 (1932): 93–95.
Whitelock, Anna. *Elizabethan Bedfellows: An Intimate History of the Queen's Court*. London: Bloomsbury, 2013.
Wildman, W.B. *A Short History of Sherborne from A.D. 705*. 2nd ed. Sherborne: Bennett, 1902.

Williams, Neville. *Thomas Howard, Fourth Duke of Norfolk.* London: Barrie and Rockliff, 1964.
Wilson, Jean. "The Noble Imp: The Upper-Class Child in English Renaissance Art and Literature." *Antiquities Journal* 70 (1990): 300–78.
Wilson, Sir Thomas. *The State of England anno. Dom. 1600.* Edited by F.J. Fisher. *Camden Miscellany.* 3rd series, vol. 16. London: Camden Society, 1936.
Wood, Anthony. *Athenae Oxonienses.* Edited by P. Bliss. 4 vols. London: Rivington, 1813–20.
Worsley, Lucy. *Cavalier: a Tale of Chivalry, Passion and Great Houses.* London: Faber & Faber, 2007.
Youings, Joyce. "Ralegh's Devon." In *Raleigh and Quinn: The Explorer and his Boswell.* Edited by H.G. Jones. Chapel Hill: University of North Carolina Press, 1987. 69–85.
Young, Bruce. "Parental Blessings in Shakespeare's Plays." *Studies in Philology* 89 (1992): 179–209.

Index

Numbers in **_bold italics_** indicate pages with illustrations

Antwerp 120, 126
attainder 63–65, 80; attempt of Sir Walter Ralegh to evade 65–67; campaign of Elizabeth Throckmorton Ralegh to ameliorate 75, 79–84; delayed enactment of Sir Walter Ralegh's 79; effect on Sir Walter Ralegh 67, 72–73, 75; patrimony and prospects of Walter Ralegh (Walter, Jr.) destroyed by 65–70, 116; *see also* corruption of blood; Sherborne
Aubrey, John: on Sir Walter Ralegh 28, 41, 67, 103, 113; on Walter Ralegh (Walter, Jr.) 111–12

Bacon, Sir Francis 136–37, 140
Bailey, Captain John 168–69
Bassett, Elizabeth 48–49, 143
Bassett, Judith 48–49
Beer, Anna 154, 189, 193n2
Bonetti, Rocco 135
Boyle, Richard, earl of Cork 168
Broad Street (London) 78, 85, 198n17
Brussels 120, 124, 126, 139
Burgh, Sir John 135–36
Burghley, Lord (William Cecil): education of his son Robert 37; precepts for Robert 33–34, 89, 91, 93; pre-eminence among English statesmen 37

Camden, William 118, 202n9
Carr, Sir Robert 83–84, 101
Cecil, Mildred 33–34
Cecil, Sir Robert 2; archive 27, 79, 196n17; cajoled by Elizabeth Throckmorton Ralegh 24–25, 79; death 117, 143; emulation of father's career 33, 37, 61; instructions to son's tutor 107; letters from Sir Walter Ralegh to 23, 25, 80, 84–85; opposition to Sir Walter Ralegh 43, 49, 61–62, 65; trained by father 37; *see also* Burghley, Lord; Cecil, Will

Cecil, Will (son of Robert): with Raleghs at Sherborne 42–43; recipient of father's largesse 104, 117, 121, 202n7
Clifford, Lady Anne 154
Cobham, Baron (Henry Brooke) 48, 62–63, 75, 94
Cork 157, 168–69
Corpus Christi College (Oxford) 104–6; *see also* Featley, Daniel
corruption of blood 64–65, 82; *see also* attainder

Drummond, William 122–30
the duel 135–36, 145; banned by King James 136, 139–40; cases judged in Star Chamber 140; denounced by Lord Bacon 140, 205n35; "*Digression*" of Sir Walter Ralegh on 136–37; lethality of 135–36; rapier vs. broadsword 134–35; social protocols 121, 135–37; test of honor and manliness 136–37; *see also* Ralegh, Wat
Durham House 22, 24, 62, 75

Elizabeth I: benefactor of Sir Walter Ralegh 10, 11, 63; deceived by Sir Walter Ralegh and Elizabeth Throckmorton Ralegh 11–12; imprisonment of Sir Walter Ralegh and Elizabeth Throckmorton Ralegh in Tower 12; leased Sherborne to Sir Walter Ralegh 21–22; memorialized by Elizabeth Throckmorton Ralegh 187; reconciliation with Sir Walter Ralegh 12, 48; service of Sir Walter Ralegh and Elizabeth Throckmorton Ralegh to 11–13; *see also* Sherborne
Erasmus, Desiderius 104, 194
Essex, 2nd earl of (Robert Devereux) 21, 59–61, 94, 191, 197

father and son relationships: James I and Prince Henry 100–101; Lord Burghley and Sir Robert Cecil 37–38; Sir John Horsey II

217

and III 43; Sir John Talbot and John Talbot 166–67
fathers' advice to sons 88–89; addressed to eldest son 89; emphasis on preservation of family estate 88; misogynistic tendency 30, 39, 95–97; *see also* Burghley, Lord; *Instructions for His Son*; Percy, Henry
Featley, Daniel 106–12, 125, 203*n*32
fencing: Sir Walter Ralegh and 135; Walter Ralegh (Walter, Jr.)'s attraction to 110, 121, 136
fencing schools 110: Leiden 128–29; London 135; Oxford and Cambridge 109–10; Paris 120; Sir Walter Ralegh's patronage of 135
Fermor, Sir Hatton 116–17
Flushing 32, 138–39
a "French Captayne" 145–46
Frost, Robert 53

Gawdy, Philip and Bassingbourne 83
Gilbert, Sir Humphrey 17, 138
Gilbert, John II 135–36
Gregerson, Linda 54–56
Guiana 8, 21, 178; second expedition to 84, 86, 149–51, 153–54, 157, 163–77; Sir Walter Ralegh's first expedition to 24–25, 27

The Hague 141–43, 145–46, 151
Hammond, Christopher (and unnamed wife) 170–71
Hawthorne, Gilbert 105–6, 114
Heinsius, Daniel 126
Heminges, John 155–56
The History of the World: copies destroyed by James I 100; incorporation of a Jonson narrative 118; Jonson's criticism 130–31; oblique comments on Walter Ralegh (Walter, Jr.) 100; publication 100, 140; signed copy given to William Trumbull 146–47; as surrogate for Walter Ralegh (Walter, Jr.) 100
Hobart, Sir Henry 86–87
Holles, Gervase 68–69, 198*n*4
Hooker, John 16–17, 105
Hooker, Peter 106–7
Hooker, Richard 105
Horsey, Sir John II 43, 45
Horsey, Sir John III 43, 45
Howard, Frances 148–49
Howard, Mr. Henry 49, 143
Howard, Henry, earl of Northampton 49, 73–74, 81, 148
Howard, Thomas, duke of Norfolk 98
Howard, Thomas, earl of Suffolk 49, 143–44, 148

James I: bestows Sherborne on Sir Robert Carr 83–84; confronted by Elizabeth Throckmorton Ralegh 82–84; criticized by Prince Henry for treatment of Sir Walter Ralegh 100–101; differences with the Prince 100–101; frees Sir Walter Ralegh offended by *The History of the World* 100; opposition to Sir Walter Ralegh 61, 164; undermines second Guiana expedition 164; *see also* the duel
Jay, Thomas 141–46
Jennings, Thomas 159–61
Jonson, Ben 19, 35, 118, *119*; cold relationship with Walter Ralegh (Walter, Jr.) 122–23, 130; drunken episode with Walter Ralegh (Walter, Jr.) in Paris 121–24; interruption of literary career 120; named tutor and governor for Walter Ralegh (Walter, Jr.) 118–20; quarrel with Sir Walter Ralegh 129–30; travels with Walter Ralegh (Walter, Jr.) in France and Low Countries 120–26

Kafka, Franz 20
Keymis, Lawrence 150, 171, 181, 184
the King's Men 155–56
Knollys, Robert 138–42, 146, 150

Latham, Agnes 57, 91
Leiden 120, 126–7, 142–43
Lillington 9–10, 193*n*2
Low Countries: duels of Walter Ralegh (Walter, Jr.) in 137–38, 141–46; site of military engagements 116, 118, 132, 138; travels of Walter Ralegh (Walter, Jr.) in 120, 125–29; *see also* Antwerp; Brussels; Flushing; The Hague; Leiden; Utrecht

Montaigne, Michel de: on his children 32; on fathers and sons 14, 50, 100
Mulcaster, Richard 35

names and naming 1–2, 7, 9, 81, 111; burden of a father's name 7, 19; Carew 77; Damerei 9, 16; Walter 18–19; Wat 193*n*3
Nashe, Thomas 68
Nerée, Richard Jean de 127
Nietzsche, Friedrich 7

Ostler, Thomasine: intervention by Sir Walter Ralegh on behalf of Walter Ralegh (Walter, Jr.) 159–161, 164, 185; law-case against father, John Heminges 154–56; law-case against Walter Ralegh (Walter, Jr.) 156–59
Owens, Judith 55, 97, 193*n*2
Oxford University: Walter Ralegh (Walter, Jr.)'s life at 102–15; *see also* Featley, Daniel; Hooker, Peter; Ralegh, Sir Walter; Whitney, James

Paris 111–12, 120–25
patrilineal values 7–8, 13, 19, 88–89; filial duty to imitate fathers 19; 194*n*30; primogeniture 15; replication of fathers in sons 18–20, 37, 45; *see also* patrimony; Ralegh, Sir Walter

Percy, Henry, earl of Northumberland 41, 89, 150, 201*n*23; negative attitude to women 30, 32, 75, 79
plague 10, 25, 77, 201*n*19
Prince Henry of England 176, 196*n*22; differences with King James 100–1; hopes of Sir Walter Ralegh dashed by death of 101; as patron of Sir Walter Ralegh 100–1, 117, 120, 149, 184; as surrogate son to Sir Walter Ralegh 100
Prince Maurice of Nassau 144–46, 151, 167

Ralegh, Adrian (half-brother of Sir Walter Ralegh), 27
Ralegh, Carew (brother of Sir Walter Ralegh) 6, 15, 66, 138
Ralegh, Carew (son of Sir Walter Ralegh) 77; birth and baptism 77; closeness to Elizabeth Throckmorton Ralegh 84–85, 183; interrogated by the crown 186; misidentified as recipient of *Instructions to His Son* 91; portrait with Elizabeth Throckmorton Ralegh **188**; restoration of family blood 49, 64, 77; from Sir Walter Ralegh 77, 177
Ralegh, Damerei 10, 18, 22, 25, 193*n*1
Ralegh, Elizabeth (Throckmorton): administrator of Walter Ralegh (Walter, Jr.)'s effects 184; correspondence with Robert Cecil 24–25, 31, 81; devotion to Walter Ralegh (Walter, Jr.) and Sir Walter Ralegh 185, 187–89, **188**, 189–92, **190**; imprisoned and banished from court by Elizabeth I 23; marriage to Sir Walter Ralegh 23–24, 73–74, 85, 152, 185; portraits **74**, 187–89, **188**; protector of family's estate 75, 79, 81–83, 184, 186 (*see also* Sherborne Manor); remonstrations to King James 82–84; service to Elizabeth I 11–13; socially isolated (with Walter Ralegh [Walter, Jr.]) at Sherborne 31–33; stereotype of her as indulgent mother 34–35, 161; subordinated to Walter Ralegh (Walter, Jr.) in will of Sir Walter Ralegh 29 (*see also* Ralegh, Sir Walter); support from her brother, Arthur Throckmorton 21, 23
Ralegh, George (half brother of Sir Walter Ralegh) 15
Ralegh, George (nephew of Sir Walter Ralegh) 167, 175
Ralegh, Katherine Gilbert (Sir Walter Ralegh's mother) 17
Ralegh, Sir Walter: ambivalence toward Walter Ralegh (Walter, Jr.) 52; authority within his family 13–15, 73–75, 84–87, 97–99, 130; belief in shared identity with Walter Ralegh (Walter, Jr.) 7, 18–19, 37–39, 43–47, **44**, 52–53, 93; belief that Sherborne with Walter Ralegh (Walter, Jr.) as birthplace and patrimony 27–29; concern about Walter Ralegh (Walter, Jr.)'s future 38, 52–60, 67–70, 88–101, 136–37, 147, 163; deviations from patrilineal custom 41, 45–46; discord with James I 185; distance from his father 14, 16–18; execution of 147, 185, 187; expedition to Cadiz 28, 42; expedition to Fayal 191; expeditions to Guiana 25, 163–77, **165**; expedition to Panama 21–23; feud with Ben Jonson 130; interventions on behalf of Walter Ralegh (Walter, Jr.) 131, 144–47, 151, 159–61; Ireland 10, 11, 170–71; 17, 29, 134 (*see also* Cork); marriage to Elizabeth Throckmorton Ralegh 21–25, 27, 29–30, 39–41, 71–75, 77, 176–77 (*see also* Ralegh, Elizabeth); patrilineal beliefs 13–14, 29, 65–67, 72, 89–90, 97; portraits (as commander of Guiana expedition **165**; double portrait with Walter Ralegh [Walter, Jr.] 43–47, **44**; matched miniatures of him and Walter Ralegh [Walter, Jr.] in Elizabeth Throckmorton Ralegh's locket **190**, 189–92); Prince Henry 100–1, 117, 120, 149, 184; provision of a patrimony for Walter Ralegh (Walter, Jr.): 26, 29, 67–70; responses to death of Walter Ralegh (Walter, Jr.) 173, 176–77, 182–84; service to Elizabeth I 11, 59, 61, 62; support of deceased retainers' dependents 170–71; trial and conviction for treason 62–63; will and testament 28–29
Ralegh, Walter (father of Sir Walter Ralegh) 14–18
Ralegh, Walter, Jr. (Wat): accounts of death 173–76, 182; ambiguous social status after Sir Walter Ralegh's attainder 67–70, 102; assault on Thomasine Ostler 157–59; attainder of Sir Walter Ralegh as loss of his patrimony and prospects 65–70, 116; burden of name 19–20; burial 178; convicted of assault against Thomasine Ostler 157–59; early life 30–31, 33–35, 41, 43; final words 179–80; as image of his father 46–47; 50–51; mockery of social customs 111–12, 122, 124–25, 153–54; model for character in Jonson's *Bartholomew Fair* 124; opponents in duels 138–46; at Oxford University 102–115 (*see also* Featley, Daniel; Hawthorne, Gilbert; Hooker, Peter); physical exuberance 108, 111, 170; portraits (double portrait with Sir Walter Ralegh **44**; matched miniatures of Sir Walter Ralegh and Walter Ralegh [Walter, Jr.]) **190**; propensity to violence 132–47, 157–59, 169, 173–76; rebellion against father's authority and that his surrogates 7, 110–111, 122–24, 130, 137; resistance to obedience and discipline 34–35; 47, 167, 175, 179; signature 114–15, **114**; similarities to Sir Walter Ralegh **44**, 111–13, 134; travels on the Continent with Ben Jonson 117–30; tutors 33, 78–79, 106–11
Roosevelt, Theodore, Jr. 19

Rudick, Michael 57–58
Rudyard, Benjamin 153, 205

San Thomé 171–73, 178, 184, 191
Shakespeare, William 50, 66, 120, 155–56, 166, 194n30
Sherborne Abbey 9, 45
Sherborne Grammar School 33
Sherborne Manor 26; birthplace of Walter Ralegh (Walter, Jr.) and his intended patrimony 9, 25–27; failed conveyance to Walter Ralegh (Walter, Jr.) 65–67; granted to Sir Walter Ralegh by Elizabeth I 48, 187; improved by Raleghs 26–27, 48; leased to Sir Walter Ralegh by Elizabeth I 21–22; Sir Walter Ralegh's last sight of 188; struggle of Raleghs to resist its seizure through attainder 75, 79–84
Sidney, Barbara Gamage 32, 40
Sidney, Sir Henry 34
Sidney, Sir Philip 33, 134
Sidney, Sir Robert 32, 40, 119
sons: breeching 32–33, 41; duty to imitate fathers 33; rebellion against fathers 100–1, 137; removal from mothers 32; as replication of fathers 18–20; 33, 37, 43–47, *44*, 50–51, 196n36
Spenser, Edmund 83, 208, 213–14
Stone, William 159–61

Talbot, John 78–79; accompanied by son in Tower 79; death 170; related to friends of Elizabeth Throckmorton Ralegh 171, 199n25; secretary to Sir Walter Ralegh 166; tutor to Walter Ralegh (Walter, Jr.) 33, 105, 166; unnamed mother 171
Talbot, John (son of Sir John) 166–67
Talbot, Sir John 166; model for Sir Walter Ralegh 166–67; in Shakespeare 166–67
Throckmorton, Sir Arthur 116–17; loyalty to Elizabeth Throckmorton Ralegh 21–22, 28, 73

Throckmorton, Sir John 138–39
Thrush, Andrew 151
Tower Hill 77–78, 104, 117, 171
Tower of London *76*; Carew Ralegh conceived and baptised in 77; depression of Sir Walter Ralegh in 67, 95; fellow prisoners with Sir Walter Ralegh 30, 32, 48–49, 62, 75; life of Walter Ralegh (Walter, Jr.) in 33, 76–79, 85; lodging for Ralegh family 75, 86; release of Sir Walter Ralegh by James I 148, 153, 163; Sir Walter Ralegh and Elizabeth Throckmorton Ralegh imprisoned by Elizabeth I 10, 12, 22–23; Sir Walter Ralegh imprisoned by King James 71; visitors to Sir Walter Ralegh 105, 139; *see also* Waad, Sir William
Treswell, Ralph (the Younger) 206n25
Trumbull, John 124, 126, 139, 146–47
Tyrwhitt, Robert 143–46, 150

University of Leiden 6, 127–29
Utrecht 141, 144, 146, 151

Waad, Sir William 77–78, 105; *see also* Tower of London
Wallace, Charles William 156–57, 159, 206n25
Wallace, Hulda 156–57, 159, 206n25
Walton, Izaak 130, 202n9
West Country: foreign to Elizabeth Throckmorton Ralegh 31; primogeniture in 15; Ralegh family connections widespread 35–36; students and tutors at Oxford 105–6
Whitney, James: description of Walter Ralegh (Walter, Jr.) at Oxford 111
Winwood, Sir Ralph 138–39, 206n11; concern for Walter Ralegh (Walter, Jr.) 142, 145, 151; supporter of Sir Walter Ralegh 138; Sir Walter Ralegh's letters to 150, 176, 181
Wotton, Sir Henry 141–42, 144–47

www.ingramcontent.com/pod-product-compliance
Ingram Content Group UK Ltd.
Pitfield, Milton Keynes, MK11 3LW, UK
UKHW041952140426
5217IPUK00015B/758